Richard H. Wilmer, Mary A. Howe

The Rival Volunteers

The Black Plume Rifles

Richard H. Wilmer, Mary A. Howe

The Rival Volunteers
The Black Plume Rifles

ISBN/EAN: 9783337292959

Printed in Europe, USA, Canada, Australia, Japan

Cover: Foto ©Thomas Meinert / pixelio.de

More available books at **www.hansebooks.com**

THE

RIVAL VOLUNTEERS;

OR,

THE BLACK PLUME RIFLES.

BY MARY A. HOWE.

—•••—

NEW YORK:

JOHN BRADBURN,

(SUCCESSOR TO M. DOOLADY,)

49 WALKER STREET.

1864.

W. H. Tinson, Stereotyper,
43 Centre St., N. Y.

John J. Reed., Printer,
43 Centre St., N. Y.

To

MY BROTHER,

·

WILLIAM HILLS,

Serving in the First Regiment of Massachusetts Volunteers,

These pages are affectionately inscribed, with a sister's earnest assurance that not
alone our country's brave defenders suffer in this our hour of national
anguish; but that many who obey no bugle call, listen to no
cannon's roar, bear, nevertheless, their full share in
the nation's sorrow, through lasting ties of
kindred and of sympathy.

CONTENTS.

———•◦•———

THE RIVAL VOLUNTEERS;

THE BLACK PLUME RIFLES.

CHAPTER I.

IN THE SUNSHINE.

SULLENLY the lowering war-cloud brooded over the thriving western city, whose marvellous growth in all material prosperity had been suddenly checked by the devastating influence of the fierce conflict, rending kin from kin asunder, and transforming friends and neighbors into vindictive and remorseless foes and assailants. The tread of armed men was becoming a familiar sound throughout the streets, while on the evening breeze, as well as day's more sultry airs, floated up from encampments in the environs martial strains from bugle and clarion, mingling with the drum's deep roll.

A body of Union soldiery had been fired upon by an excited crowd cheering wildly for Jeff. Davis and the South. The fire had taken effect on harmless pedestrians, some random shots even entering dwelling-houses to the utter consternation of their peaceful inmates,

adding fresh fuel to the flames of animosity already
raging throughout the length and breadth of the State.

A mysterious red chalk-mark had been discovered
beneath the threshold of more than one dwelling harboring inmates suspected of secession proclivities, and the
sinister rumor had been bruited round, that houses thus
designated were to be given up to plunder and pillage,
and razed to the ground under cover of night—a rumor
so terrifying to the Secessionists, that more than one
family, hastily packing up their most precious valuables, betook themselves therewith to their carriages,
leaving the city with all speed, spending the entire
night in the fields, and not venturing to return in the
morning until a servant had first been sent out in recon-
noisance, to ascertain if haply their own roof-trees remained to shelter them.

In the midst of all this fearful foreboding and deadly
virulence, one spacious mansion, the gilding of its cor-
nices fresh and bright, the paint of its frescoes scarcely
dry, echoed only to sounds of mirth and festivity. No
loud, spirit-stirring peals of music here, only those
light, airy tones inspiring languid "poetry of motion."
Who could have dreamed—to have seen these men be-
curled and be-perfumed, these women be-jewelled and
be-gemmed, floating in clouds of gossamer lace and
gauzy tissue through the mazes of the circling dance,
or exchanging with their companions that gay-hued
conversational efflorescence which is generally the
nearest approach to real interchange of thought permitted by such a scene—that outside lurked grim horror, stalked ghastly carnage, its trail the death-scent in
the air. Within the lofty apartments shone dazzling
splendor—without, crouched squalid misery grovelling
in moral mire : within was beauty, grace, fashion, the
gay, careless laugh, the polished gleam of wit foiled by
repartee as keen—without, the angry scowl of the foot-

sore guard as his eye rested on the colored lanterns illuminating the garden that separated the house from the street, or his ear caught the tones of the band, which, instead of discoursing such dulcet strains, should have been sounding forth spirited appeals to young men and old, to rise up in their might and nerve their strong right arms to valiant deeds in defence of country and home.

Let me personalize a few of the actors in the festal throng. This portly, red-faced, middle-aged gentleman, with pompous air of ownership, as who should say, " Behold the extent of my possessions, and beholding the same, be ye thereby abased," is Mr. Caruthers, the bachelor host of the entertainment ; and the exquisitely attired brunette, stylish in appearance and with coldly polished manners, calculated rather to command respect than to conciliate regard, is a younger sister who fills the position of hostess in receiving and providing amusement for her brother's guests. His eye rests not ill-pleased upon the graceful, buoyant figure of a fair young girl, whose claims to notice merit at least a passing description. She is a little above the average height, her flexile, willowy form wholly free from that wasp-like contortion of the waist (hideous deformity ! synonym with slow and lingering decay) which so utterly destroys symmetry of contour in so many of our young countrywomen. Her luxuriant amber hair falls in thick, heavy curls over a well-rounded neck, by no means of ivory whiteness, but of delicate, creamy flesh-tint. Her brow is perhaps too full and heavy for the lower part of the face, but this one scarcely remembers when marking the sparkling vivacity of the deep hazel eyes, the flitting hues of the changeful cheek, and the varying expression of the mobile mouth. Gentle and winning as were her manners, there was, nevertheless, something in her erect bearing, in the stately turn

1*

of her handsome head, that showed she was hardly the person to submit passively to a wrong or. an indignity; that those hazel eyes could flash with ire, as well as dance with mirth or melt with tenderness; that beneath that girlish exterior dwelt a high, indomitable spirit, which would bear her bravely up under trials that would crush a feebler nature into the very depths of despondency.

To explain why I thus particularize the attractions of Minnie Brandon, I may as well state at once that she is the bride-elect of the host, whose thoughts, as he listened to the playful raillery with which she parried the jesting adulation lavished upon her, ran nearly in this wise: " How perfectly at ease she seems, although this is probably the first time she ever took part in such a brilliant assemblage. She will grace well the station to which I propose raising her, and do credit to my taste and my fortune; I could not have chosen better. Sister Dian wished me to wait until the wedding reception, which will come off some time next month, I suppose, before throwing open my house for the envy and inspection of all comers. But by that time my eastern customers will be off, and I was bound to show them that we Westerners could do up this sort of thing in as good shape as they of the older cities. How poor Lucy Sears would enjoy being here! but then my fine-lady sisters would either turn her the cold shoulder, or show off her gentle, girlish, winning ways in a perfectly ridiculous light; for she hasn't Minnie's ready wit and never-failing tact to protect herself with. No, I have selected wisely—Minnie shall rule here in the high position nature has so well qualified her to fill, and Lucy I will persuade to friendship. Dear, credulous child, she listens to me as though I were an oracle, and never gainsays any word of mine. I shall have no difficulty in prevailing upon her to relinquish the claims she must now learn to look upon as null and void."

A distinguished-looking foreigner, whose silk net sash with bullion fringe, gold-bordered shoulder-straps, and the silver-embroidered spread eagles thereupon, denoted his official rank in the Federal army, came up to solicit Miss Brandon's hand for the German.

"By Jove, she is splendid," thought Mr. Caruthers, as, with courteous ease, she accepted the honor with an air which seemed to intimate that she was conferring an equal honor in return. "I suppose it is a consciousness of the high social position to which our union will raise her that makes her receive distinctions which would drive any other woman in the room half out of her senses with delight, in this quiet, unmoved fashion. Why, she couldn't be more completely self-composed if she were at home in her father's shabby-genteel parlor—horrid musty place—scantily furnished in everything but books; *they* are plentiful enough in all conscience; books in cases, books on shelves, books on tables, books on slabs, books in chairs, and books on the floor. Whatever a man wants to stultify himself for, with bolting such a lot of dead men's dust passes my poor comprehension. The clear, running stream of thought, fresh from living minds, for me. I want to read the look of a man's eye, and to watch the turn of his face when talking, that I may see if he is speaking me true, or only trying to start me off on a false trail for purposes of his own; and these signs of what one is really thinking is just what print hides, and that is why I care precious little about it, save as an advertising and news medium. But, heigho! this is not entertaining my company. I must stir round and get up some sort of small talk to suit each one. I shall be thankful when it is over, for if I didn't know it was pleasure, I should say that this laying

one's self out to amuse folks one wishes at the bottom
of the Dead Sea, and be hanged to 'em, is more like
downright drudgery than anything I've come across in
counting-room or warehouse for many a day."

If the success of an entertainment is to be gauged by
the apparent enjoyment it confers on its partakers, then
was this of Mr. Caruthers an unequivocal success.

"I hope the evening has been a pleasant one to you,"
he said to Minnie Brandon, as he handed her to the
carriage he had placed at her disposal.

"Perfectly delightful," was the prompt and animated
response.

Soon the environs—I cannot say suburbs, for in these
comparatively new western cities the line of demarca-
tion between crowded dwellings and untamed wilds is
often clearly and sharply defined, instead of being mel-
lowed and toned down by gradual process of suburban
outgrowth—of the town were reached, and a drive of
several miles brought her in front of a large, low, ramb-
ling cottage, so irregularly designed that it gave one
the idea of having been built piecemeal, and dovetailed
together by clumsy devices in the form of mortised
roof and gabled projections. With springy, elastic step
she hurried across the entry into the room where a man,
crowned with the venerable locks of age, awaited her
return.

"I am sorry to have kept you up so late, father; but
I was so enchanted with the charming gaities of the
evening, that I could not tear myself away sooner.
Such delicious music under a little awning just outside
the canvas pavilion erected purposely for the dancers,
and entered from the drawing-room through the open
French windows. I must show you over the house
some day; the paintings and the statuary in marble and
bronze you will find well worth looking at. But I have
not yet shown you the crowning proof of Mr. Caruthers'

princely munificence; behold his latest gift to one whom he delighteth to honor."

She threw off her silken *par-dessus,* and with triumphant air courted her father's critical inspection.

" A costly gift, indeed," he coldly remarked ; " diamonds in Etruscan setting of rare design."

" Yes ; necklace, cross, ring and pin. Those pokey Pike girls, who never let pass an opportunity for giving me a slight or an affront when I was meet recipient for such amiable attentions, were half dead with envy in their poor cameoes and corals."

A look of mild reproof stole to the face of Mr. Brandon, whose white clerical neck-tie sufficiently indicated the profession he had long since resigned in favor of the repose befitting his declining years and congenial to his studious habits.

" I am sorry, Minnie, to hear you use language so strongly savoring of petty malice ; the ornaments of a meek and quiet spirit far outbalance "——

" Please don't, father ; my spirits are so light, that I am like a butterfly in the sunshine, and I cannot bear a breath of chill."

" But the chilling breath of trial will come, dear child ; worse than that, the fierce blast and the howling tempest ; it is the tender plumaged butterfly wings that are soonest bruised and torn in misfortune's raging gale."

Her face clouded for an instant, but as quickly brightened again.

" You have often told me, father, that of all species of borrowing, the one in which trouble constitutes the loan from the future is the most profitless; so I will bask in the sunshine till the clouds gather and actually break over my poor head."

She removed the flower-wreath from her amber tresses, and began untwisting the slender wire that

bound rosebuds, heath and fuschias to the tiny stalk of
myrtle which had held them in durance sweet. One by
one, she placed the detached florets in a shallow, crimson glass, remarking :

"I shall press them, in order to preserve some remembrance of the happy hours that have sped all too
fleetly. Another very pleasant association is also connected with this wreath. Miss Dian Caruthers, under
pretence of arranging a loosened sprig of mignonette,
pinned this to my shoulder."

The speaker handed him a blue satin star, fringed
with red, on which was wrought in letters of pearl,
"Star of the Evening."

"The tribute was so grateful to me," she added,
"because it tended to prove that the family are not
averse to his marrying one so much his inferior in fortune and social position as myself. Think of it, father,
as soon as he can get out of business and settle up affairs
connected with it, we are to spend a couple of years
abroad. I shall see St. Peter's marvellous dome, the
bronzes of Benvenuto Cellini, the arches of Augustus
and Trajan, with all the glories of old-world art, about
which I have so often read to you. But I must away
to bed if I would be rested for the drive Mr. Caruthers
has promised me to-morrow, with the dashing pair of
bays he has just purchased. Good night."

Once in her own room, she removed the brilliants
from neck and arm, replacing them in the ebony casket
which had held them at presentation. Then withdrawing the glittering jewels, she drew them across her dainty
palm with light, caressing motion, a dewy lustre in her
half-veiled eyes, on her parted lips a joyous smile ;
giving little thought to the value of the gems at which
she gazed, prizing them chiefly for the regard which
had prompted their bestowal.

"To no other person in the wide world would he

offer gifts like these," she mentally assured herself. " I will strive, by all means, to make myself worthy of a devotion so freely given on his part, on mine so little deserved. I will improve myself, store my mind with themes for discourse, both grave and gay, that he may never tire of his choice."

In a totally diverse channel flowed the perturbed stream of her father's cogitations below stairs.

" Is the girl bewitched," he asked himself, with puzzled air, " that her simple, refined tastes should so suddenly give place to this feverish thirst for dress and display? She used to be a sensible, intelligent companion for me, reading and talking of what she read understandingly; but now she is constantly running after some novelty or other, and there is no repose about her. Can it be possible that a commonplace, matter-of-fact man like Mr. Caruthers, whose reading list is principally comprised in day-book and ledger, can have turned a head like hers? Well, more absurd things than that have happened in this odd world of ours, where the flimsiest fallacies often shut out the light of truth from our dim, uncertain vision. I think if one studies one's self to good purpose, one grows more lenient to others' foibles as one grows old. If Minnie is happy in her enchanted air-castle, why should I seek to tumble it about her ears? It does seem hard, now that she is all I have left, to see her interest so entirely absorbed in a comparative stranger, while my preferences are no longer consulted nor even remembered. I shall not so much as hint a remonstrance, however, for I have not yet forgotten the burning resentment arising from my interference with her elder sister's matrimonial plans. Poor Susan, she would have thrown herself away on a smooth-tongued dissembler, so devoid of all sense of moral propriety as to make his boasts of the mean underhanded practices by which he had bam-

boozled and defrauded everybody with whom he had
had any dealings. When I strove to save her from a
fate so wretched, she resolutely refused to see my conduct in any other light than that of an unnatural parent,
who with cruel malignity thwarted her most cherished
wishes. I forbade young Makepeace crossing my
threshold, and she met him by stealth. I explained to
her the real character of the man as the ground of my
objection to her union with him. He told her that I
despised and persecuted him on account of his humble
calling, thus establishing a fresh claim on her ready
sympathies. She inherited a tendency to pulmonary
complaint, and I noticed with alarm her slight, hacking
cough, and the too vivid flush on her cheek. I sent her
up to Lake Superior for the benefit of change. What
did he do but engage himself to work in one of the
copper mines, and contrive to see her daily! Then the
sterling integrity of her better nature asserted itself.
She awoke to a clear consciousness of her own delin-
quency in the systematic course of deception she had
been practising toward me, came straight home, confessed all, blaming herself so much that I couldn't have
added a word of censure if my life had depended on it,
wound up by declaring that she could die if need be,
but that no wrong should come to any one through her
means, and fell swooning at my feet. I could see that
she grew thinner every day after that, and as a forlorn
hope, determined to try and prevail on Makepeace to
so far modify his course of life, that I could tolerate him
as a son-in-law. I found him in a yacht on the lake in
company with a wealthy Chicago banker and his only
child, a beautiful and accomplished girl. My words of
warning and counsel the young man heeded no more
than the idle wind. I couldn't get hold of him, for he
seemed entirely destitute of that moral sense which dis-
criminates between right and wrong. 'You must look

sharp after Susan,' said he, without seeming to be aware of his own insolence, as we parted, 'for she is very impulsive and susceptible, and if she should be guilty with others, of conduct as imprudent and indiscreet as that she has shown toward me, she would certainly be talked about. Not that I shall ever betray her; you surely do not think so ill of me as to apprehend any step of that sort on my part.'

"I was choking with rage, and could have knocked the puppy down with a will. 'If you wish to blazon the fact of having won a trusting girl's affections,' said I, 'under false pretences of being what you are not, a true and honest man; and to state furthermore that as soon as your baseness became thoroughly known you was forbidden her father's premises, set about it as soon as you like, thus affording fresh evidence, if such were needed, to prove you the despicable double-dealer you are.' 'I'd no idea a clergyman of your experience ever so far forgot his principles as to let his temper run away with him in this highly unclerical fashion,' said the irreverent scoffer. I let the remark pass without reply, and we have never changed words since. He married the banker's daughter, squandered her fortune, and then deserted her. A costly monolith marks the little space of earth which is all she now needs; but her rest is not sweeter than that of my poor girl beneath the village sod.

"How my thoughts linger over the past, because the present is such a blank, I suppose. Come here, Omer, dog: you are about the best friend a man could have after all. Never longing to be gone when I want you beside me, and never obtruding when you're not wanted. Watching me, with drowsy, half-closed eyes, while I read; sober when I'm sad, frolicsome when I'm glad: I'd rather part with half my acquaintances than with you, dumb friend."

CHAPTER II.

IN THE SHADE.

PUNCTUALLY at the appointed hour, Mr. Caruthers' mettlesome bays, attached to a light, open buggy, drew up in front of Mr. Brandon's cottage. Minnie, looking as fresh and blooming as though she had not danced half the previous night, was quickly seated in the vehicle. Rapidly they spun over the road, space swiftly devoured by the nimble-footed steeds, until a half score of miles intervened between them and their starting-place. The panting horses slackened their pace on reaching a steep acclivity, when the sharp rattle of musketry, and the drums' measured roll, became distinctly audible. Mr. Caruthers and his companion exchanged startled, significant glances.

"A parade, possibly," he suggested, his look contradicting his words; "we will soon find out what is going on."

Quickening the speed of his horses by a gesture of the hand, they soon reached the summit of the ridge.

"No mock fighting here," he exclaimed. "An engagement between our forces and those of the enemy."

Minnie turned deadly pale.

"See the drivers of vehicles galloping their horses down the road; let us follow their example, and fly too, while we may."

"Don't alarm yourself, child. They have no artillery that I can see; and even if they had, we are so much higher than those long double lines of men, warring with each other to the death, that we are beyond reach of harm. We may never again find opportunity to look on a scene like this."

"Let us not look on it now. It makes my blood run

cold, this wholesale slaughter; it is no sight for a weak woman's eyes."

He darted an impatient glance at the wan, imploring face raised so entreatingly to his own.

" I wish we had come in the close carriage, and then I could have sent you off in charge of the coachman. Were you ever afflicted with that fearful feminine visitation known as hysterics?"

A glowing tinge of red flashed to her cheek.

" Never, Mr. Caruthers. I will remain since you desire it."

" That is right. I am glad to see you act as though you were gifted with at least some small modicum of common sense, which is more than can be said of many of your sex (he bowed, as though conscious of having bestowed a merited compliment). Your eyes are younger and clearer than mine; look over the plain and tell me which are our men."

" Those at the right or easterly side of the field, which slopes gradually backward to the treacherous marsh in which it loses itself. How the smoke-wreaths curl about the stars and stripes, glorious emblem of the nation's greatness, hereafter doubly sacred, doubly dear, since so many eyes beloved have glazed in death's films while guarding from stain of dishonor the hallowed emblem, consecrated by the baptism of fire through which our fathers passed, in order to bequeath us a legacy so priceless as that it symbolizes."

" Don't stop to talk of that now. Has either side gained the advantage, can you see?"

" I can see better than I can describe. Skirmishers seem more active just now than those drawn up in line of battle. Hark! what means that shrill, imperative bugle-note? It must be a signal, for the scattering troops rally in column; and now comes a perfect blaze of musketry along the entire lines. Ah! here comes one who can tell you much better than I the progress of affairs."

Mr. Caruthers turned to speak to Colonel Vanburgh, a meritorious officer, who had retired from active service with honorable scars and honorable mention, and who now hobbled up on crutches to the side of the vehicle.

"How goes the tide of success below?" asked Mr. Caruthers.

"Let me take in all the bearings of the case and you shall have my opinion for what it is worth," calmly responded the new comer, seating himself at the foot of a tree, and sweeping the prospect with a powerful pocket-glass.

"I should say they are about equally matched as regards numbers. The enemy are plucky and impetuous; but our men are firm as a rock, and stand fire better than could be expected from those so lately but raw recruits. They are gradually lessening the space, too, between themselves and the foe, leaving the wounded in their rear, to be picked up and cared for by the surgeons and their assistants."

"Leaving, also," sighed Minnie, through her tears, "many a fallen, nameless hero, who has gone nobly to a patriot's doom, and no longer needs even our pity; but Heaven grant the balm of consolation to the stricken hearts that, in speechless sorrow, mourn at home, in utter desolation of spirit, the loved and lost!"

"Brava!" shouted the colonel, tossing his cap in the air in the exuberance of approving delight; "our lines are taking the double-quick—the attacking force has always the advantage when it comes to close quarters. *Charge* BAYONET!" he shouted, with the enthusiasm of one familiar with said charge.

Suddenly his gladness was changed into desolation.

"Ten thousand perditions!" he muttered, hoarsely, replacing his cap with an air of profound chagrin, "our guards ought not to let them fall into a trap of this sort. Perhaps the guards are not to blame. There's a signal from bugle and drum, and there goes an aide from the general's staff to the battalions in reserve. It is almost more than flesh and blood can bear to pause in the midst of a brilliant charge that was nearly sure to rout the enemy, and fall back to their former position. They do so in good order, that's one comfort."

"But why should they fall back just as victory was to crown their efforts?" sharply queried Mr. Caruthers.

"Can't you see, man, those regiments of infantry marching to the relief of the enemy?" somewhat tartly responded the colonel. "I'm afraid that isn't the worst we have to dread, either, unless my wits are much at fault. There is some mischief brewing behind that scanty belt of pines skirting the hill at the opposite side of the field; if I were only a little higher up I should be able to make it out. If my broken leg, that never healed rightly from want of proper care, wasn't such a disability, I'd climb this dead pine and settle my doubts one way or the other. I will climb it, if I'm a knock-kneed cripple forever after; there will be plenty of the same sort to keep me company before the sun goes down, or I am far out in my calculations."

He tossed his crutches aside, and after more than one futile effort, succeeded in attaining the required altitude, and with it the view for which it had been undertaken.

"Pluto and purgatory! it is just as I feared," he called out from his new post of observation, " cannons, caissons and all, protected by an efficient guard. There, they have planted their battery in the place of all places where it can do us most harm. There it booms, a deadly, disastrous, enfilading fire, that makes our brave fellows bite the dust in numbers, it makes a tough old veteran sicken to think of reckoning. There comes a

fresh shower of grape and shrapnell, and the color-guard
has not escaped scathless. The flag wavers in unsteady
hands. Cheer up, comrades, never let those glorious
folds dip to traitorous rebel foe. There they float, the
stars and stripes, free to the breeze once more. Our
lines are in confusion; they break, fall back, leaving the
ground strewn with the dead and the dying; re-form,
strengthen themselves by alignment of battalions in
reserve, and once more show the enemy a bold, determined front. There go a couple of the general's aids,
who ride as if life and death depended on their speed.
I foresee their purpose. You are right, General Seit-
zel, better sacrifice five hundred of the very flower of
your army in capturing that battery, than to have your
ranks mown down in this way. Away go the detachment of infantry into the very jaws of death on their
desperate venture. Doomed, *doomed !* they know not
the strength of the force against which they are pitted.
What boots it that they form into line in separate
divisions so as to avoid the cannons' shot and shell, when
a more dreadful foe lurks for them in ambush ! Now
they are so near that the cannon's angle of elevation
hurls its missiles over their heads. How eagerly they
press forward, believing an easy victory almost won.
Suddenly from the underbrush fronting the battery
springs up a rebel regiment, discharging a volley of
musketry full in the faces of our advancing troops.
That is right, my men, flee, scatter, never risk a bayonet
charge from an exultant foe, when you are confused by
an unexpected assault, and inclined to panic through
heavy loss. Now pluck up good heart, and start fair
and fresh once more, but not as quarry for the craven
brood that still infests the brushwood. Make a circuit
in small force to the open space at the rear of the battery, cutting down all opposition in the way, leaving
the main body to occupy the enemy by feints of attack

in front. The deed is done, the gunners silenced, the battery in our possession, and a fierce hand-to-hand conflict raging between the two regiments."

"What of the main engagement in the plain below?" asked Mr. Caruthers.

"Nothing but disaster there; a terrific bayonet charge, in which our men are borne down by sheer brute force of superior numbers. They yield the ground, step by step, each one obstinately contested at countless cost. This will never do; there is such a thing as carrying bravery to the extent of foolhardy bravado. Why will they not surrender when the odds are so fearfully against them? Will they wait to be forced back into that bog, and killed to the last man?"

"Let us go; it is half killing me," entreated Minnie, shaking from head to foot, her face blanched to the very lips with an ashen pallor.

"You need have no fear," returned Mr. Caruthers; "I assure you there is not the least occasion; we are quite beyond range of the artillery, and there isn't the slightest cause for alarm; you can't be hurt, make yourself perfectly at ease on that point."

Without an added word of protest, she shut out the scenes of ghastly carnage that thrilled her weak, womanly nerves with acutest anguish, by burying her face in her handkerchief. She was roused from the aching sense of misery that had wrought her keenly sympathetic nature to its highest point of intensity, by a jubilant shout from Colonel Vanburgh.

"Here they come at last; just what we need, a powerful body of well-mounted cavalry. On, hearts of oak, on to the rescue, before the bodies and souls that still hold together have parted company. How like a whirlwind they thunder down that rolling slope, hurling themselves with resistless fury upon the enemy's right, which, with the reserve in echelon, forms into square to receive them. The horses—noble beasts, I can pity and admire them, while glorying still more in the daring and gallantry of their noble riders—obey curb and spur to a nicety, and dash, without sign of fear, upon the bristling wall of bayonets that will leave many of them battered hulks to feed carrion crows and breed pestilence in the air.

"There comes as brave a man as is to be found in our ranks, young Stanwood, staff officer, who never knew what it was to fear mortal man ; charged with orders of importance, I'd willingly lay wager, or he'd never ride that splendid black charger of his at such a break-neck gallop as to make the white foam fly from his lips and churn out from his saddle-girths. Evidently he seeks to communicate with cavalry official, or he would not thus expose himself in advance of our lines. Crack ! there goes a rifle shot from behind a vine-covered paling, and the horse's chest is crimson with gore ; a second, and this time it is the rider who is hit. Malignant fate, to shield him from whizzing bullet and bursting shell, and then yield him inglorious prey to the lurking assassin's fatal aim. The order-bearer reels in his saddle, but still keeps a firm hold of the bridle-rein. He will die like the dauntless hero he would have lived, ready to give his last breath in his country's service, straining every nerve to fulfill the commission intrusted to his charge. It is not thus decreed. He is under higher orders than those of his commanding general now. The reins fall from his loosened grasp; his head bends forward until his plumed hat nearly touches his horse's neck. He has lost all control over the animal, which leaps and plunges, maddened with pain. It rears on its hind legs, beating the air wildly with its front hoofs, then partially loses balance, is almost down, staggers to its feet, makes a single spring forward, and falls heavily, a dead, crushing weight, upon its luckless rider. Poor

Stanwood, pure patriot, unflinching supporter of a holy cause, would I were near to lend a helping hand in this your hour of direful need ; to aid in placing you where your last breath should not be quenched in suffocation."

"Peace, poor, tortured soul!" murmured Minnie, in reverent, awe-struck tones, her dim eyes blinded by unshed tears ; "Heaven's benison be thine, since earthly succor is not for thee."

"It is now the enemy's turn to cower, their own battery turned against them," called out their informant from the dead pine, in tone once more raised to pitch exultant. "Their lines are in confusion ; they break and flee in disorder, pursued by our cavalry and light troops, the others only waiting to restore order in their columns before hurrying off in the same direction. Here come medical directors with hospital attendants and ambulances, which will all be needed. Men crawl down from trees, crawl out of pits and hollows, crawl forth from brier and dingle, staring warily about them. Why cannot some of them picket those riderless horses, whose every step maims or mangles some wounded soldier? I'll hobble down to the plain myself; it isn't much that I can do, but a kind word goes a good way sometimes. I found that out when I lay half dead in a Mexican lazaretto. There were none but glum, scowling faces about me, excepting that of a gaunt old chore-woman, whom I made twenty excuses a day to see; for, though she was homely enough in all conscience, she was the only living creature from whom I received a look or word of compassion, and it is like the horror of solitary confinement to be deprived of that."

With some difficulty he came down from his post of observation, and picking up his crutches, laboriously commenced the descent of the hill, Mr. Caruthers cautiously following, and eyeing with distrust every bank

2

or bush that might screen a straggler from the scene
of the late conflict.

"What ails you, child?" asked the limping pedestrian,
of a little boy with a tin pail on his arm, who pressed
his hand to his forehead, as if giddy or sick, swaying to
and fro, and groping his way along with wavering, uncertain footsteps.

"Mother sent me to bring his dinner to father, who
has been working on the road; but I couldn't find him,
and something I didn't see struck me in the side; I'm
hurted bad."

The tin pail to which he had clung while strength
lasted was suddenly dropped. The speaker threw up
his arms, and with a long drawn gasp, a single convul-
sive shudder, fell forward a corpse almost beneath the
wheels of the vehicle.

As they neared the plain, sights and sounds of suffering multiplied about them. One wounded officer, fevered
by burning thirst, dragged himself to the edge of a stag-
nant pool, and in attempting to adjust his drinking-tube
in the slimy water to filter the same for use, lost his balance and plunged incontinently into the oozy slush,
which would have proved his burial-place but for the
united exertions of the colonel and a man whom he
summoned to his aid, Mr. Caruthers never once dreaming of soiling his spotless kids and snowy linen by prof-
fering assistance on the occasion.

A fair-haired girl was borne past on a litter of boughs;
her long lashes resting on her colorless cheek; her
heavy, dishevelled tresses falling over the pale blue
dress, which would flutter at heart-beat of hers never
again.

"How came *she* here?" Mr. Caruthers paused to inquire.

"She was out for a walk with her betrothed," explained, with grave courtesy, one of the bearers of the

rude trestle; "and I suppose they were so much taken
up in talking over plans for the future as to pay small
heed to signs of approaching danger until escape from
it was impossible. Her intended husband belonged to
the Home Guard, a splendid marksman, and when he
saw that he had really lost her for this life, he instantly
seized upon the musket of a dead soldier, crying out,
'Now, oh my bleeding country! with my whole heart
do I espouse thy cause,' and rushed into the thickest of
the fight."

Slowly they once more wended their way onward.

"Stop!" entreated Minnie, as the pale, rigid face of a
young man borne past on a stretcher riveted her gaze,
"that is Morland Ellsmead, do let me get out and take a
nearer look at him."

She sprang impulsively to her feet, and in another instant would have been on the ground if Mr. Caruthers'
restraining grasp had not forced her back to the seat
from which she had just risen.

"If you wish any inquiries made, I will make them
for you, if you will oblige me by doing nothing to render yourself conspicuous," he observed, in tones of cold
reproval.

"But Morland is such an old friend of ours," she remonstrated. "He was my father's pupil once; and we
chased squirrels in the woods, and gathered wild-flowers
and nuts together when we were children and play-
mates. He may be dying now; I *must* speak to him, I
should never forgive myself if I lost such an opportunity."

Once more she attempted to put in practice the purpose her words implied, and once more she failed to
achieve her intent.

"Understand me, Miss Brandon," he remarked, in
freezing accents; "I have no desire to see the lady who
will one day bear my name (a name of as sterling weight

as the best on 'Change); preside with grace and propriety, I hope, over a household establishment which,
for bounty and liberality, has not in the whole city its
superior; and dispense with a pride becoming to her
high station, but without any of the upstart forwardness
and affectations of oddity which are so apt to make the
conduct of those who have suddenly been elevated from
the humbler to the higher walks of life supremely
ridiculous"—

He paused abruptly, his speech arrested by a look he
could not fathom from the wide-open eyes that were
looking straight into his.

"What I mean is, Minnie," he resumed, with a voice
and manner somewhat modified, "that I do not wish to
see one, whose fair name and fame it will soon be my
privilege to guard, familiarly jostled by a motley, nondescript crowd such as is fast collecting here. A woman cannot pay too strict a regard to appearances, and
should never overstep a conventionality even, or hazard
the remotest chance of acquiring an unenviable notoriety."

To these concluding platitudes Minnie turned a deaf
ear, her whole attention being for the moment concentrated on the white, motionless face, shaded by curls of
chestnut-brown hair, that lay so still and impassive beneath her anxious gaze. A man standing near, super-
intending the arrangement of cushions and blankets
for a soldier with shattered collar-bone, noticing her
expression of eager, almost hopeless inquiry, with demeanor sympathetic and respectful, explained that Mr.
Ellsmead was not wounded, but merely stunned by the
concussion of a spent ball, which had just grazed his
head in its rebound from some obstruction in its course.
Minnie thanked her informant with grateful warmth,
and Mr. Caruthers, jerking his reins impatiently, urged
his steeds to a rapid pace.

"I do wish, Minnie," he averred, in tone irascible, as soon as they were beyond earshot of casual eavesdropper, "that you would be a little more retiring and feminine in your deportment toward strangers, especially such as do not stand on a footing of equality with us. After I had offered to make any needful inquiries, regarding the young man in whose fate you manifested such a remarkable solicitude, it was in exceedingly bad taste, to say the least, for you to still persist in making yourself the centre of observation to such a motley throng. I wonder if a woman, with the least pretension to good looks, could be so circumstanced that the vain longing to show off her attractions would not be the mainspring to her every act."

Minnie turned on him a glance in which resentment was overborne by a look of boundless surprise.

"If you think, Mr. Caruthers," she returned, in tone as cold and hard as his own, "that I am capable of being swayed by paltry motive of mere personal display in the midst of the agonizing scenes through which we have just passed, you do me a cruel injustice, and are far from comprehending my real character."

"Quite likely! it is no very transparent one," he carelessly subjoined; "and it is sometimes quite too deep for sounding by an out-spoken man like me, who uses plain words to convey a plain, intelligible meaning, and has no need of roundabout ways and means for making himself understood."

Minnie closed her eyes quickly to crush the tears that had gathered beneath their lids. She was too deeply wounded to venture any attempt at self-vindication. For miles the silence between them remained unbroken. She was the first to speak.

"I am deeply grieved, Mr. Caruthers, that I should have been so unfortunate as to shock your perceptions of what true feminine propriety requires of those who aim to practice it ; the only reparation I can make, now that I know your views on the subject, is to strive faithfully to conform to them in every particular ; this it shall be my constant and unwearying effort to accomplish."

"Is it possible *that* has been running in your head all this time?"

"Had you forgotten it?"

"Completely: I have more sober realities to fret about. This confounded secession mania is raising the very deuce with business. What with the blockade, barricades, batteries and earthworks, the Mississippi is shut up tight as a vice—no outlet for bacon and corn, no inlet for silks and wines. Pardon me, this is no meet subject of discourse for a lady's ear. Did you understand what I was talking about?"

"Perfectly, and thank you for speaking to me as though I were a rational being," she replied, with an intonation of bitterness that was thrown away on his obtuse perceptions.

"Everything is at loggerheads in the mercantile community just now," he resumed ; "my last champagne was a villianously transparent sham ; the last tobacco I bought for my meerschaum was enough to harrow a man's soul up for a whole day after smoking it; and tea and coffee are rising to an unprecedentedly high figure—how we are to live through such straits is more than I can tell. Where are the dividends from my railway shares coming from, with the rails torn up, freight and fare stopped? How am I to collect my rents, with my tenants off to the war, and their families thinking more of their own selfish interests than of paying my lawful dues? We have to run after the customers who used to run after us, and half of them aren't worth the trouble of catching at that—failing up, selling out at a ruinous discount, and skulking round, if you refuse a dividend of five cents on a dollar, in all sorts of out-of-the-way lurking places, as hard to find as a needle in a hay-mow. No very consoling fact, either, to be told by those who know the most of statecraft that we have by no means reached the crisis of the financial pressure as yet."

Once more the speaker lapsed into silence. They were nearing the cottage when, bowing with air apologetic, he said, "I have left you long to your own thoughts; I hope they have run on pleasanter themes than mine."

"I was thinking," she rejoined, in wearily dejected tone, "what a relief it was to be told that Morland Ellsmead was only stunned, not dangerously wounded."

Mr. Caruthers did not seem particularly gratified at the intelligence conveyed through this admission.

At the first sight of his daughter's troubled face, Mr. Brandon saw that the pleasant anticipations with which she had looked forward to her drive had not been realized. She gave him a sadly wistful glance, as seating herself near him, she removed her light Leghorn hat, trifling abstractedly with the heron's plume, which was its sole adornment.

"Our butterfly is not in the sunshine to-day," he quietly remarked.

"I have looked on a sight, father, that would make murky clouds on the fairest sky that ever smiled. From the top of Pine Ridge we witnessed an engagement between the National and Confederate forces. I hope my vision may never be blasted by such another sight."

"Which side was victorious?"

"Ours; but only after a severe repulse, which must have resulted in utter defeat, we were so greatly outnumbered by the enemy, but for the opportune arrival of reinforcements. When our men, horse and foot, had driven the foe from the field, we drove slowly across it.

The faces of the dead I saw wore a peculiar livid expression, the result, I think, of the fatal gun-shot wounds
through which life's tide had ebbed; it was so unlike
the look of calm, placid repose of my mother's face
when I strewed flowers on her pillow, knowing that to
their lovely tints she was blind, that through earthly
sense the sweetness of their perfume could not reach
her, and yet, urged on by a feeling I could not overcome, and would not if I could, that she did somehow
recognize and appreciate these last tributes of filial love
it was in my power to render unto her. What a sad
house was ours for the first year after she left us.   I
could not see a sable pall or a funeral procession without my eyes being blinded by tears.   I thought of so
many little kindnesses I might have rendered, and did
not, because she was so uncomplaining I never knew her
need of them until it was too late."

Mr. Brandon's eyes moistened with the tender reminiscences her words had recalled.

"Those who die by swift-winged messenger of destruction, Minnie, while nobly contending in a righteous
cause, are less to be pitied than those who sit by lonely,
desolate firesides, nursing vain, regretful longings for the
dead and buried past, which locks in its coffers the
sounds for lack of which the ear is forever unsatisfied;
the sights which alone can bring gladness to the eyes,
making the waste places of the earth to bud and blossom as the rose.   All honor and glory to the patriot
heroes who fall in defence of the Right; but sudden
death by bursting shell or sabre stroke is scarcely harder
to bear than the clinging memories which haunt the
bereaved heart with delusive phantoms of a happiness
that might have been.   Fatal the marksman's aim, but
grief has also deadly weapon, venomed shaft in its
quiver."

Minnie drew a long breath; her thoughts dwelt on

the unmerited rebuke she had received from one to whom her sacredly pledged word had yielded the right of control over her future destiny.

"The same words from other lips would have been nothing," she said to herself, "but I have so worn my heart on my sleeve for him, that it is very bitter to receive a blow in return for my trust."

"What is it, Minnie? Have you kept back from me any cause for your unusual disquietude?" asked her father, noting the look of extreme despondency stamped on her expressive features.

She started, colored violently, and stammered a scarce coherent reply. Not even to him could she reveal the words of cold reproval, forgotten by their speaker almost as soon as uttered, which rankled sorely in her thoughts. She was learning that embittered lesson which all but the shallowest natures must, sooner or later, learn—to suffer and be still.

—•••—

CHAPTER III.

CHANGEFUL SKIES.

ONCE within the sanctuary of her own chamber, she takes from her dressing-table the jewel-casket already mentioned. What wills she with it? Surely her heavy, tear-stained eyes will not regain their lustre through the sparkle of gems. Full well recks she of this, as, placing the casket in a small walnut-wood box, and adding to its contents a locket, a miniature at which she does not even stop to glance, she slides the same beneath her bureau, saying to herself, "There let it remain for the present."

Nearly a week elapsed before Mr. Caruthers again came to the cottage.

"I can hardly stop to sit down," were almost his first words; "for I'm so harassed by business cares that I have hardly a minute to spare, and fairly filched time to run down and ask after your health."

"It was very kind of you, I'm sure; but how did you come? I do not see your horse or vehicle."

"I left the horse in the shade of the walnuts yonder, it is so sunny here."

"As you are in such haste, let me drive a mile or two with you on your return; I would like the walk back."

"I should like nothing better than to have you go; very good of you to offer, I'm sure; but, unfortunately, I have a friend with me, and must defer the pleasure of a drive with yourself to a more favorable opportunity."

The slight confusion in his manner did not escape her penetrating glance.

"Only a young relative," he explained, in reply to her look, for she had asked no question; and turned to lavish voluble praise upon the shrubs in full bloom beneath the window. She gathered him a bunch of these gorgeously tinted censers of sweet incense, and then accompanied him as far as the garden-gate, where he bade her "Good-day" in a tone so decisive, that she was strongly inclined to the belief that he was fearful of her accompanying him farther, and desirous of baffling any such attempt on her part. Filled with a vague distrust, which was all the more tormenting that it had no tangible base on which to rest, instead of returning to the cottage, she made her way to the top of what was known as Sugar-Loaf Hill, commanding the view of a long stretch of level vale, through which wound the road leading toward the city. She had acknowledged to herself no definite purpose in toiling up the ascent, but her eager glance across the extended valley would have betrayed to acute observer the clue to her secret motive. Her gaze rested on the object it had sought; there were the dashing bays creeping along at a snail's pace, hardly consistent with their driver's recent lament at being unable to snatch more than briefest respite from harassing business cares, and by his side, the drooping blue feather in her charming hat, jauntily looped up at the rim, distinctly visible, sat a lady in whose conversation, judging from his attitude of rapt attention, he was deeply interested.

Slowly and sadly Minnie wended her way homeward, oppressed by cause so slight or so subtle as to defy all attempts at mental analysis or verbal embodiment. The next day she accompanied her father in a drive to the city, and on a crowded sidewalk caught a brief glimpse of a lady in jaunty hat with drooping blue feather, who carried in her hand the identical bunch of scarlet geranium, ever-blooming rose and scented laurel she had herself presented to Mr. Caruthers the previous afternoon. This little incident, trivial and unimportant though it seem, was yet sufficient to poison for its beholder every fount of joy. From the maze of suspicion and perplexity into which it threw her, she found herself utterly powerless to escape.

The deep, strong tones of Mr. Caruthers' voice, as he came up the garden-walk with her father late in the week, half disarmed her of her doubts; surely that frank, outspoken voice would never convey to her message of guile or deceit. She met the speaker with a look of the keenest scrutiny, which he returned with one of smiling good humor.

"I have just come from Marchmont's greeneries, and here is a bouquet—monstrous in size, but selecting from such a wealth of sweets, I couldn't make it smaller—which I had the gardener cut expressly for you. Here are scentless roses, blue, white and purple campanula, and camelias, which are good for nothing but to be looked at; it is amongst these carnations and heliotrope blossoms that you must seek for perfume such as you will never find in odor-cases. These passion-flowers are said to speak a language intelligible to the initiated, of which I am not one; pray enlighten my ignorance, Miss Brandon, from the fullness of your own knowledge."

"I am quite as uninstructed in floral lore as yourself," she returned, unable to throw off the slight shade of restraint that still chilled her manner; noticing which, he redoubled his efforts to cheer and enliven her.

"I will not ask you to go with me for a drive to-day," said he, "our last experiment in that line not having led us into scenes that could exactly be called inspiriting; but please favor me with your company for a short walk."

Without demur she acceded to his proposal, and they strolled forth arm-in-arm. Having been long accustomed, through motives of self-interest, to the close study and observation of mankind, and dealing with a character as transparent and free from art of guile as was that of his companion, he was not slow in ferreting out the cause of her uneasiness, and applying efficacious antidote.

"One reason for my visiting you to-day," he carelessly remarked, breaking ground by cautious and guarded approach toward the theme which he well knew to be uppermost in her thoughts, "is. to solicit your kind offices in behalf of a young *protégée*, a distant connection of mine, who comes amongst us an entire stranger to our habits, ways and customs. Miss Sears may be neither very brilliant nor very learned—that last fact rather a desideratum in a woman, I think—but she has such a flow of spirits that you can never tire of her; I never heard an ill-natured word from her lips, and she is so sweet-tempered, that on acquaintance you cannot help liking her."

Minnie's look said as plainly as words could have spoken, that she was not indisposed to resist the effect of said allurements, and that all sweetness from that flower unseen might as well be wasted on the desert air as on senses steeled like hers against their bewitchments. Mr. Caruthers saw the mistake he had made in praising one woman to another, already half disposed to regard her as a rival, and hastened, so far as lay in his power, to retrieve this vital blunder.

"Let me tell you something of Lucy Sears' antecedents, Miss Brandon, that you may see how utterly forlorn her condition would be if it were not for the friendly aid I felt it my duty to bestow on the lonely orphan girl who would otherwise have been thrown penniless upon the uncertain charities of a selfish world. Her father, Gregory Sears, was one of nature's oddities, who lacked nothing in the way of intelligence and ability, excepting common sense. I don't suppose he was to blame for the infirmities that seem to have been born with him; but they were the cause of great tribulation to his parents. He was quick and apt at book learning and soon knew more than his masters in that line; but set him to swapping jack-knives or jews-harps with the biggest noodle in school, and he was sure to get the worst end of the bargain. His father, who was a grazier in a small way, used to set him to watch the cattle and sheep, but generally found him in some shady nook, book in hand, its margins all scribbled over with rhyme and his wits gone wool-gathering to the ends of the earth, where his sheep might have been too, for all his interfering to prevent."

"Then he was a poet," suggested Minnie.

"I suppose so, poor fellow; he couldn't help it — always star-gazing, and so falling into the open pitfalls

lying unheeded at his feet. Of course he fell in love,
as the phrase goes—your improvident, sentimental
dreamer always does that—with a white-handed, lily-
browed, inefficient sylph, who rapt him into the seventh
heaven of Elysium by reading the 'effusions of his
muse,' as she called his jingling metres, with the air of
a tragedy queen on the stage (I don't mean that she
raved and stamped, and tore her hair like Lady Mc-
Ghastlin after she had poured a drop of melted lead in
her husband's ear, but she did the pathetic to a turn,
with real tears in her eyes), and she encouraged him to
publish his rhymes. Quite naturally, the operation
proved a losing one on his part; for, though the newspaper critics said one wouldn't be likely to fall asleep
over the book, which found a ready local sale, and
wasn't very bad stuff to take, if one got weather-bound
at a country tavern or any other out-of-the-way place
where a billiard-room or a bowling-alley was an unat-
tainable luxury, he lacked the enterprise to place it
properly before the public and make it pay. After his
marriage, affairs were far from mending; for his wife,
who could sweep the streets with the air and the grace
of a seraph, knew just as much, no more, no less, than one
of those celestial beatitudes about anything in the way
of useful employment. A more comfortless, ill-arranged
home than poor Gregory's I never saw.

"I offered him a situation as clerk in a branch house
at New York connected with our firm. He was a good
penman and quick accountant, the only trouble being
that nothing would cure his mania for dabbling in verse.
With a whole string of charges waiting to be entered on
the books, he would. as likely as any way, be found up
in the loft, on a pile of gunny-bags, putting meadows
green and running brooks into lines chopped of an equal
length, and bringing up with a certain similarity of
sound. It was this habit of losing himself in his own

fancies that indirectly caused his death. He was so inconsiderate as to lose himself in a brown study directly
beneath the scuttle, down which, from an upper story,
the boys were lowering a large quantity of heavy merchandise. They got tired, I suppose, didn't adjust
the ropes as carefully as they ought in handling such
weighty boxes; one of them slipped from its fastenings
before it had half reached the ground floor, and striking
Gregory on the head killed him on the spot.

"I went to New York as soon as I heard of the accident, and found the young widow—she did set her life
by him, there's no mistake about that—in a truly piti-
able condition, violent hysterics alternating with complete prostration of the nervous system. There never
was a woman worse calculated to push her way upward
in the world, or to do anything in the way of earning her
own livelihood. I couldn't help pitying her, though
she provoked me out of all patience by constantly parad-
ing her grief to the friends for whom she sent as soon as
she was able to receive them, and to whom she talked
volubly of the virtues of the deceased and her own irre-
parable loss, shedding torrents of tears the while.. The
grief that spends itself in words is not the kind that cuts
deepest, I'm inclined to think."

"You are right," assented Minnie; "it is the unspoken sorrow whose betrayal would lead to humiliation
or abasement in one's own self-respect, to which sympathy
would give but an added pang, that eats like iron into
the soul. It is only in deeds brought about by wrong
and dissimulation that this intolerable sort of endurance,
unshared and unsolaced, becomes imperative in a proud,
self-reliant nature."

He glanced at her a little uneasily, and resumed, in a
lower tone:

"Your eyes accuse me, if your words do not. You
surely would not have had me, the only person living on

whom they had the shadow of a claim, leave the widow
and her fatherless child—Lucy was only ten then—
with the wolf almost at their door? Easily swayed by
generous impulses yourself, I made sure you would approve rather than condemn the same in others."

He had struck the right chord at last, and the vibrations responsive to his touch were exactly what he could
have wished. She was ashamed of the suspicions she
now accused herself of having entertained without a
shadow of cause; and in her eagerness to atone for the
injustice of which she supposed herself to have been
guilty toward her companion, she passed at once to the
opposite extreme of boundless trust, for which she had,
perhaps, as little reason as for the cankering doubts that
had poisoned her peace. He was not slow to perceive
the advantage he had gained, nor to act upon it.

"I do most warmly approve your generosity," she
hastened to assure him; " it is just the sort of nobly-dis-
interested act I should have expected from you under the
circumstances."

"Thanks for your good opinion. We will not pursue
the subject further. I cannot suppose that you will
feel toward utter strangers anything like the degree of
interest with which I regard those I have been so fortunate as to befriend."

"Pray go on, Mr. Caruthers, I will not look upon any
one whom you call friend as a stranger. Mrs. Sears
and her little daughter were left in dependent circumstances, I gathered from what you said."

"The furniture of their lodgings, a few books, a half
dozen prints or so, and their clothing, were all they
could call their own. I tried to make her understand
her true condition, and to find out her plans for the
future; but if she had any understanding, I couldn't
draw it out; and as to plans, I could take my oath with
a clear conscience that she need never plead guilty to

any such indictment. When I asked her if she intended to remain where she was, she said it made no difference where she lived, or what became of her, now that she had nothing left worth living for. 'But you must live somewhere,' said I. 'I trust my sojourn in this wretched world may be short,' said she, beginning to cry; 'and if by any sort of drudgery I can obtain the bare means of subsistence, the humblest shelter, and the coarsest fare, I shall be more than content. Henceforth I shall look upon life as a burden to be borne, not as a good to be desired.' She stuck so to generalities, that I had to pin her down to a plain question, by asking her if she thought she could earn her own support if I could prevail on some of my friends to give the little girl a home? Didn't she rave then? asking me if my heart was as hard as the nether millstone, that I could think of separating a widowed mother from the only dear object she had left upon earth. I had a great mind to leave her to settle that point at her leisure, and I would have done so, only I knew she was just gull enough to run through her small possessions in the briefest possible time, and come upon my hands more destitute than ever.

"I had a small tenement vacant in Troy, which I offered her, rent free, promising to superintend her removal to the same if she would go at once. She made as great an outcry at the idea of being carried away from her friends and her husband's last resting-place, as though I had been trying to wrong instead of to benefit her, but finally closed with my proposal. I left her comfortably settled in her new quarters, with a supply of fuel, and provisions that would not need hasty replenishment. 'I shall soon obtain some sort of employment,' were her parting words, 'when I shall at once cancel my indebtedness to you, as I wish to be under no obligations to one who never appreciated my precious Gregory's matchless gifts; and instead of placing him

in a position whence his untrammelled spirit could have
flown. on pinions free, to the vaulted empyrean, bound
him down to the performance of such taskwork as more
common natures might as well have fulfilled."

" An odd way of expressing gratitude, it seems to me."

" So I thought ; she appeared to be so much in dread of
lowering her dignity by acknowledging the receipt of a
favor, that she resolutely persuaded herself none such
had been conferred.   I received a letter from her within
a month after reaching home.   She had been learning
to make thin vests and coats, she wrote, from a widow
woman and her daughter, to whom she had given their
board in return for instructions received.   She understood her *trade* (the word she underlined, as though I
were somehow to blame for her being forced to apply
it to herself.) perfectly, and could obtain plenty of work
from the shops.   The only trouble was she could not
sew rapidly enough by hand to compete with those who,
by the help of sewing-machines, could stitch up seams
in as many minutes as it took her hours to do with her
needle.   If she only had some friend of whom she could
borrow fifty dollars to purchase one of these invaluable
assistants to female toil, she trusted soon to be able to
repay what she owed me with interest.   She actually
proposed selling her watch to raise the needful sum, as,
she said, a poor person could get along without the time
of day, but the means of gaining a subsistence were in-
dispensable.   In reply, I ordered one of Ladd & Web-
ster's machines to be boxed up and sent to her, hoping
it would bind her over to keep the peace for ever after.
It didn't answer the purpose long.   The next letter I received was such a high-flown mess of rodomontade
that I couldn't for the life of me make out what the
woman was driving at.   She talked of inspiration, and
the soul of art ; of low. grovelling natures, that had no
affinity with those goaded on in an erratic, comet-like

orbit of eccentric course by the divine afflatus baser spirits could never fathom or comprehend. Then she had lots to say of Michael Angelo, and several other old painters who died years ago; and I concluded, as she didn't see fit to explain her purposes in an intelligible manner, to go on to Troy myself, and see what new hobby the widow had started off on this time.

"To Troy I went; and the instant the slipshod servant girl admitted me, I was conscious of the same aspect of untidy discomfort that had always somehow pervaded Gregory's home. The entry smelled of frying-pans and rancid gravy drippings, and the curtains of the room into which I was shown were yellow and dingy, the carpet ragged and soiled, and the filthy table-cloth furnishing entertainment for ravenous squads of vagrant flies. I was kept waiting half an hour, and then such a figure as presented itself to my astonished view! Wearing a nondescript article of calico attire—a cross, I should say, between a tunic and a dressing-gown—over grey flannel trousers, red velvet slippers with pointed toes, and on its head a blue cloth cap trimmed with tinsel."

"Had the poor creature really lost her senses?" asked Minnie, with apparent interest.

"It is my impression that she never had any to lose," was the cool rejoinder. "There were some rough sketches done on Bristol board, the glasses kept in place over them by a binding of brown paper, hanging against the walls; and, to show a becoming interest in all that pertained to my charming relative, I asked if they were little Lucy's handiwork. 'By no means,' said the widow, tart as a snapdragon; 'a mere child like her could no more comprehend the mysteries involved in the study and composition of high-art productions like these, than a sign painter could illuminate an ancient missal?' 'Are they crayons?' asked I. 'Monochromes,' replied

she; and offered to take them down for my closer inspection. I objected to putting her to the trouble, for I
had had enough of the wretched daubs; but as she had
made up her mind that I was to pass critical judgment
on them, pass judgment I did, to the best of my ability.
'This,' said she, 'is Poudalinne, a lovely peasant-girl of
Bretagne. Did you ever see such hands on a living
person?' 'Never,' said I; 'but I have seen them wonderfully like on the wooden dolls I used to buy little
Lucy.' She snatched away the portrait, and put another
in its place. 'This,' she explained, 'is Medora, watching, by night, the return, which will not happen in time
for her to see it, of the bandit chief who is her lord. See
how picturesquely her long floating hair streams out on
the pinions of the passing breeze!' 'It seems to be in
a dreadful snarl,' said I, 'and she will tear it half out
by the roots before she ever gets a fine-toothed comb
through it.' 'Don't, I entreat,' said she (not Medora,
but the widow), 'take views so prosaic of incarnation so
poetical. A work of art is to be looked at in an ideal
light, don't you perceive?' 'Not exactly,' said I; 'I
take things as they come, and if the light in which a
picture is placed comes through dingy, floppy curtains,
I can't alter the fact, as I see.' She gave me a look that
didn't seem quite friendly as she whisked Medora off my
knee, and put a female who seemed on the point of
going raving distracted in her place. 'Of what does
this remind you?' asked Cousin Lucy, drawing herself
up with something of the old tragedy air. 'Of a woman
with a dislocated neck,' I answered, 'her head is so
twisted over the left shoulder.' To my surprise, Mrs.
Sears seemed rather pleased at my reply. 'I thought,'
said she, 'that the subject of this monochrome had been
so faithfully and vigorously treated that it would provoke
you into the betrayal of some strong emotion, either of
admiration or repugnance—the latter, perhaps, being ·

the more appropriate tribute to the power of the artist, who wrought out this female figure as an impersonation of Horror. Examine the lineaments more closely; isn't every feature instinct with that passion that curdles our blood and makes our flesh creep?' . 'Ten times more natural than life,' said I; 'the figure really seems as though it might step forth, in actual bodily presence, and use those sharp finger-nails to evil purpose.' Then I seriously advised their exhibiter to throw the ugly-visaged harpies amongst the rubbish to which they rightfully belonged, and offered to send her on some really well-executed engravings from my own collection. Instead of appearing pleased at my proposed gift, she put her handkerchief to her eyes and threatened me with a lachrymal shower, which I dreaded above all things. I thought I would try the effect of a compliment, by way of averting the impending storm. 'Have your own portrait and that of your child taken,' I suggested ; 'for why should your walls be disfigured by these scrawny, hollow-eyed ogresses, when beauty and grace are so handy for portrayal ?'

"She caught the bait readily ; said that her good looks were nothing to her now that the only eyes she cared to please were closed forever; that she did not expect me to approve the new project she was most anxious to carry out. I had never appreciated poor Gregory's talents, and she had no reason to hope for a greater display of leniency toward her own. I begged her to explain her project at once ; and she told me that she found needlework a most irksome employ-ment, and would much prefer painting pictures instead. I asked if the sewing-machine had not worked well, and she confessed that she never could learn to manage it so as not to waste thread, crook needles, skip stitches, and make such fringed seams that the shopkeepers found fault with her work and refused to employ her. 'My

heart was not in my task,' said she; 'but, in bodying
forth, with the pencil's magic touch, the ideal creations
of my husband's lofty genius, I shall find active call for
all my higher faculties. In the first place, however, it
will be necessary to go through a regular course of instruction. I would like to take lessons of Madame de
Friponne—forty dollars a quarter is her price for tuition
—who sometimes sells a single painting as high as three
hundred dollars, and earns a handsome support by her
art. If you will lend me a helping hand now, at the
outset of my new career, you shall be repaid out of the
first profits it brings me in.' Of course, I was delighted
to comply with a request holding out such tempting
prospect of a rich return ; so I became responsible for
the painting lessons, and only heard occasionally from
the artist for the two succeeding years.

" At the end of that time, business calling me on to
New York, I went a little out of my way to call on the
widow. While several blocks distant I heard the rattle
of piano-keys from Mrs. Sears' sitting-room, mingling
with two voices, tenor and treble, according with about
the effect one would naturally expect from a hurdy-
gurdy and a corn-stalk fiddle playing in concert. I
found a foreign-looking man with thin, sharp features,
an eye like a live coal, and long, black hair, parted in the
middle, acting as grand performer in the instrumental
accompaniment to this concatenation of sweet sounds.
The widow, too, seemed quite rejuvenated, with frills
to her gown, shamrock bracelets on her arms, and all
sorts of odds and ends on her head. The music stopped
on my entrance, and the long-haired pianist, with a
profusion of smiles and gestures, bowed himself out of
the room. 'Who is that fellow?' I asked. 'That gentleman,' replied Mrs. Sears, with severe dignity, 'is Professor Anglocini, my music-teacher, and this piano is
his. His charges for instruction—none but the first.

families can afford to employ him—are usually considered exorbitant; but out of regard to my reduced circumstances, he has treated me with the utmost liberality. I may say that my lessons actually cost me nothing, as it is very little more trouble to cook and lay the table for three than for two; and I only give him his board in return for his invaluable services.' 'But who provides the means for furnishing household supplies?' I asked, confounded at her cool way of stating the case; and inclined to the belief that, instead of being the shallow innocent I had taken her for, she was about as long-headed a schemer as a man could well have to deal with. 'Thank you,' said she, 'for reminding me of a subject about which I have been very anxious to consult you. These vulgar trades-people have become so insolent and pressing in their demands, that I most earnestly beseech of you to find some means of relieving me from their persecutions. You cannot imagine how excessively annoying it is to a woman of refined sensibilities to be waylaid and accosted in the street by a clamorous dun. I have suffered more in this way than I can possibly describe to you. Only think of it—I had planned a cosy little dinner-party, simple soups, birds, sherbet, sangaree, ices, and fruits. in honor of the arrival of some distinguished Italians, friends of the Professor. I had my best gilt dinner service, a birthday gift from my lamented Gregory, with the silver-plate hired for the occasion, on the side-board, when who should make his appearance, with a bill as long as your arm, but the provision dealer round the corner. He was very civil and smooth-tongued, so was I, and thought I had smoothed down his ruffled plumes; but conceive my overpowering resentment, when the heartless wretch had the unparelleled effrontery to come back with an officer, and march off with plate, dinner-set, and all. Of course, the owner of the silver looked out for his property, but my gilt service was gone forever ; and no one can imagine the intensity of my mortification in being obliged to pass soup to a gentleman so thoroughly accustomed as is the Professor to the formula of well-bred observance, in a bowl, with latten spoon as accompaniment.'

" Instead of attending to her twaddling prate, I inquired how much and how many she owed, and found I had some pretty heavy bills to pay on her account. I paid them, there was nothing else to be done, since I had undertaken the burden of their support ; but I had no idea of being almoner to a pack of make-shift foreigners, who got their living by their wits. My sweet cousin abused me like a pickpocket when I proposed removing her to a cheap boarding-house ; declaring that she should have nothing left worth living for, if I interrupted her in the prosecution of her musical studies. I told her they would soon get to be an old story with her, and she would tire of them as she had of making pictures. No, she said ; painting she had been forced to resign because she found it was seriously impairing her eyesight, while the odors of the colors was undermining her health ; but to music she was deeply anxious to devote herself for the sake of her child. Little Lucy had an aptitude for rhythm and vocalization, which, if properly cultivated, she might one day turn to good account. ' My constitution,' pathetically stated Gregory's well-preserved relict, ' has been so shattered by repeated blows of misfortune that I am unfitted for continuous effort, and can look forward to nothing better than becoming a useless cumberer of the ground, a burden upon society at large, perhaps, if the friends in whom I may have vainly trusted should prove false in this my hour of sorest need. Having nothing further to hope for myself in this weary world, I would devote the declining remnant of my days to the task of so developing my daughter's talents, as to make them best contribute to her own maintenance, thus sparing her that galling sense of dependence which is, and must continue to be, the blight and bane of my existence.'

"There is gratitude for you; she would graciously condescend to accept from me the means of support, all the while petulantly bemoaning the hard fate which had subjected her to the humiliation of submitting to obligation so unwelcome. Obligation, did I say? she felt nothing of the kind. She was one of those essentially selfish persons to whom you may give ninety-nine times without any shadow of return; but, refrain from giving the one hundredth, and see what a crop of enmity your favors will have sown for your own special reaping."

"You have spoken thus far only of the mother," suggested Minnie, with slightly rising color, "while it is the daughter of whom I am most curious to hear."

"I saw very little of the child during her mother's lifetime, but when Mrs. Sears went off in a rapid decline, I was left with an awkward responsibility on my hands, considering my bachelor estate. What was I to do with a pretty, petted, wilful, attractive girl of fifteen? I asked the question a great many times, always failing to gain any satisfactory reply."

"Then she was quite a charming person, this young Miss?" interrogatively suggested Minnie, the slight quiver of the muscles about the mouth betraying the anxiety with which she awaited his response.

"I do not know how she seemed to others. To me, her lively flow of spirits, her disposition to make the best of everything, even her harmless little affectations of a spite and malice it was not in her gentle nature really to entertain, afforded me an unfailing fund of amusement, and kept the old house from knowing a dull moment while she was in it."

3

"To what house do you allude?" asked Minnie, with an air of cold restraint.

"To the old family mansion in Orland Park, where my mother had kindly consented to receive the orphan, and superintend the progress of her education, which had been sadly neglected, so I was told. Lucy would have got along well enough at the Park, if she had had only my mother to deal with; but my stately, punctilious sisters were bent on disliking my ward from the first, and reproved, brow-beat, and lectured the poor child till she hadn't a minute's peace of her life. They were pinks of propriety, bound up in rigid conventionalisms which no earthly motive could have induced them to overstep; she danced, and sang, and laughed, and chatted in utter defiance of those stringent rules of etiquette which were their law and gospel. I was at my wits' ends, trying to steer a clear course between the two factions. There were never-ending complaints of her unformed manners and peculiar ways, which I did not much mind so long as Lucy kept up good heart and showed no signs of falling a victim to this petty tyranny."

"What did they see in her behavior to provoke such repeated censures?" Minnie curiously inquired.

"Nothing worthy of death or of stripes, so far as I could make out," was the careless rejoinder. "She loved pleasure better than study, which was natural enough at her age and with her cheerful temperament, and hid 'Jane Eyre' and 'My Novel' under her French exercises, reading the stories by stealth. When practising at the piano, she would slip aside her 'Zauberflote,' or some operatic gem, and rattle off some noisy reel or hornpipe, winding up, perhaps, with 'Sweet Youth of Lochrain,' and 'Peggy on her old Black Cart.' Then she had a habit, when she came in from a walk, of tossing her hat into one chair, her scarf into a second, and her gloves and parasol into a third, giving the room an appearance of disorder which Dian couldn't tolerate. She had a fancy, too, for running into the neighbors, bareheaded, and with bare arms and shoulders, and for singing on the balcony, which my sisters insisted that she did solely for the purpose of attracting attention from passers by. She chatted at the area gate with the ice man, the dirt-boy, or anybody else who would give her back a pleasant word or smile, and horrified Dian by tossing forget-me-nots to her music-master, and playing polkas on a jews-harp for the servants to dance by in the kitchen. None of these were legally indictable offences, you perceive, but they shocked my sisters' sense of decorum, until they declared that my ward, as they persisted in calling Lucy, was so hoydenish and underbred that she was scarcely presentable to persons of ordinary refinement. They began to treat her with cold, stinging slight and neglect. When she opened the piano, they retreated to the most distant part of the house, as if to avoid its sound. She was requested to study in her own dressing-room, and was rarely sent for to meet any of their visitors. If a pleasure excursion were planned, she was never asked to make one of the party. When they went out for a drive, she was not offered a seat in the carriage. In a thousand ways she was made to feel that she was an unwelcome interloper, who had no rightful or recognized place in the household.

"Business called me to Liverpool. When told that I must leave her for a time, the poor girl cried as though her heart would break, and begged to go with me. Compliance with such a request was simply out of the question, and I told her so. She readily acquiesced in my decision; she never was one of your self-willed vixens, bent on carrying their own purposes at all hazards—at least she never attempted to thwart any plan of mine.

"I was away from home two months, and on my return I noticed a great change in Lucy Sears. She had grown quiet, reserved, womanly. She was not looking well either, and her eyes showed frequent traces of weeping, but she made no complaints. My sisters treated her with the same studious coldness as heretofore ; but she betrayed no token of annoyance at their undisguised antipathy. I resolved to send her away to boarding-school. I supposed she would be delighted at this arrangement ; but, to my surprise, she entreated to remain where she was. 'I will not get in your sisters' way,' she said, with a humility that touched me to the quick, 'if you will let me stay ; but pray do not send me quite away from the only friend and benefactor I have in the world.' It was a hard case for the lonely orphan to be sent amongst entire strangers ; wasn't it, Miss Brandon ?"

"Very hard," she returned, in her most frigid manner, " when she seemed to have been so warmly attached to her guardian."

"It was no more than natural, when he was the only person to whom she could turn for kindness or comfort," admitted unsuspecting Mr. Caruthers. "After this implied admission of a preference so flattering, I was necessarily bound, as a man of honor, to remove her from an influence which might become too powerful for her to resist, and so wreck her happiness without the least fault committed on her part."

Minnie flashed at him a glance of anxious, troubled inquiry, which he was too much absorbed in his own reminiscences to observe.

"I was firmly convinced that, for her own sake, she must go. I wrote to the principal of a seminary, and arranged terms for her board and tuition ; but when I saw how Lucy grieved over the prospect of our immediate separation, I exerted myself to the utmost to relieve her despondency. 'Keep up good courage,' said

I, 'study hard, perfect yourself in all the modern accomplishments, attend carefully to the precept and example you doubtless will receive, in grace of manner and elegant ease of address, which I lack, but which the future Mrs. Caruthers must not be deficient in.' Was I to blame that she put a construction on my words they were never intended to convey? She took it for granted that there was some sort of tacit understanding between us; and as I could not, without a gross violation of all rules of gallantry, humiliate and mortify her by explaining and correcting her mistake, there was nothing left for me but to humor it as best I might, trusting to time to unravel the tangled web of fate."

" Leaving her in the meantime to the fancied security of a false trust, which absence might but strengthen !— was not this a cruel kindness, Mr. Caruthers?"

" Absence was quite as likely to efface all remembrance of the youthful attachment she had so unguardedly betrayed; and that would have put matters all right at once."

Minnie's cheek flushed and paled as she ventured her next suggestion : "Then your own feelings were not in any way involved in the result of this experiment you were trying on those of your ward."

" I beg your pardon, Miss Brandon ; I am a plain man, and like plain speaking. I do not quite catch the drift of your last remark."

" I mean that—if the regard you had reason to suppose this inexperienced girl entertained for you stood the test of time and absence, what course would you have adopted in such contingency ? Would you have awakened her abruptly from her dearly-cherished delusion? or would you have fulfilled the expectations you knew your words had raised ?"

"That would have depended on circumstances," he replied, with an air of careless indifference.

"I am not to be thus easily baffled," thought his fair querist, both cheek and eye brilliantly aglow.

"In what circumstances?" she dauntlessly persisted.

"I am quite unable to tell, as they never occurred," he curtly replied, somewhat irritated by her pertinacity. "I have spoken of my own personal affairs much more freely than is my wont, in order that you might know, if any exaggerated rumors concerning the subject that I have been explaining—to your satisfaction, I hope—should reach you, exactly how much and how little credence to give them. I dare say there was no occasion for my raking up the past in this fashion; but I always aim to have every transaction of mine open and above board. Let those who will, stoop to trick and chicanery, it is not my way."

———•◆•———

CHAPTER IV.

GATHERING CLOUDS.

It was with a heavy, depressing weight on her spirits that Minnie Brandon returned to the cottage. The lurking demon of doubt had crept into the pure Eden of her faith; left its trail on the sweet lilies of her trust; tainted all the odor-laden air with its pestilent breath.

She sat down at the open window, heeding nothing of the sights and sounds passing about her, every faculty of her being concentrated in the effort of recalling every word, tone and look accompanying the recent conversation between herself and Mr. Caruthers. The entrance of her father with a couple of letters, one directed to herself, disturbed her profitless musings. With languid,

listless air, she broke the seal to her epistle, unfolding a
closely-written sheet of note-paper, presenting, when
held at a little distance, the appearance of a most delicate and elegant specimen of chirography, but proving,
on closer inspection, very difficult of decipherment.
Thus its contents ran :

"Miss Brandon :—I have a very serious reason for
penning you these few lines, which I have lain awake all
night thinking over, hoping you will excuse the liberty,
as I am not acquainted with you, and never, to my
knowledge, so much as laid eyes on your face. But for
all that, I have something to say to you that ought to be
said, and the sooner it is over with the better for all our
sakes. I consider it my solemn duty to warn you against
placing your affections upon Mr. Caruthers ; and if you
don't heed my warning, there is no telling where the mischief will stop ; for I am very resolute and determined
when once I set about a thing, and I shall leave no stone
unturned to defeat the machinations set on foot to sunder
the ties binding me to my affianced lover. You had better give him up of your own accord, otherwise he will
be taken out of your toils in a way that will make no
end of gossip and scandal. I send you this note, hoping
that mild measures may serve my purpose ; but despise
these, and set me at bay, if you dare ; I have no fear of
being worsted in the end.

"Excuse me, I did not mean to threaten you ; let me
state facts, and you will see that my claim on Mr. Caruthers is older and more firmly established than yours.
Our engagement has lasted three years, and is at this
moment as binding as ever it was. Our wedding-day
was appointed last autumn ; but, an unavoidable cause,
that could neither be foreseen nor prevented, occurred
to postpone it—only to postpone it, mark you—and I
haven't a shadow of doubt that fate will prove more
propitious when the appointment is renewed.

"That was a terrible evening for me when I looked through the lace-curtained window, where the blind was not quite drawn down, and saw him doing the honors of his splendid new house with such a grand and lofty air, knowing, as I did, that my rightful place was by his side. I felt better when he told me that he didn't know I was in the city; as, indeed, he didn't; for I had not apprised him of my coming, fearing he would oppose it, and so frustrate my purpose of being near him. I have no intention of returning to Troy, although he strongly urges my doing so, as he thinks I should be safer there than here, until these war-clouds blow over. I am willing to run all that sort of risk for the sake of the delightful society he so kindly devotes to my entertainment. I ride out with him every day, and not an evening passes without my seeing him.

"I close by warning you, afresh, to beware of striving to beguile my promised husband away from the true and faithful allegiance he owes to me. Even if your arts did in some sort succeed, the day that brought you such success would be an evil day for you. We are strangers now; Heaven grant that we remain so; we could never meet as friends. I do not sign my name, not because I am ashamed of it, but because you would be none the wiser for reading such signature."

Minnie folded this strangely worded epistle, with a look of added perplexity on her troubled face. Her suspicions pointed at once to Lucy Sears as the writer, and she carefully noted and compared several striking coincidences between Mr. Caruthers' confession and that conveyed to her in epistolary form. "He can find plenty of time to devote to her, while to me his visits are of the briefest," she said to herself with untold bitterness.

"You have bad news, I fear," said Mr. Brandon, with mild solicitude.

"Not exactly news," she returned, with wearily dejected air, "at least, I hesitate to receive it as such
until I know who sends it. I shall make every effort in
my power to ascertain the truth or falsehood of the
accusations contained in this anonymous letter; if they
be false, I will do injustice to no one by repeating them
—if true, you shall know all if I have the heart to tell
you."

"An anonymous letter," repeated Mr. Brandon; "the
most contemptible mode of sending barbed shafts from
hidden shelter that was ever invented. Depend upon
it that the writer who sends accusations he has not the
manhood to substantiate by his real signature, has no
very creditable motives for withholding the same. Do
not give yourself a moment's uneasiness from cause so
entirely undeserving of notice. I have news more re-
liable which will call me away to Chicago for a few
days. But with marauding parties ready to start up at
every turn, I dare not leave you here, with only old
Chloe as protector. Perhaps you would like to pass the
time of my absence with the Caruthers." She shook
her head.

"Miss Dian is housekeeper for her brother, at present,
and nothing would induce me to take any step that
might be construed into the appearance even of an
attempt on my part to court his society. Leave me, if
you please, with my mother's cousins, Miss Honour and
Wilhelmine Courcelle."

"Two single women, all by themselves; not much
safer than leaving you here."

"They are such bold, resolute, self-reliant persons that
I shall have no fears with them; besides, their house is
so far from any ordinary line of travel that it is not
likely to be molested. My casket of jewelry I shall
carry to Mr. Caruthers, requesting him to lock it up in
the safe with his plate."

2*

"Why not put it in the blind closet leading from the cellar-arch? M. Moellon designed that hidden recess specially as a place in which to secrete his valuables."

"In case of fire my casket would be lost. I would rather leave it as I first proposed."

One reason for her persistence in this plan was, that she had resolved on showing the letter which had so deeply disquieted her to Mr. Caruthers, watching the expression of his face while he read the missive, and drawing therefrom her own conclusions as to the truth or falsity of these anonymous revelations. "Let me but know the worst," she said to herself, "and I will call up my best fortitude to meet it; but this wretched state of uncertainty and suspense I will not submit to a moment longer than is absolutely necessary."

On reaching the door of the mansion from which she had last issued in mood of festal mirth, she was permitted by the servant, who recognized his prospective mistress, to pass directly to Miss Dian's dressing-room, where the latter, before a tall Psyche glass, was, with minutest care, arranging the folds of her robe to more harmonious flow. Her brother was out of town, she said, and readily agreed to take charge of the casket until his return. When Minnie started for home the former accompanied her for a short walk. Up the broad thoroughfare, down which their promenade extended, dashed a pair of spirited bays, whose driver was in the thoughts of both pedestrians. Minnie caught sight of a fair smiling face shaded by drooping blue feathers, as her companion tried to hurry her beneath an ivy-covered archway. The young girl maintained her ground resolutely.

"If you know, Miss Caruthers, the lady driving with your brother, please to tell me who she is."

Miss Dian hesitated, scarcely knowing what reply it would be most desirable to make.

"I already have her name," desperately ventured Minnie; "I merely wish to know the estimation in which you hold her. Your brother seems to consider her a very charming person, whom I could not fail to like on acquaintance.

"There is where he and I differ," asserted Miss Dian, with warmth. "Lucy Sears is a pretty-faced, soft-mannered, selfish shallow-pate, gifted with the same sort of cunning as other inferior animals. I cannot deny that she can be very amiable—when it suits her purpose. It suits her purpose to be all honey and sweetness to my brother, and so she always wears velvet gloves for him. He thinks it is for him alone her blandishments are exerted. Fool! I have seen her put on as many airs and graces to fascinate the music-master Kilby paid for flirting with her; at least, that was the main accomplishment she acquired from him. Strange how much sooner even men of sense, in other matters, take to a pretty simpering woman than to one who knows enough to conduct herself like a responsible human being."

"Did Mr. Caruthers ever make her direct proposals of marriage?" abruptly asked Minnie.

"Heavens! don't startle me with such a preposterous suggestion. What sort of a figure would she cut in a family like ours? Absurd! incredible! Never allude to the possibility of such an occurrence again if you do not wish to seriously offend me. Her silly chatter amuses him, that is all. Come back and remain with me while your father is away, and we will make the house so gay and lively that all outside attractions shall pale in comparison."

"I am in no mirthful mood," pleaded Minnie; "I cannot come."

"Not when it is to rescue Kilby from the arts of an unscrupulous schemer, who will leave no means untried to bind him to her interests?"

"Not even for that. Mr. Caruthers is old enough to
know his own mind, and to act upon such knowledge.
He has the right to select the society most congenial to
him; if that does not happen to be mine, there is no
help for it. As to stooping to court the attention he sees
fit to bestow on another, nothing would induce me to
adopt a course so derogatory to my own dignity and
self-respect."

"The love cannot be very strong that can thus easily
be overmastered by pride."

Forbearing all reply to the covert reproach conveyed
through these words, Minnie took brief leave of her companion, and, with an air of unruffled composure, proceeded on her way. It was not until her feet once more
pressed the greensward a considerable distance outside
the city's limits, that she gave free scope to the bitter
tears wrung forth by mortified pride and slighted regard.
It was only for a brief space that she groped her way
along, half blinded by passionate weeping, half choked
by stifling sobs, then, drying her eyes, her step grew
firm and her look composed, as she said to herself, "It
is better to suffer through another's wrong-doing than
through one's own—to be sinned against than sinning.
My father was right when he said that no one whose
conscience rose not up in accusation against him could
experience the deepest wretchedness of human woe."
Before reaching home, she had overcome every trace of
emotion; but an acute observer might have remarked
that in her whole air was a tinge of unusual sadness,
marked by an added expression of gentle deference toward the parent she revered.

When tea was over, she proposed reading aloud to
him, and, with a look of gratified expectancy, he threw
himself on the couch, prepared to listen. From the
works of the grand old masters of English song, lining
the book-case, she took down volume after volume, cull-

ing extracts here and there as fancy prompted—
extracts, by some subtle instinct chosen, permeated
through and through by plaintive outgush of human
grief from some chastened soul, striving in vain yearn-
ing to soar upward on wings of finite melody, if, haply,
it may catch but faintest echoes from those infinite har-
monics to whose entrancing strains earthly perceptions
are sealed for all time. Unconsciously she read these
outpourings of a sorrow which none can escape, but not
all can express, with a depth of feeling, an earnestness
of appreciation, which attracted her father's notice.
Raising himself on his elbow, he closely scanned the
reader's face.

"Something must have gone seriously wrong with
her," thought he; "it is only through afflictions of our
own that we learn to enter, heart and soul, into those of
others."

She paused, gravely thoughtful, as she finished the
perusal of Hood's "Song of a Shirt," quietly remarking,
"It must be most wearing, wearisome effort, the ill-paid
drudgery, the never-ending toil by which the poor
needlewoman, by slow stitches, earns the scant pittance
that keeps body and soul together; but the heart may
be heavy with its own bitterness where no physical want
is known."

"Life, you will learn, Minnie, as you know more
of it, is no holiday gift to even its most favored possessor. We must all fight the good fight of faith with
the evil that is within us as well as without. Our
spiritual weapons are to be kept bright by constant war-
fare with the sins that do so easily beset us; and yet, in
the midst of the conflict we must daily wage, we have
also to watch narrowly, lest, in such strife, we sacrifice
all the sweet charities of life—the meekness, patience,
and long-suffering which would lead us to bless even our
enemies, and to minister unto their needs, if sick or in

prison, even though we may have been the chosen instruments for inflicting on them God's vengeance for wicked misdeeds."

" If I ever learn to be patient and tolerant like yourself, it will be through much tribulation," Minnie frankly admitted ; " at present, any sort of treachery or double-dealing rouses in me the most unqualified resentment."

He waited for her to proceed ; but, fearing that some unguarded word might betray the secret source of her uneasiness, she remained persistently silent.

With undefined purpose of fathoming the motive for her reserve, he asked, " Did you see Mr. Caruthers to-day ?"

" Not to speak with him?" was the laconic reply.

" How did it come to pass that you met without speaking to him ?"

" It is not easy to call out from a crowded side-walk to a gentleman driving up a thronged street," returned Minnie, with a disingenuousness for which she heartily despised herself.

The sound of wheels on the carriage-sweep outside sent a rosy flush to her cheek. Had Mr. Caruthers, on learning of her father's contemplated journey from his sister, come to urge her remaining with them during his absence ? Chloe opened the door to admit a small boy with bill for repairing hay-cutter. Sick at heart from effect of chimerical fancy, as unsubstantial as bursting bubble or evanescent rainbow tint, Minnie stole away to her own room, hoping in sleep to lose the aching sense of unrest she could not otherwise hope to escape.

Next morning there was a little flutter of expectancy in her manner as she glanced toward the road at the sound of every vehicle that chanced to pass ; but as noontide drew near, and she gradually settled into the conviction that he would suffer her to depart without any attempt at explanation or leave-taking, a look of unwonted pride and resolve stamped itself on features generally a reflex to all kindly and gentle emotions.

Throughout the long drive conveying her to the temporary place of abode she had chosen, she maintained an almost unbroken silence. Her father, noticing her abstraction, soon desisted from all efforts at conversation, saying to himself, "She must work out life's problem in her own way. Heaven help her; I can't. It is the human lot to learn wisdom through no teacher save hard experience."

Not thus forbearing those two notable housewives and sagacious managers of ploughing and planting, sowing and reaping, Miss Honour and Wilhelmine Courcelle, who would have scorned to claim protection from any living being, deeming themselves fully equal to the task of asserting and maintaining their rights, as well as redressing their wrongs. Industrious, frugal, indomitable of will, with decided opinions of their own, which they were not at all backward in promulgating, in season or out of season, any indulgence of sentiment was likely to meet but scant favor from the elderly, matter-of-fact spinsters. Jealous of any innovations upon the customs which had descended to them with their estate from their immediate ancestors, no carpets covered their well-waxed floors, no modern furniture was permitted to oust from their time-honored places the comfortless oaken chairs and leather-covered benches, and no fresh print disputed possession with the wretchedly-executed family portraits staring woodenly from the walls. Stanch Unionists, their sharp-tongued assaults on those inclined to sympathize with the insurgents won them enemies by the score. Perhaps a glance at the well-thumbed contents of their book-shelves may give a more accurate impression of their mental habitudes than could be otherwise conveyed in form as concise. Here is the "Bee-Keeper's Manual," "Hints for Rearing Young

Stock," "Every Man his own Veterinarian," "Insects injurious to Vegetation," "Fertilizers best adapted to different Soils," "Notes on the Use of Nitrates and Ammonia in Agriculture," "Essay on Irrigation," "Directions for Grape-culture," "The Horticulturist," "A Treatise on Political Economy," "Condition of the Laboring-Classes in Great Britain." "Monarchy, Autocracy, and Democracy," "Spitalfields Weavers and Cornwall Miners," "Statistics of English Domestic Service," "Prince Albert's Address to the Servants' Provident Society."

It will be perceived by this brief glance at the Misses Courcelles' supply of reading material, how eminently utilitarian the taste directing their studies. Minnie was not long suffered to remain idle. "Come, and make this yeast with your own hands," directed Miss Honour, "that you may know how to impart to a servant, if need be, so useful a piece of information. It is well for the mistress of a household to understand all these things, even if she has not so much as to turn the silver faucet supplying her daily bath. We wait upon ourselves from choice; but we know what it is to be served like ladies—to be perfumed in fine laces and brocade, with one servant to fan away the heat and another to brush away the flies—we know what it isn't, too; it isn't good for low spirits or dyspepsia; so we harden our hands, bronze our faces, strengthen our muscles, and lengthen our lives by wholesome toil. Who questions the wisdom of our course?"

"Why make us out worse than we are?" asked Wilhelmine. "Why not confess that, in all this pinching and saving, we act from a higher motive than any which could arise from mere personal aims?"

"As Minnie's mother was a Courcelle, it may not be amiss to comply with your suggestion," returned Miss Honour, with dignity. "It was my father's life-long

desire to manumit his slaves; but as most of them came
to him by way of dower with our mother, there were
unsurmountable obstacles in the way of his carrying
out his purpose; which he died bequeathing to us. His
intentions we could easily have fulfilled by disposing of
this place; but could we let Pré-Fleuri, which our great
grandfathers made to bud and blossom as the rose,
pass into the hands of strangers? Not if any means of
ours could prevent it. Pré-Fleuri, without the curtail-
ment of a single acre, shall be handed down to our
nephew Falkland Courcelle, the only male survivor
bearing the family name. God willing, we will also
leave our servants free, and with some provision for the
future; if they would only work half as hard as we do,
this might easily be effected; but they would rather
take their ease when they can get it, living from hand
to mouth, than to lay up store for the rainy day, which
they never think of so long as the sun shines. Now,
there's Jim, weighs two hundred, and is tough as a
rhinoceros; with the exception of what I lay out for
his clothes, I promised him the whole of his wages to
put by as a fund to accumulate for the support of his
wife and children. I thought the idea of working for
himself would spur him on to make the most of his
opportunities, but he is less diligent and faithful in
others' employ than he was in ours. I have often asked
myself if generations of forced servitude have destroyed
all tendency to thrift and self-reliance in many of our
colored population; if they have been so long habituated
to look to a master for the supply of all their wants that
they are no longer animated by a desire for freedom
and the means of obtaining an independent support
sufficiently strong to make them put forth their best energies to grasp the same.

"I hardly think this can be so, for why did Prince
Albert, of blessed memory, deliver an address, in which

he declared 'the largest of all the classes of her majesty's subjects in England is the class of domestic servants,' to the 'Servants' Provident Society,' if they had not needed stringent reminder of the duty of making suitable provision for their declining years? That they do not make such provision is proved by the fact that a majority of their number look forward to nothing better than an old age of pauperism, with the almshouse, perhaps, as final place of refuge when their laboring days are over. None of my people must ever be allowed to sink into a state of beggary and destitution like that."

" What do you want, sir ?"

This curt interrogatory was addressed to a cadaverous looking individual, seedy and threadbare of garb, slouching of gait, scowling of brow, and repellant of mien, who had approached unseen, and paused outside the window.

" Something to eat," was the equally curt rejoinder.

" Why should an able-bodied man like you beg, when our quota is not made up, and Government needs every arm that can be raised in its defence ?"

" I sprained my ankle by a fall three days ago, all that time I have spent dragging myself thus far toward home.   Give me a piece of bread or I shall faint with hunger by the wayside."

" Isn't that the rebel uniform you have on ?"

" I scorn to deny my colors ; I am heart and hand with the cause of our young republic."

" Then, go starve; or get your bread from the traitors you serve."

" Beware, madam, beware."

" Beware of what, insolent vagabond ?"

" Beware of turning a famishing man empty-handed from your door ; beware of the heavy curse with which he would repay the pittance withheld from his sore necessities."

"Do give him something, Cousin Honour," intreated Minnie, with troubled, anxious look.

"Not a crust," was the inflexible rejoinder, "will I bestow on one who has served in this wicked and causeless rebellion."

With a fierce malediction the man turned away.

"I would not like to have any one give me a look like that," said Minnie, with an air of extreme discomposure.

"I've learned not to be scared before I'm hurt," was the indifferent reply. "The fellow has enough to do looking out for his own forage without seeking to do me an ill turn."

The speaker left the room on household cares intent. Looking from the window, Minnie saw the stranger pick up a cob, on which a few kernels of corn still remained, and crushing the same beneath the heavy hilt of his dirk, devour them with apparent voracity.

"He shall not go away with fierce hunger gnawing at his vitals, if I have to suffer myself to prevent it," thought she. "I know that nothing here is mine to bestow; but I can go without my dinner—that is mine while father pays my board—and without wronging any one, give the hungry man the benefit of my abstinence."

Hastening into the pantry, she hurriedly prepared some sandwiches, and adding to the same a slice of cheese and a strip of honeycomb, speedily overtook therewith the forlorn outcast. His rugged face softened as he accepted her simple offering, and while he lunched off the grassy mead, she folded a thick, impervious leaf, plucked from the velvet plant, into the form of a cup, and filling it from a running brook, presented it to her guest for the nonce. On resuming his walk he was pleased graciously to observe,

"If you should ever stand in need of a rebel's aid,

even though it should be mine—Lambeth, don't forget
the name—I hope it may be as freely given as that you
have rendered unto me."

When the dinner hour drew on, Minnie quietly saun-
tered forth for a walk, hoping by this means to avoid
the embarrassment of unwelcome questioning. On her
return she was met by Miss Honour with the tart injunction, "You must learn to be punctual at your
meals, or you won't fare very well while you are with
us; we never keep the table waiting for anybody."

"I am very glad, Cousin Honour, that you did not
break the rule on my account; when I am not punctual
at my meals, it is because I prefer going without them;
you are not to give yourself the least trouble on that
score, it would annoy me if you did."

Minnie spoke in a mild, even tone, as with air serene,
she commenced hemming a cambric band.   -

Miss Courcelle relented.

"My remark was merely intended as a caution for
the future," she said, deprecatingly; "living a life of
monotonous routine, my sister and I, it is but natural
that we should grow methodical in our habits, and for
the short time you are to remain with us, it will be
easier for you to conform to our ways than for us to
change them."

"Most certainly," assented Minnie, "I will endeavor
in all things to adapt myself to the mode of life most
agreeable to you."

"Spoken like the sensible girl you are; let the past
be overlooked; come out with me and get some dinner."

"I beg your pardon, Cousin Honour; but I have
already told you that if I had cared for my dinner I
should have been here at the appointed time."

"Are you sick, child?"

"Perfectly well, I thank you."

"You needn't thank me, there's no occasion; I never

knew a porcupine temper before amongst the Courcelles. Is your father an irascible sort of person?"

"My father is a gentleman," averred Minnie, with a slight show of resentment.

"And yet his daughter is so waspish that at a word of reproof she flies into a pet, and like a peevish, self-willed child balked of its whim, sulks and fasts the whole day long, and will be bought over to good behavior by nothing short of sugar-plums and penny trumpets."

"I assure you, once for all, that I am not in the least inclined to sulk; and as to my fasting, I have a reason for that which is perfectly satisfactory to me, but which I could scarcely explain to your satisfaction."

Miss Courcelle was not accustomed to being baffled and mystified in this way, and her ire rose accordingly. She descanted fluently on the social evils wrought by ill-judging almsgivers who encourage vagrancy and pauperism by their indiscriminate gifts, bestowed alike upon those who were ready to lay down life in their country's defence and those who were striving, by any means, fair or foul, to rend it asunder. Not that any of her strictures were addressed to Minnie, whose presence she studiously ignored, even at tea-table, failing to extend to her those little civilities ordinarily incident thereto. It was in sadly dejected mood that the weary girl betook herself to her room for the night.

As she sat with her head bowed on her hands, her reflections were far from inspiriting.

"I verily thought I was doing a good and charitable deed in practising an act of self-denial for the benefit of a famishing fellow-creature; but Honour has so confused my perceptions of goodness and mercy by persistently harping on the folly of encouraging vagrancy and the criminality of giving aid and comfort to the enemy, that I am half persuaded my conduct has been rather reprehensible than otherwise," pondered the bewildered girl.

"Good intentions are certainly meritorious, so far as they go, but there are so many ways of carrying them out! and if one happens to take a wrong one, or even a misstep in a right, down one plumps into the very depths of despair. If one could only do exactly as other folks do, it would be a great saving of perplexity, though it must be fearfully irksome and humdrum to be all trudging along together in the dusty, beaten highway, when the wild birds are singing, the cool dews sparkling, and the water voices rippling sweet, in the scented hedgerows hiding, mayhap, a thorn, to pierce over venturesome hand. How I have flattered myself that my intelligence was quite equal to that of the average of womankind; now, I incline to the belief that that opinion was nothing more than a snare and a delusion calculated to entrap me into the commission of all sorts of absurdities which I should have avoided if I had entertained a more moderate estimate of my own faculties. I have been simply wise in my own conceit; there is no blinking the fact, which won't become the more pleasant from fearing to look it full in the face. How sure I was that I had secured the strong, deathless regard that was to be my shield and safeguard for a lifetime—now I am sure of nothing save the unspeakably dreary present. Not a line have I received from Mr. Caruthers, not even so much as an inquiry after my welfare, since I came here, although our wedding-day is appointed, and my bridal robe, with its laces and flutings, lays half finished on my bed at home. Neglect is the portion meted out to me, devoted attention quite likely being reserved for another. I never exchanged words with Lucy Sears, but I feel capable of hating her desperately."

There was a light tap at the door, followed by the immediate entrance of Miss Courcelle.

"Here is a letter marked 'With dispatch,'" said she, "so I brought it you at once."

A brilliant glow flashed over Minnie's tell-tale face as she took the welcome missive, with the instantaneous conviction that it came from him who held her thoughts in sway. She could not read it with those cold, unsympathetic eyes upon her, ready to note every trifling change of expression. Finding she had nothing to gain by prolonging her stay, Miss Honour considerately terminated it. With beaming glance Minnie examined her letter's address, which was in the handwriting of her father. The first revulsion of thwarted expectancy chased the roses from her cheek, then she reproached herself bitterly for the filial ingratitude of which she had been guilty, in casting aside as of little worth, the loving-kindness which had crowned all her days with blessing, while remembering but too faithfully one who gave not faithful remembrance in response.

She broke the envelope with listless languor, possessing herself of the contents inclosed.

Mr. Brandon had been ill with a feverish cold, which had greatly aggravated the bronchial affection from which he had been long a sufferer. He had reached the city on his return journey, and would have driven out for her that afternoon, but fearing the effect of the chill night air, had concluded to wait until morning, when she might look for his early arrival.

Full of a tender compunction for the little thought she had bestowed during his absence on one who had watched over her own welfare with untiring solicitude, she retired to rest.

No sweet dreams soothed her light and broken slumbers. Men's hoarse voices, a woman's cry of distress, startled her from sleep unrestful; both voice and cry were real.

CHAPTER V.

NO RAY OF CHEER.

THE burning smart in her eyes on awakening, Minnie
at first assumed to be the result of having "cried herself to sleep;" but quickly became aware that her room
was rapidly filling with a dense smoke. Terror gave
speed to her movements as she hastily dressed herself.
Her chamber was in a wing at a rear angle of the house,
to the front of which she could only gain access by descending one flight of stairs and ascending a second.
She opened the door and stepped upon the landing,
caught a glimpse of the fiercely darting tongues of
hungry flame lapping the staircase mouldings, shut out
quickly the heavy suffocating volumes of smoke envelop-
ing her, and sought some safer mode of egress. Softly
raising a window commanding a partial view of the
main body of the dwelling, she saw a number of horses
tied to a railing near the barn; heard Miss Courcelle's
stifled cries for help, piteous appeals for mercy—cries
and appeals answered by cruel taunts and mocking,
brutal jibes that sent a creeping sensation to the roots
of her hair, filling her with an overpowering desire to
escape from those capable of utterance so revolting.
She could hear the loud bang of doors, the fall of heavy
footsteps below, and felt that there was no time to be
lost in effecting her retreat.

Closing the window as noiselessly as it had been
opened, she cautiously raised the one at the gable end
of the room, crept therefrom to the roof of a porch adjoining, reached the ground by aid of a grape trellis,
and was away on fleet step she knew not, scarcely cared
whither, if she might but evade detection, avoid pur-

suit. The sky was partially overcast; but the moon, occasionally emerging from its cloudy screen, gave sufficient light to prove that she was traversing the shortest and most direct path leading to the sparsely wooded upland slope where she hoped to find safe refuge until dawn, which could not be far off. She had soon more light than was at all desirable. The devouring flames had twined in fiery folds about the upper portions of the dwelling, towering heavenward in the majesty of resistless might, casting a lurid glare on objects far and near. Dreading discovery and capture above all else, she glanced eagerly about in search of a temporary hiding-place. Assuredly, near the place where she was standing, there was formerly a shepherd's hut; true, but its site was now blackened by a smouldering heap of ruins, and what had been its tenant hung dangling, a lifeless mass, from a lower limb of the Chickasaw plum-tree, which in life had been the old man's pride and delight.

A dilapidated sheep-pen afforded the covert she sought. Scarcely had she availed herself of its shelter, when a low, regular sound on the ground beside her added greatly to her alarm. More triumphantly leaped heavenward the earth-fed flames, illumining with more vivid glare all the landscape round. By this added light Minnie saw, with a shiver of terror, that she was standing beside the sleeping figure of a man wearing the Confederate uniform. She could even detect the outlines of his musket, the glitter of the unsheathed knife grasped in his hand.

With bated breath and cautious tread she stole from her transient place of shelter, and swiftly sped toward the wooded slope. The shades of night deepened about her; the roof of the burning house had fallen in, and the moon was veiled in a fleecy cloud. Hark! is it the sound of a footstep she hears in close pursuit? Trembling with fright, every nerve strung to its highest

4

pitch of intensity, every muscle strained to extremest effort, she paused not to ask herself if her pursuer might not be a phantom of her own overwrought fancy; but, without so much as turning her head over her shoulder to convince herself by sight that it was no hideous delusion inspiring her with vain terrors, she fled straight on toward the sanctuary she had first proposed to herself as a goal.

The wood is almost gained. Beneath the shelter of a low-hanging branch of a hackberry-tree she safely passes; but in flying the ills she knew, she has given no heed to those she wot not of, and is first reminded of the same by finding herself in the powerful grasp of a manly arm.

Her stifled shriek was instantly suppressed through affect of the reassuring whisper: " Hush! you are safe; it is I, Morland Ellsmead."

The act of stooping to utter those whispered words in all human probability saved the speaker's life, as a musket-ball whizzed through the empty space his head had just previously occupied, and lodged in the splintered trunk of the tree behind him. He bore her, half fainting with terror, to the protecting shelter of a shelving bank, and leaving her there, crept cautiously and stealthily back, peering with strained and eager gaze at every suspicious-looking object that might by any possibility resolve itself into a lurking assassin's form. Failing to discover any trace of his late assailant, he returned to the terror-stricken fugitive, whose forlorn helplessness furnished claim indisputable on every kindly office in his power to render.

" Do not leave me," she entreated: " I am so thankful to be in charge of one I can fully and freely trust."

The assurance of perfect confidence, thus unwittingly conveyed, fell as gratefully on the ear of her listener as genial sun-ray on plant benumbed and chill.

"Hush! an incautious sound may bring destruction on us both," he said, warningly, in tone so subdued that it was only by an effort that she caught the import of his words.

He pressed his hand firmly, in token of silence, on the restless, trembling foot that, with unconscious flutter amongst the dry leaves on the bank, might have betrayed their proximity to lurking foe. She instantly controlled this outward token of inward tremor, and only the night wind's gentle plaint breathed through the catalpas of sadness and of sighing.

A faint streak of grey in the east betokened the coming dawn; and by its aid she was able to discern objects which had hitherto escaped her observation. Grasping her companion's arm, she pointed, with a thrill of apprehension, to the crouching figure of an armed man who was gradually nearing them by slow and guarded approach.

"Only a companion sentinel," exclaimed Mr. Ellsmead; "there are a long line of us belonging to the outposts in the rear. That is a signal of danger he is giving me. Hist! that slight stir in the leaves may be forerunner of fatal blow."

"It is but the wind moaning through the catalpas."

Enjoining silence by gesture imperative, he crept away from her, taking advantage of bush, tree, shadow and hillock to mask his stealthy advance. A few minutes, and he was lost to her sight. Her heart beat audibly, as with anxious longing she awaited his return.

The piercing call of a night-bird rung shrilly forth on the silent air, instantly succeeded by the sharp report of a musket.

A sensation of tingling pain shot through her nerves. Had she looked her last on Morland Ellsmead? Welcome sight, that of his returning figure. She gave him her hand frankly, in words, few and glowing, expressing her joy and relief that he was still un-harmed.

Passing her, he approached the next sentinel on guard sufficiently near to communicate with him by means of telegraphic signals from the hand, receiving similar telegram in reply. With a heavy sigh, as of one re-lieved by the performance of a duty painful but inexor-able, her companion resumed his weary watch. He climbed a tree somewhat overlooking its fellows, and with a powerful pocket-glass swept the prospect for miles around. Day was breaking fast, and afforded him clear view for his fruitless survey.

"We are seldom molested after this hour," said he, on his descent; "I may venture now to ask what brought you here at such a time?"

"The house where I was stopping with relatives, while my father was away at Chicago, was set on fire by rebel guerillas, I suppose, and I fled for dear life."

"That, then, was the flame I saw reddening up the whole southern sky?"

"Quite likely. Now let me ask you a question, Mor-land. I heard the report of a musket while you were away from me. What did it mean?"

"It meant that I had traced the prowling villain who shot-at me to his secret skulking-place; and I did not forget the brave comrades who have been picked off from our line by this sharpshooter's aim."

A prolonged shiver shook her frame.

"You are more than half afraid of the man who, for any cause, defaces form created in his Maker's image," he doubtfully suggested.

"It is not that, Morland; but an enemy defeated is an enemy no longer, and it is terrible to think of a fel-low-being wrestling alone with his death-agony, while we are so near."

"Set your heart at rest on that point. I startled him

from his lurking place by a ventriloqual trick nature gave me the faculty for practising, and—my aim was sure. I know better than you, because through stern experience, the fearful responsibilities of a soldier's life; and knowing, I do not shrink from accepting them even when it comes to taking the life of others or to rendering up my own. One can do no more than yield up life for a friend, and for one's country—the dear, native mother earth that smiles at us through tears and flowers, feeds us from her bounteous stores, clothes us in coats of many colors, and when we have done with her gracious gifts, folds us tenderly away in the last close embrace mortal may know—when torn by faction, wounded in the house of its friends, one can do no less. Deeds committed in individual self-defence, however unjustifiable, in themselves considered, are sometimes pardoned, nay, approved, for the sake of the motive prompting their commission; but when it is the national existence which is at stake, how much more heroic and exalted the incentive impelling those rallying to the rescue, to sacrifice on the altar of country every blessing that country has given; all that makes life precious; life itself, if that alone will serve the country's needs. From no mean, mercenary motive; for no cause less sacred than that which fires the ardent patriot's breast, would I consent to battle unto death with those who are foes to me through the simple reason that they are foes to a government which has not only ruled its own people with mild, beneficent sway, but has provided happy refuge for thousands of the oppressed from foreign lands, who now bring brave hearts and willing hands to the support of their foster-land. But enough of this; if you supped on horrors, that is no reason why you should be forced to breakfast on the same. I hear you are to be married soon."

He could not have introduced less grateful topic of discourse. She merely bowed an affirmative.

"I never should have sought you to ask the question; but since opportunity so kindly befriends me, pray gratify my curiosity by telling me why you singled out Mr. Caruthers from all other adorers as the favored individual to be blest with that little monosyllable outside barbarians might sigh their lives out in vain to win."

The inflated style in which this query was proposed, by reminding her of the continuous neglect she had received from one who held her plighted troth as though it were a gift scarce worth the holding, stung her to quick and impatient retort.

"Do talk like a rational being, Morland. The train of adorers you so liberally bestow on me is but a myth of your own fancying. Scatter the shadows that people your dreams; it can be no difficult task."

"Your word is law. Presto! change! begone! There they vanish; but here remains Mr. Caruthers; why, in preference to all the others, was he made the happy recipient of your life-long regard?"

"Must I tell you again that 'all the others' didn't care a straw for me? He did, or seemed to do so. If that isn't a good reason, I can't help it; I don't keep the commodity ready cut and dried to dispense in justification of every step I take. Men reason from the head, women from the heart."

"Ah! then this is an affair of the heart."

Her cheek flushed and her eye lit; but she vouchsafed no verbal reply to this indirect query. He saw that he had disconcerted, possibly provoked, her, and changing his tactics, arming himself with the lighter weapons of gay *persiflage*, he returned with renewed zest to the attack.

"I can fancy Mr. Caruthers making out schedules of lading, examining invoices of merchandise, fingering drafts, acceptances and bills of exchange; but imagination utterly fails when I try to put my mind's eye on

Mr. Caruthers enacting the *rôle* of sighing swain and beseeching lover."

"I don't see why you should put yourself to the trouble of any such uncalled for stretch of fancy," Minnie dryly retorted.

"Very true; when you can so easily render unnecessary any further blundering attempts in that direction. Take pity on one of the uninitiated, and give me some vague idea of the terms in which our brave wooer urged his successful suit."

"I have half a mind to quarrel with you seriously, instead. Mr. Caruthers is no sighing swain, no love-sick boy to make a fool of himself by prating of sickly sentiment; he just asked me in straightforward, manly fashion to marry him, and that was enough."

It was now Morland's turn to redden with resentment called forth by the unwonted bitterness of her tone, and the contemptuous emphasis he thought she had placed on the word "boy," intended, so he supposed, as scornful reminder of the fact of his having recently attained his majority. Piqued and indignant, he was thrown off the strict guard he had hitherto maintained over himself, and to his lips leaped hasty, impulsive words he regretted almost as soon as spoken.

"It would not have been enough," he asserted with warmth, "if I had been in Mr. Caruthers' position. I pity the man with soul so dead that he can't talk sentiment and act it, too, on fitting occasions. Given Mr. Caruthers' opportunity, I should inevitably have made a fool of myself by saying, 'I love you,' Minnie, before venturing on the proposal that would have sealed my fate."

She drew a little aside from him, with an air of quiet, womanly reserve.

"I beg your pardon, Mr. Ellsmead, but this topic is distasteful to me; we will change it, if you please, for another."

The topic was dropped abruptly instead of being exchanged for another. Mr. Ellsmead concealed his embarrassment by turning his back on his companion and examining the contents of his cartridge box, while saying to himself, "A most precious noodle am I; I needn't have told her that I should inevitably make a fool of myself if opportunity were but given; any dolt might predict that without the help of astrology."

"Now, that it is nearly sunrise, I think I might return to Pré-Fleuri," proposed Minnie, with ill-concealed uneasiness.

"Return to the site of a house that has been burned; across a district infested by guerillas; absurd! the third relief will soon take our places, and then I will give you in charge to the sergeant or corporal who will, without doubt, be able to devise some means of restoring you to your friends."

She opened her eyes wide in startled wonderment.

"Have I been guilty of transgressing any of your laws and regulations by coming within your lines, that you propose surrendering me to official control?"

"That is the best means I can devise for ensuring your safe departure."

"Thank you; but when my father, who comes to carry me home this morning, finds only a heap of ruins in place of the house where he expects to find me, he will be deeply anxious on my account. I must prevent this by being on the spot to explain to him what has happened. I am not afraid, by daylight, to cross the open fields alone; I would much rather do so than subject you to the awkwardness of explaining to guard officials the cause of my accidental appearance here."

"Then I will accompany you to the end of my beat, and protect you while you are within range of my musket; more I cannot do."

She rose instantly, and he walked beside her, silent and sad, detaining her a moment at parting.

"We may never meet again, Miss Brandon; pardon my thoughtless, ill-considered speech; and give me some word of kindly farewell."

"It is I, Morland, who ought rather to entreat your pardon for veiling my real feelings in utterances whose inexplicable bitterness you quite naturally resented. I was so sore at heart that your light words were as a sharp probe from which I shrank. Grateful remembrances for your timely succor, I shall always cherish. Goodbye."

From leafy covert he watched her retreating figure. The golden sunlight flooded vale and slope, but day's lovely radiance was lost on him for the shadow that lay darkling at his heart.

"Young, admired, with a brilliant marriage in prospect, she is yet unhappy," thought he; "would that I had the right to claim her confidence, to comfort and console. It is well, I suppose, to proclaim the vanity of riches, and to inveigh against the same, but there are cases in which filthy lucre alone can act as counterpoise to the happiness of a man's life. If I had possessed but a tithe of Caruthers' glittering dross wherewith to provide her a fitting home, he would have found an earnest and determined rival in his path. I richly deserved the rebuff she gave me, and like her none the less for having had the sense and spirit to bestow it. Strange that she, of all women, should have found her way here, when I have so scrupulously avoided her ever since I discovered that she was coming between me and my own thoughts, in a way that left me fit to think of nothing else. She is wondrous fair, and I must forget if I would be free."

She stopped at the sheep-pen whence, scarcely two hours before, she had fled in wildest dismay, and through the chinks at its side, surveyed the smoking embers marking the scene of the fire. It was nine

4*

o'clock when her father arrived, by which time a number of neighboring farmers had collected in little knots,
talking excitedly. From one of these Mr. Brandon
withdrew, as his daughter approached, saying hurriedly:
"Let us go, child; this is no place for you."

She noticed that his hand shook as he helped her into
their gig.

"Did you learn," she asked, "what became of Cousin Honour and Wilhelmine?"

"I did, Minnie; but there is no use in speaking of
what is all over. They are beyond reach of harm now,
and there is no need of harrowing up my feelings by
recounting deeds of brutal fiendishness that will, sooner
or later, recoil on their perpetrators if there is justice on
earth or in Heaven."

"I see that you are looking pale and worn," she subjoined, instantly taking the cue he had given. "Was it
bad news that called you to Chicago?"

"Yes; news of the fatal illness of a tried and valued
friend. Do you remember Dr. Thornton?"

"Quite well. He was a liberal Christian gentleman,
as ready to encourage real worth as to rebuke fraud
and pretence; his wife was a true gentlewoman, too."

"She is in great affliction now. Her husband
breathed his last on the very day of my arrival, and she
is left in destitute circumstances. The doctor was
always too generous for his own good. To the needy
but meritorious students of his Institute, his charges
were almost nominal; he endorsed for friends and lost
heavily by the process; and the disease of which he
died was contracted in gratuitous attendance on a
deserted outcast to whom no one else acted the part of
good Samaritan. She came on with me as far as the
city, where she purposes renting a small house of Mr.
Caruthers—she is a relative of the family, she tells me
—and supporting herself by taking boarders."

"What, then, becomes of the Medical Institute of which Dr. Thornton was head?"

"It will be closed for the present, and I shall take charge of one of the departments—its duties will not be burdensome, or consume too much of my time—when it is reopened; that is, as soon as you and Mr. Caruthers are married, *if* you ever are."

The significant emphasis he placed on this doubt-implying particle made her sicken with apprehension of what was to follow. She strove to start some other subject of discourse, no matter what its theme, so it trenched not on the one topic to which she dreaded even to allude, and forced herself to the utterance of those trivial platitudes so often used to conceal the gnawings of hidden pain.

In the close companionship of home, Mr. Brandon could not fail to note the great change that had come over his sole surviving child. Her moods were changeful and uncertain, corresponding with the feeling of doubt and uncertainty shrouding her future. Periods of forced and fitful gaiety surrendered without apparent cause to attacks of profound depression. Shunning him in a measure, when with him she read aloud for his gratification, or kept up an incessant flow of small-talk that baffled his penetration and allayed the anxiety her pale face and drooping gait might otherwise have occasioned.

Mr. Brandon, having occasion to go to the city, invited his daughter to accompany him, an invitation she promptly declined.

The instant she caught a glimpse of him on his return, she said to herself, "He brings me ill tidings, and I am not prepared to hear them with composure. I cannot meet him quite yet; I must have time to steady my nerves—to school myself into listening to whatever he may have to tell, without betraying that wretched weak-

ness to which, until I was tried and found lacking, I
thought I had too much character to yield. To what
depths of self-abasement have I fallen when I can thus
be moved at thought of one who gives no thought to me.
I could despise myself for so feebly submitting to this
galling chain of bondage; but self-loathing cannot be
mine to bear so long as the knowledge of my infirmity is
safe in my own keeping, and the darts of ridicule, cold
comment or contemptuous pity cannot be levelled at
me. I shall bless the day in which I can return his
neglect with an indifference that is not feigned; but such
victory comes not yet."

"Minnie," called Mr. Brandon, from the foot of the
staircase, "I have something particular to say to you;
come down."

"I knew it," thought she; then to him over the
baluster, "I will be with you in a minute, father."

Dashing the tears from her eyes, and laving them
from the contents of her water-basin, she descended with
tranquil air, a snatch of song on her smiling lips, to the
sitting-room. So little do we often know of the real life
of those whom we meet daily at the social board, with
whom we share the same sheltering roof, and to whom
we deem ourselves bound by closest ties of kinship and
of confidence.

"I saw Mr. Caruthers in the city to-day," her father
remarked, exactly as she had expected he would remark.

"Let us not talk of him, please. So long as he does
not see fit to intrust to me any information regarding
his plans and movements, I would rather hear nothing
of the same, not even the mention of his name."

Mr. Brandon noticed that, though her voice was
steady, her accent firm, her face was white and rigid
with unflinching effort at self-control. With impulse of
tenderest compassion, he drew her to his side.

"Do not suppose that I am blind, and cannot see what

you are enduring, dear child; you may suffer and give no sign in words, but I discover your grief, and share it, for all that."

"Don't degrade me in my own esteem by pitying my weakness," she began; but, finding her lips quivering and her eyes filling, she abruptly withdrew the hand he had taken, and hurriedly returned to her room, where he heard her pacing to and fro with restless, disordered step. He, too, walked the room with perturbed air.

"It is unaccountably foolish of her, so sensible as she has always seemed," he discontentedly soliloquized, "to distress herself so sorely from such a cause. I can't help pitying her for all that; I had youthful illusions myself once on a day. Oh, me! what long years have gone by since then."

At tea-table it required all the self-command of which Minnie was mistress to carry out the customary forms of observance, and to direct the flow of discourse into its ordinary channels. After asking a second time for a cup of tea, Mr. Brandon received, in compliance with his request, the sugar-bowl and a spoon-holder, an oversight he considerately rectified without directing her attention to the same.

—•••—

CHAPTER VI.

DISENCHANTMENT.

WHEN Minnie took the evening paper to read aloud to her father, as was her wont, he frustrated her purpose by remarking decisively—

"The reading can wait, I wish to talk with you now. Mrs. Thornton I found settled in her new home at Belherbe, a quiet little snuggery just beyond sound of city turmoil, and she wished me to say to you that she was anxious to receive a call as soon as you could possibly make it convenient to come her way."

" I will certainly call on her the first time I go in town."

" You had better go to-morrow; I make it a special request that you do so. There is no use in striving to buoy yourself up with false hopes; cast aside everything in the way of factitious support, and face the facts of your actual position with that calm self-reliance which you are capable of summoning to your aid in an emergency like the present. I am sure no daughter of mine will ever sacrifice the womanly dignity which is her shield and guard by complaining of any man's neglect, or by pining for the regard that is not willingly bestowed."

Scalding tears were in Minnie's eyes, a burning glow on her cheek, as, with unfaltering accent, she replied, " I make no complaints, and intend to make none. You shall see, as soon as the first shock of surprise is over, and I have accustomed myself a little to the possibility of all my air-castles being shattered, that you have not overrated my powers of endurance. Give me time, and you shall have no cause to reprove me a second time for any show of weakness."

" Heaven knows, dear child, that my words were not spoken in censure or reproval."

" I am sure of it; you are too kind to be harsh; but I am so sore at heart that what is meant as balm acts as bane. Have patience awhile, and I will bring no discredit on your name."

" It is not of my own name or my own credit that I am thinking; they rest on too firm a basis to need props of support; but solely of what is for your best interests. If I could further these by any course of procedure calculated to place the relations between yourself and Mr.

Caruthers on a happier footing than the existing one, without lowering you by throwing you at his feet as suppliant for compassion, I would undertake the office at a minute's warning; as matters stand, I cannot see my way clear to the accomplishment of any such purpose. Do you agree with me on the subject?"

" I ought to, but I feel as well as reason. I have not released Mr. Caruthers from the promise binding him to me; I hope it may not come to that. This girl, Lucy Sears, has many claims on his kindness and attention; an orphan, she has been accustomed to look to him for support, as her mother did before her. She is deeply attached to him, an attachment he regrets and humors without reciprocating."

" Why, then, is he so much with her?"

" She courts his society, and came on here in opposition to his express wishes."

" Who told you this?"

" Mr. Caruthers himself."

" Let me advise you, Minnie, not to be over credulous regarding any man's professions; but when his words and deeds do not tally, sift and weigh the latter much more carefully than the former. It is cruel, I know, to shake thus your faith in human goodness; but better the bitter rind enfolding the kernel of truth, than the false fruit, fair to the eye, but turning to ashes in the mouth. I repeat, be not over credulous."

Next forenoon found Minnie Brandon in the plainly-furnished sitting-room of the doctor's widow, a tall, thin, dark-haired woman, whose expression of quick intelligence redeemed her face from the charge of positive ugliness.

" Your father called on me yesterday," said Mrs. Thornton, " and I sent for you to come to me, although I should not have done so, steeped in sorrow and unfit for companionship as I am, if I had not had something of importance to communicate."

Minnie was in the act of thanking the speaker for the
kind consideration manifested in her behalf, when she
started with surprise at sight of a miniature, lying on
the table near, a seeming counterpart to one she had
often slipped inside her belt.

" Mr. Caruthers is a relative of yours, so 1 am told,
Mrs. Thornton."

" True ; but that miniature does not belong to me."

" To whom, then ?"

" To a young lady who is boarding with me ; her
name is Sears."

" Can you tell me how this picture came in her possession ?"

" It was Mr. Caruthers' gift ; she has others of far
greater value bestowed by the same hand."

" Pray tell me all you know or suspect at once.   This
dealing forth your information by driblets only keeps
me on the tenter-hooks of suspense. Speak straight
out, and let me know the worst I have to dread."

" As you will.   In all human probability Lucy Sears
will one day become Mrs. Caruthers ; and I, for one,
think her admirably well qualified to fill such position."

The speaker was shocked at the effect of her words.
Minnie turned deadly pale and clutched at the table for
support. Mrs. Thornton handed her a bottle of salts,
and she revived from the momentary attack of faintness
that had nearly overpowered her.

" Excuse me, Mrs. Thornton ; you placed the fears
I had scarcely admitted, even to myself, so suddenly in
tangible form before me, that I could not help recoil as
sudden ; there will be no recurrence of a similar nature.
You know the relations subsisting between myself and
the original of this miniature ?"

" Yes ; and knowing, deeply deplore the same."

Minnie looked her surprise at this singular admission,
so strikingly at variance with the felicitations she had
been wont to receive on her approaching bridal.

"Even more on your own account than on his," persisted Mrs. Thornton; "I regret that any lasting tie should bind you one to the other. You make friends and companions of your favorite authors; he would fall asleep with such dull companionship. You are sensitive and high-wrought; he so phlegmatic that he would hardly feel a blow which would crush you. He would lacerate your feelings in a thousand ways without even being aware that he had hurt you, and instead of resentment or remonstrance, you would brood over his unintentional slights, magnifying them into cruel wrongs perhaps, until you lost the gay vivacity that was your principal charm in his eyes, losing which, your last hold on his affections would be gone. I have studied him closely, knowing that you were engaged to him, during the evenings he has spent with us, and it is my firm conviction that you could not have selected a more unsuitable partner for life."

"Then he spends part of his evenings with you?"

"Not particularly with me; it is the society of Miss Sears that he seeks. Every spare minute he can snatch from business cares is devoted to her. You must have suffered severely from his neglect; how much harder would it be to endure if you were his wife, and he always trying to escape presence irksome to him."

Minnie assumed stately, almost resentful air; it was bitter enough to know herself neglected for another, too galling quite, to be reminded in plain words of fact so unpalatable.

There was a soft rustle of silk on the stairs.

"She is coming down," said Mrs. Thornton, in a low tone; "now you will have an opportunity of seeing what she is like."

"Do not introduce me," Minnie hastily entreated.

A pretty, fair-haired blonde, with well-cut features and a delicately tinted complexion, glided gracefully into the room.

"I believe I left my miniature on your table, Mrs. Thornton; ah, here it is. I am so worn out with belaboring that horrid piano, that I am going out to refresh myself with an ice. Dear me, what a relief it would be if some accomplishment would come in fashion that would not require such a tedious amount of application as practising. If Mr. Caruthers should call while I am out, please say to him that I have gone to the confectioner's (he knows which one), and that I have earned my ride by working like a galley-slave for two mortal hours at that tiresome instrument."

"Do not hurry away, Miss Lucy, but sit down and help entertain my young friend, Miss Bur-r."

"Delighted to entertain Miss—I beg pardon—did not quite catch the name. Lovely weather, isn't it? Did you see the parade of the lancers yesterday?"

"I did not have the pleasure of witnessing the spectacle," replied Minnie, watching with absorbing interest every change in the dimpled face, every turn of the symmetrical figure beside her.

"Then you missed a sight well worth beholding. I proved my patriotism by being in the street nearly all day, and waving my handkerchief in answer to repeated huzzas till my arm fairly ached with the effort. Such splendidly burnished spears—I wonder if they kill folks with them—with the sweetest little flags floating from their shafts. I should have enjoyed the sight amazingly, if a horse hadn't stepped on the back breadth of my best silk; it will be such a fearful job to turn it upside down."

"You must feel a strong interest in the struggle at present convulsing the nation," suggested Minnie, regarding her companion with a look of doubtful inquiry.

"Oh, intense," was the prompt response. "I went out to Camp Bolivar, the other day, and the hideous cavalry I saw there, mounted on caissons and galloping round the field, belching forth flame and smoke, gave me such a turn, I hardly got over it all night. You should have seen the prancing and curvetting of the officers' chargers; it was almost equal to the equestrian scene in the Hippodrome, where somebody or other I remember to have seen in mythology, drove a chariot with four horses a-breast. There were quantities of infantry, too, drilling in squadrons and pontoons all about the camp. So sad-to think of their being sent off to be shot at. I do wish the authorities would listen to the emancipation plan, and make people stop killing each other."

" Then you are in favor of immediate emancipation or abolition," suggested Minnie, in some confusion as regarded the speaker's meaning.

" O dear, no. I think the abolitionists, with a finger in everybody's pie, are worse than all the other parties put together. But we are really drifting into politics, and as we don't have to vote, and as nobody cares a fip what we think about national affairs, where is the use of our muddling our heads over what doesn't concern us? What do you think of my new hat, Mrs. Thornton?"

" I liked the one with the blue feathers."

" That does very well as a plain, serviceable article, but this is perfectly captivating; I positively went into raptures at the first glance of it through the shop-window in which it hung. Look at this gorgeous plume, three shades of purple tipped with Solferino, and this purple velvet puffing banded with gold and fastened with a clasp of amethysts. Excuse me, Miss ——, for not wishing to discuss politics with you; but to tell the plain truth, I get as puzzled trying to understand what all the fighting is about, as I sometimes do over a piece of music in six flats, where the naturals and accidentals are enough to drive one to distraction."

Minnie rested her face on her hand with a weary air, making no attempt to resume the conversation.

The wearer of the gorgeous hat rose to depart.

"If Mr. Caruthers should come, Mrs. Thornton, oblige me by telling him that three garnets are gone from my buckle, and he must have them replaced, as I can't live without it, for it fits all my belts, and I can't wear his miniature without a belt; don't forget that part of the message, as all the rest hangs by that. I left the buckle on my bureau after all—I must run up for it."

A bitter smile curled Minnie's lip as she watched the bland and smiling speaker as she tripped lightly up the staircase.

"And that is the woman who has robbed me of my rest, and stolen away my peace. A rare bit of art, that reference to his miniature."

There was a ring at the bell, the door opened, and a man's step sounded through the hall—a step that set Minnie's cheeks aglow and her heart tumultuously astir. Mrs. Thornton hurried out to receive her landlord.

"Come in, Mr. Caruthers."

"No, I'm obliged to you; I cannot leave my horses. Is Miss Sears ready to go to a military review with me?"

"She was about starting for a walk, and has run up stairs; she will be down in an instant."

"Very well; I hope you are thoroughly comfortable in your new domicile. Report to me any needed alterations or repairs, and they shall be promptly attended to."

How those hearty, cordial tones called forth echoes from the past which still in Minnie's faithful memory fondly lingered. His next words struck cold and chill on her ear, and the sweet echoes of lang-syne died away in plaint of ineffable sadness.

"Here comes our queen of violets, all purple and gold. Who could resist such a powerful battery of charms?"

Minnie struggled for breath as though she had been undergoing the tortures of suffocation, pressing her hand over her mouth to repress the sobs that almost forced themselves from her lips. A short allegory she had read when a child, came unbidden to her thoughts. Thus it ran : A party of pilgrims set forth from a bleak and sterile plain for a fair and fertile land, rich in abundance of all things good for man. A chart was their only guide. Their way was rugged, painful oft, sometimes shut in by flinty rocks, sorely wounding their tender feet, and at others rendered nearly impassable by thickets of bramble and briar that cruelly lacerated the hands raised to put them aside.

All the while that these pilgrims, footsore and weary with plodding onward in their toilsome way, forced thus their painful march along, they could clearly discern the sights, detect the sounds of the tempting Vales of Pleasaunce to which the mountain slopes bordering their rugged path descended on either side. There, in spicy groves, the false and fickle sirens sang in tones of entrancement so delicious, that the unwary ear, athirst for the unheard harmonies audible only to those loosed from fleshly bonds, turns eagerly to quench its thirst from the sparkling cup whose dregs are death. There, too, in course nearly parallel to the rough, mountainous pass they trode, ran delightfully sheltered avenues, bordered by clustering shades, where birds of golden plumage toyed and lingered—bordered by marble grottoes, where bloomed floral gems of subtlest potency, and where Bacchante proffered cup of circean spell. And it came to pass that many of the pilgrims, faint with the burden and heat of the day, turned with longing eyes toward the bowers of ease and indulgence, whose varied allurements placed in marked contrast the barren waste in which their rugged pathway seemed interminably to lose itself, saying to themselves, we will but step aside for a moment to screen ourselves from the

noontide sun, and to slake our thirst at these sparkling
cisterns, which our chart says are broken and hold no
water, but whose contents we will test for ourselves.
So the worldy-wise speakers turned aside, with purpose
of speedy return; but it was not until sated with revelry,
cloyed with sybaritic luxury, that they bethought them
of retracing their steps; but trusting to treacherous
guides, they failed in their attempt, never rejoining the
faithful few who struggled on through all opposing
obstacles, reaching, with the scar of many a conflict in
proof of their unblenching valor, that fair land where
those that mourn shall rejoice, and they that weep shall
be comforted.

Not much of an allegory this; but coming to Minnie's
remembrance as it did at a moment of sore trial, it
soothed and strengthened her.

"I have still an object, one as high and holy as any
to which mortal can aspire, to live for," she said to herself. "If my steps have been uncertain and blundering, no irretrievably false one have I yet taken, and
henceforth I must be doubly on my guard against such.
If Mr. Caruthers wrongs me; I am not to let such wrong
eat out from my better nature all those sweet and
gentle charities, without which woman is a monster.
Neither am I to hate the rival, who has never intentionally done me a harm, and never consciously looked on
my face."

"How do you like the young lady's appearance, now
that you have seen her, Minnie?"

"Have they gone, Mrs. Thornton?"

"Yes; five minutes since, and I have spoken to you
twice without receiving any answer."

"Pardon my inattention. I do not think Miss Sears
is a person I should select as a friend," replied Minnie,
striving to express her real opinion freed from all tinge
of bitterness.

"Do not let prejudice blind you to facts. So far as I

can see, she is singularly good-humored and warm-hearted, with amiable and engaging manners. I know your characters are wholly dissimilar; but if she drinks less deeply than you of life's draught, she thereby escapes the lees you are sure to quaff."

"It was not of her depth or shallowness I was think-ing. One values a friend for goodness and worth, aside from all considerations of intellectual excellence, and it is in respect to the former that I think Miss Sears lack-ing. Why does she put on those pretty little affected ways, if it be not to hide what she really is?"

"Those airy, sprightly graces are just what Mr. Caruthers finds irresistibly attractive."

A slight contraction showed for an instant on Minnie's brow, but she rejoined quietly, "No manner conveying the impression of hollow insincerity can ever be attrac-tive to me."

"I fear you are still cherishing a feeling of resentful dislike toward one who does not deserve it. Lucy Sears saw and loved Mr. Caruthers years before he ever made your acquaintance, bestowing on him a regard as great as he was capable of returning. It was you, not she, who made the fatal mistake of over-estimating his real character, of exalting him into a peerless ideal; and I, who look through the calm eyes of a disinterested spectator, do earnestly assure you that Miss Lucy's intervention is a blessing to be grateful for, rather than an evil to deplore, as it saves you the slow misery of seeing charm by charm unwind from an illusion dearly cherished, but an illusion still."

Minnie drew a long breath, while a look of deep dis-quiet rested on her saddened face.

"I almost lose the sense of my own identity at times, Mrs. Thornton; so secure as seemed my future, but brief space ago, and now I'm all afloat on a chopping sea, with neither rudder nor compass as guide. Tell me, is

nothing true under the sun? Did charm by charm
unwind that robed *your* idol?"

Low and tremulous the faltering response :

"I made no mistake in my estimate of the sainted
dead, whose departure has to me brought Heaven
nearer."

" Pardon my thoughtlessness," entreated the contrite
Minnie ; " in the selfishness of my own sorrow, I forgot
that you had a far greater to bear."

" Let us not talk of that, or I shall be unnerved quite.
We will speak instead of what it nearly concerns you
to know. A confidential clerk, a relative of Mr. Caruthers, was accidentally killed in a branch house connected with the firm in this city, and he supported the
widow and orphan until the death of the former. Then
a brother of Mrs. Sears, a graceless knave, I have been
told, who keeps a billiard saloon and bowling-alley in
one of our southern cities, thought he could turn his
niece's beauty and vivacity to good account in his own
interests, and did his best to ingratiate himself with her
and induce her to accompany him to his southern home.
In this design he would probably have succeeded, if
Mr. Caruthers, knowing him to be wholly unfit for the
trust he sought to assume, had not foiled his plan by
carrying Lucy to live with his mother and sisters. Such
a turmoil as this step created! The Misses Caruthers
were models of elegant and fastidious propriety, and
Lucy, it must be acknowledged, was something of a
hoyden, and by no means inclined to submit with do-
cility to the restrictions of a rigid code of manners. She
was pronounced coarse, illiterate, underbred ; and there
was no end to the slights and annoyances she was forced
to undergo.

"A girl of your acute perceptions and high spirit
would never have remained, no matter what the penalty
of escape, where such stinging affronts were of daily re-

currence; but Miss Lucy is sensitive only to actual personal discomforts, and never frets over ills that, to a mind of finer mould, would be almost unbearable. Indeed, she is extremely even-tempered, and I never heard her make use of a harsh or angry expression to, or of, any one. When Mr. Caruthers discovered that there was to be a never-ending succession of petty persecutions for the poor girl as long as she remained with his family, he sent her to the Female Seminary at Troy—an obligation she would not so readily have accepted had it not been understood between them that her education was to fit her for the position she would one day occupy as his wife. That such understanding mutually existed I have positive proof."

"You do not mean to tell me that such understanding has existed from that time until the present?"

"I could not satisfy you in regard to that point; but I can tell you what it is much more essential for you to know, that it would have been better for all parties if such understanding had continued to exist. As I have intimated before, she will make him a much more suitable partner for life than you, with your best endeavors, ever can. She looks up to him as a woman should to the man she marries; chronicles his every serious remark as though it were the utterance of an oracle, to be religiously preserved, and finds food for mirth in what seems to me the perfection of dullness. Excuse me for reminding you that my work in the kitchen remains at a standstill while I am up-stairs, and that although I would gladly urge you to prolong your stay, pressing duties forbid me the pleasure. Let me advise you to write at once to Mr. Caruthers, not with reproaches or upbraiding, but in the mild terms your own sense of discretion would naturally incline you to adopt, and release him from the engagement still binding him to you. This, under the circumstances, is much the most dignified

5

course for you to pursue, as it will spare you the mortification of being actually deserted, thus depriving gossip
of its sharpest sting in the shape of hypocritical condo-
lances and simulated pity, which you might otherwise
find very galling to endure."

As Minnie raised her parasol, on reaching the sidewalk, a scrap of paper loosened itself from the fringe and
fluttered to her feet. Picking it up, and bestowing on
it a hasty glance, she placed it in her card-case.

On reaching home, she proceeded to put Mrs. Thornton's advice in practice, by writing Mr. Caruthers a note
releasing him from all ties binding him to herself.

The scrap of writing she had picked up from the sidewalk recurred to memory, and she hastened to examine
it—nothing of special interest, one would say, only a
list of feminine purchases—laces, gloves, pinking, per-
fumery. Word by word, letter by letter, did Minnie
compare the list with the anonymous communication
previously described—the hand-writing in both was the
same.

" If I had any doubts before," she said to herself, " this
sets them all at rest. Lucy Sears wrote me that letter,
and certainly her epistolary and conversational style are
widely at variance. How prettily she mouths her words
in speaking! as one who could manage to perfection
the Dorrit-governess mode of prune-and-prism surface
address; but in writing, where she has nothing to gain
by the assumption of winning gentleness, she can threaten
with the sharpest, and put forward her claims without
mincing matters in the least. Not one particle of faith
have I in her artlessness, which is a mere blind to screen
her plotting and scheming. She boldly accuses me of
practising wiles to keep Mr. Caruthers in my toils, and
it is generally your over-suspicious person who best de-
serves to be suspected.

" I have written Mr. Caruthers that I give him up of

my own free will; I do *not* give him up of my own free will, and I will never tell him that I do. He may be false to me, but I will never be false to—myself. It may, as Mrs. Thornton says, be the most dignified course for me to dismiss him; but am I to sacrifice truth for the preservation of my dignity? Heaven forfend! Shall mine be the hand to place any obstacle opposing his return in the way of the frank, free-hearted gentleman, who is so interwoven with all my plans for the future that it seems one long stretch of blank desolation without him? I will do nothing of the sort. I could find it in my heart, even now, if he would but throw off the hallucination that enthralls him, and come to me with perfect candor of confession and acknowledgment, to overlook the past; to trust and believe in him, as I was once so happy in trusting and believing."

Long she sat in saddest musing, then tore the note she had been writing into tiny bits, saying to herself, as she scattered them from the open window, "Thus pass away my shattered hopes unless his hand bind them together once more." Gathering up the half-finished bridal robe, with its costly laces and delicate needlework, she carefully laid it away in an unused drawer with the apostrophe, "There rest thee ever, unless thou canst become joyous instead of grievous reminder."

Day after day dragged by with such a wearisome sameness that she was strongly disposed to believe that any sort of certainty would be a relief in comparison with this lingering torture of prolonged suspense; these ever recurring doubts and fears; the sudden gleams of hope quenched as suddenly in moods of despondent gloom, which, at times, made life seem a burden to be patiently endured, rather than the most glorious boon ever bestowed on creature by creator divine.

She was walking on the broad veranda, several days later in the week, watching the rosy, purpling twilight

shades curtaining the west, when a gentleman she at
once recognized as Mr. Caruthers' legal adviser rode
slowly up the avenue hedged in by Osage orange, and
throwing the reins on his horse's neck, approached her
with courteous greeting.

"You will come in and see my father, Mr. Auverne?"

"Not unless you fear taking cold out here. I have
but few words to say, and will not detain you long. I
am not used to wasting time in beating about the bush,
but when I have a thing to say, put it in as plain words
as I can find to serve my purpose. A certain client of
mine, you will readily surmise who, is placed, by an odd
complication of circumstances, in a most trying position,
from which you alone can extricate him."

He paused, looking his listener full in the face, as if
to discover the impression his first words had produced.

Her heart beat high and her color rose as she firmly
rejoined, "I shall be happy to do anything in my power
toward relieving your client from any embarrassment
he may be enduring on my account. Have the goodness to explain, at once, what it is I am required to do."

"I will come directly to the point at issue, as you request. When Mr. Caruthers made you proposals of
marriage, he never contemplated the possibility of any
occasion arising that might render such proposal im-
practicable of realization. Such occasion has arisen in
the shape of an entangling correspondence, carried on
years ago and almost forgotten, with one Miss Lucy
Sears. Most unfortunately for my client, these letters
distinctly admit the fact of his engagement to their recipient, which gives her counsellor the whip-hand over
us. In spite of this drawback, I think we might even-
tually have brought the young woman to some reasonable species of compromise by settling her at a fashionable watering-place on a fair retiring pension; but, as
ill-luck would have it, her uncle, keen as a brier and as

unscrupulous a knave as ever breathed, must turn up just in time to frustrate our well-concerted plans."

" Then Mr. Caruthers really desires to break the ties binding him to the young lady you speak of."

" Desires nothing more earnestly, I do assure you."

" And I must confess that I can see no way in which any effort of mine can absolve him from redeeming his pledged word to another woman."

This remark, proving to the wary advocate that he had thus far rather damaged than advanced his client's cause, drove him at once to the adoption of a new course of tactics.

"Suspend judgment, if you please, until you have heard me through, when you will be better able to form a correct estimate of the side issues involved in this case. This Vanwaring, uncle of contestant, carried on a lucrative business in the billiard and ten-pin line at Mobile; but, in an evil hour, he had the ill-breeding and execrable taste, and be hanged to him, to utter sarcastic and offensive remarks regarding the Southern Confederacy when there were none but Confederates near to listen—addlehead, to quarrel with his own bread and butter!—and, as a natural consequence, after receiving pointed allusions to a coat of down maintaining its consistence through adhesion to viscid woof of pitch-pine extraction, is drummed out of town, and, of all places in the world, turns up here, where his absence is a desideratum most devoutly to be prayed for. Breach of promise suit—ten thousand dollars damages—is what the fellow threatens; and, more's the pity, he has the means at disposal for putting his threat in practice. This amount, large as it is, Mr. Caruthers could easily have raised, and treble the sum, in ordinary times; but he has met with heavy losses, in ways I need not stop to specify, of late; and in the severe financial crisis at present paralyzing mercantile enterprise, it would be far from convenient for him to undertake the prosecution of an expensive law-suit."

A look of wounded pride, of affection scorned, turning to gall and bitterness the love turned back to prey upon itself, stamped itself on her white and rigid face.

"His mere convenience," thought she, "outweighs any considerations for my happiness. It was in his own well-being that all his purposes centred; mine centred there too; this was no exchange, it was a robbery; he took the cream of my life and made me no return. This is a wrong for which there is no redress, whose betrayal, even, is a burning shame to woman. I must bear it without resentment or demur; it cannot last forever."

"You are not attending, Miss Brandon, to what I wish to ask for my own satisfaction, from no other motive. I desire distinctly to state a very simple question. If Mr. Caruthers should think best to recognize and carry to its usual ultimatum his engagements with the woman who holds him in her power, would you resort to effectual method of interference with such procedure?"

"The woman who holds him in her power!" repeated Minnie, with painfully bewildered air.

"Pardons, a thousand, Miss Brandon; my words were not intended to convey the impression that you do not equally hold him in your power; what I am anxious to ascertain is, if you have any intention of exerting such power in a manner detrimental to my client's interests, if any advance step of his in an opposing direction should place him at the mercy of such mischance."

"Why should you make suggestions to me in that blind way, Mr. Auverne? It is for suspected criminals such wary cross-questionings are usually reserved. I treat you with the frankness due a friend; and you return the same with the cautious diplomacy one uses to keep an enemy at a safe distance. If you will speak to me in the plain terms for which you recently avowed a preference, you shall have reply as plain."

" Be it so. If Mr. Caruthers should conclude to make Lucy Sears his wife, should you indict him for breach of promise in a count of your own?"

Minnie's pale cheek flushed crimson.

" I understand your meaning now, thoroughly, Mr. Auverne, and you shall have a straightforward answer according to promise ; but first I beg that you will deal as openly with me when I ask if Mr. Caruthers originated the inquiry you just now made. Does he wish to know if he can be on with the old love without fear of trouble from the new?"

" Your question is wholly irrelevant, I do assure you, wholly irrelevant."

" Is it a fair rule that demands free reply to your questions, while mine are answered or put aside at your option?"

" But it imports you nothing to know whether I pursue these inquiries solely to gratify my own curiosity, or to satisfy "——

He paused, at a loss for fitting terms in which to conclude his assertion.

With a bitter smile curling her lip, she completed the sentence for him.

" Or to satisfy my client as to the probability of your attempting to wring from him some portion of his fortune in case of certain contingency. You view this case, Mr. Auverne, exclusively in its professional aspect, while I see it through the refracting medium of my own feelings. It imports me much to know whether you are interrogating me in accordance with his instructions, or simply from motives of your own."

" I have no personal motives whatever influencing my present course, my conduct being wholly controlled by a reference to the advancement of my client's interests ; I do not see how these can be prejudiced by imparting the information you are desirous of obtaining. It is Mr. Caruthers who wishes to know whether, if the contingency to which you but now alluded should occur, you would institute legal procedure against him in your own behalf."

The color slowly faded from Minnie's face, and her firm, upright attitude gave place to one of dejected languor.

"It is too true," she sadly admitted to herself, scarce heeding her companion's presence, "that I have been tormenting myself all this time over an illusory creation of my own fancy; and I am too thankful, at last, to be thoroughly disenchanted. Mr. Caruthers accused me, not long ago, of overstepping the bounds of strict feminine decorum, in addressing a remark or an inquiry to a stranger; but I will never be guilty of pursuing a course that would subject me to the notoriety I would as soon die as brave. What! *I* to provoke critical comment from crowded court-room while seeking golden balm for a wounded heart! *I* parade my wrongs and be laughed at as lovelorn damsel wearing the willow for truant swain! *I* make myself a study for eyes as coldly curious as those of the naturalist welcoming fresh specimens of ichthyosaurus to his fossiliferous treasures! No; I have neither reparation to seek, nor injuries requiring redress. I have been the victim of my own amazing stupidity, for which I alone am to blame. I need the pity of no living being; and I would resent nothing more deeply than any display of a compassion which, in my case, would be an unequivocal indignity. Come into the cottage a moment; I wish to write a brief note which you will do me the favor to convey to Mr. Caruthers."

Bowing assent, Mr. Auverne followed her into the house. She wrote a few hastily-penned lines, presenting the same for the lawyer's perusal.

"There's the answer I promised you, sir. I am ready

to seal and direct as soon as you have given it the sanction of your approval."

He read as follows:

"Mr. CARUTHERS:

"Dear Sir—I do voluntarily, of my own fullest and freest accord, release you from all ties hitherto existing between us. Permit me to offer my most sincere felicitations on your prospective union with one whose winning attractiveness will, I trust, efface any unpleasant reminiscences that might otherwise associate themselves with your memories of the past.

"Believe me, when I tell you that I now see what I might sooner have discerned, if I had not hardened myself against conviction, that I should have made you a most unsuitable partner for life; and I rejoice at the accident, if there be such a thing, that has severed the relations between us. I make this admission in no spirit of bitterness or upbraiding; acknowledging, with deepest contrition and humility, the false impressions by which my conduct has been swayed. I have acted on erroneous data, having formed incorrect estimate of your true character; and I hasten to make the only reparation in my power, that of confessing my mistake and releasing you from the obligations which have become burdensome to both.

"If a sadder, I trust I am a wiser woman, and remain as ever   "Your kindly well-wisher,
                                    "MINNIE BRANDON."

Mr. Anverne rose with an air of the utmost complaisance, briskly preparing to take leave.

"Really, Miss Brandon, you have done this very handsomely; not sacrificing your own dignity, and sparing us all cost and trouble. I thank you in my client's behalf."

5*

"I have no claims on your gratitude," she rejoined, with proud humility. "It was not to spare my own dignity or Mr. Caruthers' convenience that I wrote; but to speak the truth, or what seemed such to me; and to atone, so far as might be, for my own blunders in this miserable affair."

The lawyer smiled blandly, as he drew on his lavender gauntlets.

"A little quixotic in your notions of justice and self-abnegation yet, I see. Well, for a young person, that is better than to err in the opposite extreme; for it is a fault time will be sure to correct—yes; a fault on which years and experience will be sure to act as infallible specific."

She turned from him with slightly impatient gesture, saying to herself, "Time has not corrected the fault in my father, and while I have his example before me, I shall never believe in the necessity of growing selfish as one grows old."

CHAPTER VII.

RIFTS OF BRIGHTNESS THROUGH DARKSOME GLOOM.

For a few days, aimless and listless, Minnie groped her way blindly along through the shattered fragments cast about her by the downfall of the unsubstantial fabric of hope in which she had lately accustomed herself to dwell. The society she had once sought with avidity, she now as persistently avoided. Gentle, uncomplaining, unwearied in attentions to her father's comfort, toward all others her manners wore an icy chill, calculated to check prying and inquisitive remark. The faintest allusion to Mr. Caruthers was sufficient to make her trebly guard every approach to her confidence ; and many a word spoken in unaffected sympathy she construed as expression of contemptuous pity, and resented accordingly.

She was not one to yield supinely, for any protracted period, to influence so depressing. Her own personal griefs paled into insignificance in contrast with the frightfully accumulating evils wherewith the monster rebellion was scourging the land ; her own aching sense of disappointment and loss was partially forgotten in efforts to aid those who were risking all that man on earth holds dear in upholding the nation's honor, defending the nation's life. Coarse denims afforded her an unwonted species of needlework, while strong grey flannel passed nimbly through her fingers ; and she learned, alas! to fashion snowy robes for cold, insensate forms—precious memorials of what has been.

Weeks came and went in sad succession, finding her busy hands never idle. Her employment was one calculated to make her soberly thoughtful ; and she was no longer forced to mask a heavy heart by countenance of smiling serenity. The truth was gradually dawning on her perceptions that life was no holiday gift to be trifled away at the option of its receiver, but a sacred loan, for whose improvement we are held strictly accountable. In deciding on any course to be pursued, her first question was no longer, Would I like it ? but, Would it be right ?

Thus she sat and sewed and thought, one bleak and gusty winter's eve, when dead leaves rustled drearily along the drear earth, and the voice of the wind was like a sick child's wail. Mr. Brandon had been suffering for several days with a severe sore-throat; and Minnie, after having applied a fomentation of hops, was bidding him good-night on the stairs, when the rapid tread of horses' hoofs smote her ear.

Extinguishing the night-candle she held in her hand, she darted back to the room they had just left, raised the window long enough to convince herself that there were at least a dozen horsemen approaching the house, closed and refastened the window, hastily rejoining her father.

"The guerillas!" she whispered, quaking with apprehension.

"It may be that it is only forage and plunder they seek; if so, we had best hide ourselves. The barn and ricks are easily found."

"Better lose them and all else than life; in the brick cellar-arch, with the heavily clamped oaken door, we shall be safe. Poor old Chloe, what is to become of her?"

"Never mind her; she belongs to the privileged race, and will not be harmed by either side."

At sound of a loud knock at the outer door with a whip-handle, the speakers descended hastily to their chosen places of refuge. The creaking of boots and the banging of doors soon gave evidence that the marauders had effected an entrance.

"Hark!" whispered Minnie, clutching her father's arm, "there is a step on the cellar stairs."

A cautious and stealthy step it was, gliding nearer and nearer, until a ray of light streamed beneath the door of the arch. Speechless with apprehension, Minnie's grasp unconsciously tightened on her father's arm. The soft coal and kindlings were only separated from them by a brick wall. Was the house to be set on fire? She breathed more freely as the step retreated, passing up the stairway. Short the respite granted for self-gratulation. Half a dozen men were soon ransacking the cellar.

"Here is a likely place to look for valuables," cried

one, striking with his musket the door of the arch. " Ah, ha ! what is this ? A trapped fox, by the knave of clubs ! Here is a key in the lock; hunt up your pincers, Jack, and be spry about it ; let's see whether it is an elk or a coon we've run to earth."

Noiselessly Minnie abstracted the key from its ward.

" Great good that does you," called a voice outside. " Here, give us a charge of powder, Jack, and I will try the metal of this lock."

There was an explosion, succeeded by a violent shake at the door. The lock had been blown off; but a strong iron bolt was still firmly secured in its socket. A heavy stick of timber was procured to aid their operations in battering down the door.

" They will soon be in here," whispered Minnie to her father. " You must hide in the dark closet ; for, if discovered, they would hang you to the first tree."

" But you ! remember Honour and Wilhelmine !"

" They had made themselves obnoxious by bitter denunciations of the rebel cause amongst its supporters, before whom I have been very guarded in my remarks. Quick, or it will be too late."

She grasped the row of shelves at the end of the arch, when, swinging forward on hinges, it disclosed a narrow cell lined with brick and closely cemented. Reluctantly, and in compliance with his daughter's urgent entreaties, Mr. Brandon passed behind the shelves, and suffered them to be swung back to their original position.

The door partially gave way at last, and a man in grey uniform, with light moustaches, and audacious, rollicking swagger, sprang through the opening.

" By my certes, a fairer prize than I had hoped to capture," he cried, with a bold glance of admiring insolence. " Here's to our better acquaintance. Drink to me with thine eyes, sweet, and pledge me in sparkling draughts."

"Shame on you, Brent, for insulting a defenceless woman," remonstrated one of his followers.

" Now, a murrain seize upon thee, incomprehensible dolt, for the foul-mouthed suspicion crossing thy lips! Talk of insult, when knightly devoirs make the staple in the order of exercises. Heed not his loose tongue, my charming Amarylla, but bless the fate that threw you into the hands of one who never yet refused to fly to the succor of beauty in distress. You are frightened, over-come, poor trembling fawn, let me reassure you, let me offer my arm as support."

Minnie shrank from him with uncontrollable aversion. To be sure she had not provoked the wrath of any by stric-tures on the rebellion; but this availed her naught while in the power of a man whose love was greatly more to be dreaded than his hate.

" Don't be coy," he said, with a slight frown. " A soldier's rough courtesy is not to be lightly scorned. Give me your hand, or I will take it."

Knowing resistance to be worse than vain, she submit-ted to his escort up the narrow stairway.

While the cottage was ransacked for purposes of waste and pillage, Mr. Brandon's horse was saddled and Min-nie seated thereupon. So great was her dread that her father might emerge from his hiding-place and be cap-tured, or that the house might be fired and he left to perish in the flames, that apprehensions on her own ac-count assumed, for the moment, a place of secondary importance in her estimation. It was only on riding off with the pillagers that she awoke to a clear sense of her forlorn and helpless condition, aggravated, as it was, by assiduities she dared not resent from her special captor. They had passed, without interruption, two or three miles on their way, when a horseman from the roadside called out, in imperative tone, " Halt, friends, and receive orders."

"Our chief!" ejaculated Brent, in a tone of extreme surprise. "We are all here, and await orders, Lambeth."

"Lambeth!" cried Minnie, with a sudden thrill of joy and hope; "that is the name I was bidden to remember. Help me to escape! restore me to my home!"

"This is in palpable infringement of plain commands, Brent. How comes it that this young woman makes one of your number?"

"I entreat of you absolution without too stringent confession, or the severe penance of forsaking the error of my ways. Of a verity this young damsel is blessed not only with a comely countenance, but hath fair gifts of speech, which, with time and opportunity, I shall teach her to employ unto my edification. In alleviation of the rigors and hardships entailed by our nomadic style of life, you surely would not interdict the solace of"——

"Have done with this foolery," sternly interposed the chief of the band. "Would you stop to have out your joke with the hangman's noose preparing for your neck? We are tracked, pursued; away to the rendezvous—the lime-stone cave on Rathben Bluff. I will be there almost as soon as yourselves. Quick! begone!"

Waving on his men with gesture imperious, he seized Minnie's bridle-rein.

"Where is your home, young woman? Tell me in few words; I've not an instant to lose."

In concise phrase she gave him the information he sought.

He accompanied her within sight of the cottage, wheeled, then curbed his horse for a few words at parting.

"Bid me God speed, benefactress mine; for you know not the dangers from which I have rescued you. My

ways are of the roughest, my deeds not what they should
be; but I have not deserved ill of you, for I have not
rendered unto you evil for good. It is years since I saw
a preacher's desk, or listened to a preacher's warning;
but, taking my text from your acts, this say I unto you,
If thine enemy be an hungered or athirst, not even a
cup of cold water, bestowed in pure charity, shall fail
of its reward."

"I will treasure your words. God speed you to the
right!"

On reaching the cottage, she dismounted and hastily
entered the front door, which stood wide open. All was
still; no one astir, no light in the house. Groping her
way to the kitchen, she lit a candle and proceeded therewith to the sitting-room, where broken chairs, tables
smashed and overturned, torn books, and shattered
shelves and cases, afforded vivid reminder of rebel
raid.

Hurrying up-stairs, she rapped at the door of her
father's sleeping-room. There was no answer. She entered the chamber and found it tenantless, the bed not
having been disturbed. Could it be that the dark closet
had been so long closed that its air had become un-
breathable, and that in escaping the hangman's rope he
had met death by suffocation?

With flying feet, she made her way to the cellar. The
doors were all open, even to the inner one of shelves,
which concealed nothing. Through every room in the
house she searched; but to no purpose, her father was
not to be found. Old Chloe had slept undisturbed
through all the din, and undisturbed Minnie left her,
returning to the stable, unsaddling her horse, and leaving the animal in comfortable quarters for the night.

Deeply anxious on account of her father's inexplicable
absence, she was not in the least inclined to sleep; and,
after closing and fastening the doors, she sat down by

the sitting-room window, where the mournful wail of the unrestful wind mingled not unfitly with the restless surging of her own perturbed spirit. Long, and fraught with many a nameless terror, were the leaden-footed hours. Her heart leaped to her throat at sound so slight that, under ordinary circumstances, it would have passed without notice.

Her ears do not deceive her now; that is surely the sound of horses' hoofs on the hard-trod avenue. On the alert for any contingency, and determined not to be surprised by friend or foe, she darted from the house, and, making rapid detour of the barn, took shelter behind a clump of junipers, whence she maintained strict outlook over the approaching horsemen. They were three in number; and, greatly to her relief, she detected the tones of her father's voice addressed in friendly remark to one of his companions. There was no further occasion for concealment. Father and daughter expressed mutual delight at being assured of each others' safety. By the light of a lantern, speedily procured, she saw that yet another craved her welcome. It was Morland Ellsmead's hand that cordially grasped her own.

"Let us adjourn to the house while the horses rest," proposed Mr. Brandon.

"Morland can stay if he likes," returned the third of the trio, the son of a neighboring farmer; "but, as to my poor nags, they have to work carting sand to the brick-kiln all day to-morrow, so I must be off. Good-night, or good-morning, rather."

The remaining three entered the cottage together. The story of Minnie's safe return was soon related. Then Mr. Brandon explained that, leaving his retreat in time to ascertain the direction taken by his daughter's captors, he had roused the neighbors and started in swift pursuit. For several miles they found little diffi-

culty in tracing the marauders, but farther on, it was
only by close and careful scrutiny that they could detect
the prints of the horses' hoofs, which disappeared altogether on nearing the base of the river-side bluff.

Minnie turned on their guest a questioning look,
which plainly asked, " How came you to be of the
party ?"

" I will explain all in the morning," he replied to her
glance ; " but your father is quite worn out now ; leave
me on guard here, while you both seek needed rest."

" There is no need of your staying up to watch,"
demurred Mr. Brandon ; " we have always a spare bed
for a friend."

" I dare not risk the acceptance of luxury so unusual,
in which case I should be sure to oversleep. It is now
three, and I must leave at six."

" Then make yourself as comfortable as circumstances
will allow. Take a nap on the sofa ; there is one arm
and a cushion left. My throat is like a fresh scald from
this irritating night-air ; but what of that ? we are all
safe, for which I am devoutly thankful. Dear me !
what good did these vandals find in destroying what
was nothing to them, much to me ? Here is an anno-
tated edition of Paley, invaluable as a work of reference,
torn and mutilated in a most barbarous fashion."

While Mr. Brandon was bemoaning the fate of his
long-cherished volumes, and striving to restore contents
to covers from which they had been rudely sundered,
Morland Ellsmead, holding open the door for Minnie to
pass, murmured, scarcely louder than a whisper, " Thank
Heaven, you are safe ; I would have risked my life to
serve you."

She responded by a grateful look, and passed up the
stair-case with a smile of pleasure wreathing her lips ;
sorely wounded by slight and neglect from source
whence she had least expected it, this sincere avowal of

interest in her welfare, of earnest, respectful sympathy in her behalf, fell like balm of healing on the aching spirit pining in secret over unprovoked wrongs.

The varied causes of excitement she had undergone precluded all possibility of sleep, and she was early astir. Believing herself the only person awake in the house, she stole noiselessly down-stairs, but as her foot touched the entry carpet, the outer door opened, and Morland Ellsmead gave her morning salutation.

" I have been out to look after my horse; it is very kind of you to let me see you before I go."

A delicate tinge of carmine dyed Minnie's cheek.

" I knew you had to leave early, Mr. Ellsmead, and I am going down to the kitchen to hurry Chloe's preparations for breakfast."

" Time enough for that when I have explained to you how I happened here. In five minutes I can tell you all; and, in all probability, I shall not soon have a chance of speaking with you again. I want your advice; I need it."

" Mine, oh! Morland, when my own footsteps are so wavering and uncertain that I have oft to retrace them with bitter pain."

" Happy for you that they are not irretraceable. Now sit on the sofa beside me, and teach me to bear my burdens as patiently and uncomplainingly as you bear your own. My period of enlistment expired yesterday; I have been offered a salary of fifteen hundred a year as agent in a woollen factory, and I have been offered thirteen dollars a month to serve as private in the ranks of a brigade recruiting for service in a southern field. Give me your counsel; shall I go or stay?"

" Does the country need you?"

" The country needs me; and I have no ties; not even those of friendship to hinder my departure."

" There you do greatly err; my friends are not so

many but that one stricken from the roll makes grievous loss ; and yet, at risk of having one friend the less,
if any word of mine could encourage him to volunteer
in country's defence, such word, no matter what the
cost of speaking it, should not be withheld."

Beneath the eager scrutiny of his searching gaze, her
eyes drooped and the carmine deepened to crimson on
her cheek.

" A fair promise, freely given ; now will I test your
power of fulfillment.   Three words I spoke to you, once,
for which you gave me merited rebuff ; should I repeat
them, would your reply be still the same ?"

" Do not trouble yourself by vain repetition ; I have
the words quite by heart."

" Because my lips spoke them ?"

" Because your lips spoke them, Morland."

" Repeat them yourself that I may be doubly sure
memory has not played you false."

Crimsoning to the very temples, she gave the triple-
worded countersign he sought.

Tones commingling as gently as odor-laden breeze
sighing through sweets of woodland bloom, transformed
that homely cottage parlor into realm of fairy enchant-
ment for its occupants.   Swift sped minutes all too fleet-
ing—minutes burdened with harmony delicious from
that old, old song that first floated on the golden airs of
Paradise.

" How time has flown, Minnie ; I must leave you,
and leave much I wished to say unspoken."

" Wait one moment, Morland, I must tell you this.
The sacred cause that claims your best services, claims
mine also.   It is but little I can accomplish : but let
me earn the record—' She hath done what she could,'
and it will be well with me.   We weak women cannot,
like you, strike strong blows in defence of the right, but
we can, at least, spend our best energies in care and

tendance of those who are brought, helpless and suffering, from the battle-field, which is no place for feminine
tread. My father is going to Chicago; I am going to
St. Marc Hospital."

"To St. Marc Hospital, one of the largest and most
crowded in the vicinity! oh, Minnie, you know not
what you do; you who have been so guarded in the
seclusion of home; so delicately and tenderly reared,
to be brought in contact with coarse, even vicious
natures, to have your motives misconstrued, to"——

"Hush, Morland. Are you to be exposed to the
fierce breath of battle-roar, to deadly rifle and musket-
hail, to thirsty blade of gleaming steel, to seething rush
of cannon ball, while I sit supinely down, the winds of
heaven not permitted to visit my cheek too roughly?
Woman was created, if I have read my Bible aright, to
be faithful help-meet unto man; does she fulfill the purpose of her being, if in his hour of sorest trial, through
mere stress of conventionalism, she is induced to forfeit
her dearest earthly prerogative? Our greatest generals
are subjected to misconstruction and to contumely,
and why should I shrink from enduring, in my own
humble degree, my lot and part in the deep anguish
which afflicts the land, and every true child of the soil
in its borders?"

"I glory in your patriotism, Minnie; but it seems to
me there are ways in which you might make yourself
useful, without depriving yourself of the shielding and
protecting influences of home."

"Providence has seemed to open a way for me in a
different direction. Listen while I tell you how; and,
oh! Morland, give me an encouraging word, if you
can, as I don't quite see my way clear; and it is very
hard, at times, to take the responsibility of deciding on
my own course of action. Dr. Waldo, who attended
my mother in her last illness, is now directing surgeon

at St. Marc's, where he wishes me to come, not as nurse, for there is a sufficiency of male attendance in the sick wards, but as directress in the preparation of extracts, infusions, the herbal restoratives and medicaments he long ago taught me to compound; permitting me to search the woods and fields for anodyne and alterative, instead of sending me with a Latin prescription to the apothecary's for less harmless draught. I have bidden you God speed in your loftier sphere of effort; Heaven knows the words sending you from my side, mayhap forever, were not easily spoken, and will you be less generous in bidding me haste onward in the way duty bids me tread?"

"If it be duty that beckons you onward, Minnie, heaven forbid that hand of mine should place stumbling-block in your path. Be true to your own sense of right, and there is no fear of your being false to me."

He drew out his silver hunting-watch.

"It lacks but three minutes of my hour for starting; I must not linger here."

"I forgot your breakfast, Morland; how shall I apologize?"

"No apology is necessary; I, too, forgot it."

She walked with him as he led his horse down the orange-hedged avenue. In almost unbroken silence they traversed the way, which had never seemed so short. The rustic gate which must witness their parting was reached all too soon.

"Farewell, Minnie, my own; if I am stricken down by sabre-thrust or cannon-ball, I shall be content to be tended by no hand but yours. Pardon, my last words shall not be of theme so gloomy. Let us rather look forward with hope to that glorious hour, when this unnatural antagonism between those who should be friends and brothers, happily overcome, our union may be consummated with that of these now alienated States. I shall perform my duties all the better for knowing how faithfully you will cling to yours ; and if, mayhap, I look on your face for the last time, there is a fairer land of promise where time, the destroyer, cannot come."

" I will keep your words as talisman, if my own life-task should seem ever over-burdensome when I am left to bear it alone."

He drew a plain gold ring from his own and slipped it on her finger; it was much too large, and she returned it to him.

" I have no need of any such reminder, Morland ; your photograph will remain faithfully mirrored in my remembrance, though no sun-rays stamped it there. Neither do you, I trust, need any parting token to bring me to your thoughts."

" But one, Minnie, one keepsake for memory only— voiceless token from unsullied lips taken—thanks ; I'm away."

She watched his receding figure with contending emotions of pride, regret and tenderness, until it disappeared over the brow of a gently undulating slope. Once more, with strained vision, she caught sight of him making his way up the opposing ascent. He saw her, too, and removing his cap, waved her parting salute therewith. With brimming eyes she returned the signal.

" Gone, gone ; and if he should never return, could I ever forgive myself for having spoken the words that gave him to the noblest cause for which man ever fought and died. He came to me for encouragement ; I gave it him, but who is to encourage me ? My words bade him hie forth to—

‘ The glorious strife which is the joy of men—’

but had I counselled him to hours of silken ease, when
his brave brethren are pouring out blood like water for
the regeneration of the land, would he have spoken to
me as he has spoken, words that will be mine for al
ages to come, no matter what the future may have in
store for me? I understand, now, how Hector's patriotism overcame his affection, so that he could say to
Andromache, at parting—

> 'I could not love thee, dear, so much,
> Loved I not honor more.' "

CHAPTER VIII.

CORRESPONDENCE.

On the afternoon of the day on which she had parted
from one whom she seemed to have won and lost in an
hour, she received from him the following brief note,
which certainly had no merit, so far as literary ability
was concerned, to commend it to the repeated perusals
it received:

"My dearest Minnie:—On parting from you this
morning, my courage broke down entirely, at thought
that no link of communication was left between us. I
must hear from you; positively *must*. There is no
knowing to what infection you may be exposed at
St. Marc's, and if you do not write me a favorable
account of the place, I shall not consent to your remaining in it.

"Excuse that blot; there are four wide-awakes playing euchre on this bench, and they joggle so I can't write straight, and gabble so I can't think straight either, for that matter.

"I have been sworn into service, and have received my new uniform. There goes tap of drum for dress-parade. Two minutes, prithee, before 1 fall into line. Confound the rub-a-dubster! he is newly appointed, and delighteth in exercise of a little brief authority. I inclose you the number of our regiment, and will send you address in full as soon as our companies are lettered. Pray write to—

"Yours until death,
"MORLAND."

"True as steel," she said to herself, on folding this brief epistle. "Strange that writers should parcel out plays into artificial division of comedy and of tragedy, when, in real life, there is usually in each day's experience a combination of both."

Minnie had thought, on returning to the cottage, to explain to her father, as soon as practicable, the new turn of affairs in her own destiny; but the bronchial derangement from which he had been suffering had been so much aggravated by anxiety and exposure that for several days he was unable to swallow, or to speak a loud word, and she could do nothing save guard him from intrusion, and insure him the undisturbed repose on which nature insisted while making unavoidable repairs.

Even when he was able to take his usual place in the sitting-room, his daughter shrank from entering on a theme which might agitate him, thereby retarding his recovery. She was spared the embarrassment by a new and unexpected move on his part.

"Sit down beside me, child, while I talk over with you the perplexities it is but right you should know and

6

share. Last week I had what I considered an ample income to support our plain style of living; this week,
my circumstances have so essentially changed that I
don't see quite clearly what course to adopt. The powder factory in which my fortune was principally invested,
and from which my annual income was chiefly derivable,
has been torn down by the rebels. The damages fall
mostly to my account, as the Insurance Offices are naturally shy of taking risks on buildings covering highly
explosive merchandise. Now comes the claim on my
patriotism, much quickened, I own, by the ruffianly assault of a few nights since. We have been so much
accustomed to the peace and security conferred by our
free government that we prize it no more than the free
air of heaven; but the hour has now come when every
loyal supporter of the Law and the Constitution must
fly to their support, or be content to go down with them,
and be buried in the ruins from which chaos and anarchy
will spring in rank and noisome growth. I, for one, am
fully ready to assume my share of the national burden.
Recruits for Union service are rapidly filling our ranks;
arms will be supplied with all possible dispatch; but to
make these latter available, ammunition must be in
equally abundant supply. This is where we are lacking,
and forms my motive for desiring to rebuild the mill
without a moment's unnecessary delay; it is want of requisite funds alone that stays my hand. The bears have
control of the Brokers' Board at present, so that I should
not realize half their intrinsic value from the forced sale
of bank and railway shares; there is no means of raising
the requisite amount, that I can see, save through a
mortgage, as heavy as it will bear, on this place. If
you were provided for I should not hesitate an instant
in adopting this course."

"Then do not hesitate an instant now. I am young
and strong, and quite as ready as yourself to submit to

any sacrifice that would conduce to the country's welfare. If Morland Ellsmead returns safely from the southern expedition on which he is bound, he will seek your consent to our marriage. While he is devoting his best energies to cause so glorious, think you I should be content to sit supinely down without contributing my mite to the National Treasury? I only await your permission to take my place at St. Marc's, as assistant in preparing comforts and delicacies for its sick and wounded inmates. Here comes Dr. Waldo, who first proposed the plan to me. I will leave you to discuss the matter with him."

"Good morning, Miss Brandon," said the doctor, briskly entering the room; "I have come for your decision, agreeably to promise."

"I have decided in the affirmative, on condition of your obtaining my father's approval," she returned, effecting a hasty retreat.

Mr. Brandon remained long enough at the cottage to make such dispositions of his estate as were necessitated by his new project, and then took his departure for Chicago.

Minnie had been long enough installed in her new office to learn that it was no sinecure, when a letter, written on a half sheet of soiled and crumpled paper, was placed in her hand. Thus she read:

"DEAREST, MINE:—As there is to be a mail-bag made up by the regiment, I claim the privilege of raising my quota toward filling its columns.

"We are halting now, after a forced march of thirty miles, on our way to join the main corps of the Western Army. We are made to feel, every step of our progress, that we are in an enemy's country. Not even a glass of lemonade or a basket of fruit do we dare to take as gift or purchase, from fear of being poisoned;

and any man straggling from the ranks does so at peril
of furnishing skull as football for rebel pastime. In
passing through woods—luckily for us, the trees here-
abouts are generally tall, without low branches or underbrush—our advance-guard and flankers have to be
every instant on the alert. In open, unobstructed
plains, the cavalry deploy for our protection; bridges
we enfilade with our guns, and in passing through vil-
lages, which we avoid when we can, without making
too wide a circuit, we plant our heaviest artillery in the
most advantageous positions for being conspicuously
viewed by the villagers. Some grow reckless under this
continued exposure to imminent danger; but I never
looked so warily to every step as now that each one may
be my last.

"Tell Mrs. Burt that her son, who marched at my
left hand, gave me his musket to carry while he ran for
a drink to a brook which he saw through the poplars,
and he has not since been seen or heard from. He will
probably turn up in some rebel stronghold.

"I send you my address, the name of the town being
one which we shall, in all human probability, reach in
a couple of days. After that, I know nothing of our
intended destination, as we are not informed of our
commander's plans.

"I must close now, as I am only off guard four hours,
and there is a button to tighten on my coat, the brass
pieces on my equipments to brighten, even if my gun
doesn't need a touch from emery paper.

"Send me some word of cheer, Minnie; and believe
that, at each remove, 'my heart untravelled fondly turns
to thee.'

"Heaven bless and hold thee in most sacred keeping.
                              "Yours, devotedly,
                                        "MORLAND."

Weary and dispirited as she was, this letter inspired its recipient with fresh energy, and she at once set about her reply, which is here given entire:

"MOST VALIANT KNIGHT:—I was so fatigued and exhausted by all the labors of the day that I thought no luxury could be comparable to that of resting my tired head on my pillow; but you have proved my mistake by giving me the opportunity of communicating with you through written channel, an opportunity I improve with delighted alacrity. Not that I am complaining of fatigue, mind you, as I am bound to you by still closer ties through knowledge that this most glorious cause of a country's salvation claims your best powers as well as my own.

"You ask of me some word of cheer. How shall I give it, Morland, when I know not but that, even as I write, some mortal peril may be lying in wait for you? Will it cheer you to know that I hold you ever in fond and faithful remembrance, thinking of you not only each day but each hour, and many times in the hour? Shall I tell you that the letter you stole time from hours which should have been given to needed repose, to indite, is more precious than gold of Ophir—more dearly prized than gem from richest mine? Are you smiling at my extravagance? Be it so; if I can provoke you to mirth I care not, though it be at my own expense?

"Possibly it may interest you to know how my days are passed. Mrs. Stanton, a widowed sister of Dr. Waldo, is our principal directress, and a most stringent disciplinarian. We have each our duties to be performed at all hazards; my position, it seems, is that of maid-of-all-work, as I turn my hand to everything, from making a broth to stitching a bandage, or writing a letter for some poor fellow who craves memorial from some true heart as do I from one I believe my own.

"I rise at five and make my toilette, so inelaborate that it is, perhaps, not beyond dull masculine comprehension, so I will describe its most salient peculiarities. First, retrenched skirts without the least pretense to voluminous flow; for in meeting each other on the stairs, a dozen times a minute, no one desires to claim exclusive right of way. Then comes a dress of grey serge, which does not rustle, and is easily kept clean. Now comes the crowning abomination in the way of offence against good taste with which Mrs. Stanton, in the plenitude of her power, has seen fit to afflict her long-suffering handmaidens. Curls, for cooks, she deems wholly inadmissible; nets are a pet aversion of hers; so we are reduced to the wretched alternative of wearing the most excruciatingly unbecoming lawn caps envious malignity ever devised. Well, I don't care, since—you are not here to see; but with all humility be it written, earthly vanities are so far from having palled on my taste, that if I should catch a glimpse of you coming up the linden walk in plain view, instead of setting my cap for you, I should toss it into the nearest corner, and resort, at once, to every outward adorning that might give me grace and comeliness in your eyes.

"What folly is this! Candidly, you are disposed to far over-estimate me; and although it is very flattering to be exalted to a higher place in your esteem than my own worth justifies, truth is always best and safest in the end. I must spare you the violent revulsion you would be sure to experience if you should stumble, without any preparation of previous warning, upon the unwelcome fact that the woman on whom you had been lavishing your heart's best riches had nothing but her truth and constancy to recommend her, and was a very ordinary specimen of humanity after all.

"All this space, and only my toilette completed!

You have no idea what a variety of capricious likes and dislikes, in the way of food, we have to consult in compounding refections for the sick wards. One poor fellow, who is wasted to a shadow with pulmonary consumption, has lived on scraped sweet apples for a month; a second takes nothing, as his digestives lack the vigor for attempting functional action, but the expressed juices of meats; a third, who is almost speechless with incipient laryngeal paralysis, can swallow nothing but stimulants; while a fourth contrives to subsist somehow on narcotics, soda and lemon juice. The pervading spirit of manly fortitude and resignation with which they submit to the suffering and deprivation inseparable from their lot, acts as effectual check to any complaints in which I might otherwise be inclined to indulge.

"In one respect, I have striven to copy the example of the hospital surgeons, who, whatever their own individual trials and perplexities, permit no trace of them to become apparent to their patients. Dr. Waldo will perform the most grave and critical operations in the amputation room, and then with air as blandly disengaged as though he had just risen from couch of cushioned ease, go from cot to cot addressing to occupant of each some cheerful word of soothing or encouragement, falling like gentlest anodyne on spirits sore through sympathy with material ills.

"I wished to give you a list of my employments throughout the day, but space fails me.

"Pray do not expose yourself rashly, for the country needs every one of its brave defenders, and evil (which Heaven avert) befalling you, would be, to me, as though it had fallen on myself.

"Remembering how precious is every assurance of your continued safety, do not withhold the same from

"MINNIE."

Scarcely more than a week elapsed before she received the ensuing response to her epistle:

"MY DEAR GIRL:—I told you once that, given the opportunity, I should inevitably make a fool of myself, and as you were graciously pleased to furnish the occasion, I have attested my veracity by making the most of it. Can you imagine a man cutting up capers that would do credit to a confirmed idiot, and going into raptures over a mere sheet of paper covered with daintiest sweeps and curves, just because it happened to express some feelings of kindly interest in behalf of your humble servant? Of course, you can conceive of nothing so ineffably absurd; let us have done with such puerile nonsense.

"Do not expect anything in the way of caligraphy from me, as I am sitting on a stump, using a tin plate as writing-desk, with the boom of artillery practice sounding in my ears.

"We have had a brush with the enemy, which might have been a serious affair if it had occurred earlier in the day, which it would have done, if our original plan had not been modified by circumstances I have not space to detail. The treachery of a negro guide, who decoyed us into a well-planned ambuscade (the sort of thing that the insidious foe always does plan well, for it must be conceded the Southron is as far ahead of us in subtle trick of strategy, as European southron has shown himself over northern opponent, from the time that Spanish diplomacy outwitted Briton's astute queen to the present, when a wily Gallic hand directs the moves of a continent's chess-board), came near resulting in overwhelming disaster.

"It was within an hour of sundown; the main body of our division had safely passed a dangerous defile, which its baggage train with its convoy was about to enter, when from a large cave, whose entrance had been so artfully concealed as to have escaped the notice of lynx-eyed vidette and patrol, poured forth the enemy in force, and after unmasking batteries, gave us a tempest of shell and canister, and swooped down upon us, yelling like so many—beg pardon—d——s incarnate. Our regiment formed part of the reserve held back in case of emergency like the present. We were ordered to stack knapsacks and prepare for immediate action. The enemy had the advantage of us in being fresh, while we were spent with a weary day's march, and had eaten nothing since mid-day. The object of the attack soon became apparent; it was the wagon train our assailants were bent on capturing; the last thing to lose in a region where all forage which could not be removed was destroyed to prevent it falling into our hands. We forgot there was such a thing as being hungry and tired, and fought like tigers; not one of us but would as soon have died as seen our subsistence stores go to the sustenance of those greedy cormorants. The enemy's guns were but indifferently served, or we should have been terribly cut up. As it was, many of the horses attached to the train were shot, and if we had not had spare horses to fill their places, our loss would have been irremediable. I must tell you the last we saw of our personal gear. A parcel of negroes, Confederates in collusion with our false guide very likely, had taken possession of our knapsacks, and were scattering about and destroying such articles as did not suit their immediate needs. One brawny son of Ethiop had crowned his woolly pate with a bright-colored fatigue-cap, and strutted round in great pomp and circumstance, clad in a bugler's scarlet suit which had tickled his barbaric taste.

"When we had kept the enemy at bay long enough to give the convoy a fair start in advance, you should
6*

have seen us run, the cavalry and light artillery bring
ing up the rear. Talk of the double-quick ! quadruple-
quick, and sextuple-quick was all that saved us to fight
another day.

"I think the climate must agree with me, as I slept
on the ground last night, without either blanket or over-
coat, and feel no ill effects from the exposure ; on the
contrary, am blessed with an appetite which is much
better than comfortable, considering the scantiness of
the rations doled out by our commissary.

"I cannot request you to write me, as I do not know
where to ask you to direct. You shall hear from me as
soon as I can remove this obstacle to our correspondence, and pray respond promptly to

"Yours most faithfully,

"MORLAND."

Several weeks passed before Minnie's eyes were again
gladdened by sight of the handwriting which had grown
familiar through much repetition of vain reading. I
transcribe the missive which gave to her eyes fresh lustre, to her cheek an added tint of bloom :

"CARNROSVILLE, *Jan.* 20, 1862.

"BEST REMEMBERED FRIEND :—I have been through
such an exhaustive process of labor and fatigue since last
I wrote you, that I have scarcely sufficient vitality left
for the mental effort of giving you an account, even the
most cursory, of the difficulties we have had to overcome in reaching this place. Since the affair of which
I wrote you in my last, and for which the general of
the division complimented our gallantry, our regiment
had seen much duty on the rear-guard, which has been
peculiarly exposed to the sharp shooting of the guerilla
bands forever prowling on our flanks and rear. I do
not know what it is to fall asleep with that sense of

security which is indespensable to any repose worth the name ; and as a consequence, my slumbers are so disturbed by visions of attack and assault that they do not refresh me, and I am weary all the time.

"We took this town after a slight show of resistance from the inhabitants ; and I belong to the detachment left to occupy it, as it is of considerable strategic importance, owing to its railroad junction affording us line of communication with base of supplies.

"The women here belong to such a species of nondescript as I never saw before, and hope never to see again. Ignoring all the graces, they are ready to aid the fray by those underhanded means which weak cunning suggests. If they wish to throw off the guards with which chivalry protects them against life's severer ills, let them fight us on equal terms—meet us in fair and honorable conflict, as I, for one, am strongly opposed to having my head broken by missiles from a chamber window, or to being knocked down with a rolling-pin and dispatched with a skewer. When the gentler sex proves false to its benign mission, and aggravates instead of softening asperities quickened to unwholesome growth in troublous times like these, let it expect an exceeding bitter penalty for its betrayal of sacred trust. When I look at these fierce inciters of deadly strife, it is to turn, in thought, with tenfold tenderness to one who would gladly spur us on to deeds of high emprise in patriot struggle ; but whose hand, bearing to us merciful healing, will never come armed with rod of wrath.

" Do you remember Gustave Ashmore, captain of our company, and as big a poltroon as ever breathed ? A supercilious fop, whose equipments are not likely to be tarnished through use, and whose chief military accomplishment consists in showing a clean pair of heels to the enemy; he has been promoted to a majorship, and his place bestowed on a lily-livered milksop who happened to be well connected, and brought letters of recommendation to our General from influential relatives at home. Well, I have not been sparing of myself in the country's service; I have never fled from the post of duty because it was the post of danger; and yet, if I return, I fear I shall bring but few laurels to lay at your feet. I have neither patronage nor the impudence needful to push on my way to advancement, and it is sometimes hard to stand aside in the ranks and let a worse man step into the honors he has never earned.

"Our detachment is so small for the performance of the duty assigned it, that we are all overworked. Our labors will be lightened when we have finished throwing up a fort on the hill overlooking the junction. When I say fort, do not imagine heavy ramparts with bastions of solid masonry, for that would give you an erroneous idea of our stronghold, which comprises two or three acres of ground, is walled in by logs, with embankments of earth on the inside reaching a little higher than a man's head. Outside, a moat, fifteen feet deep by twelve in width, extends, or will when completed, around the structure, which is octagonal and will look tolerably formidable when our thirty-two pounders are mounted. If you did but know the labor dire I have gone through delving in this hard soil! My hands have been so blistered that I could scarcely handle a musket; face and ears are blistered too; for the sun already runs high, and I miss my havelock sadly, as it cannot be replaced.

"I fear this is but a drowsy production, and well it may be, for—pardon lack of gallantry implied by the admission—I have been surprised off guard, by more than one nap since commencing the above. Send me some coveted assurance of undiminished regard, and you shall receive no lifeless response. No one who has not ex-perienced it, can fathom the intensity of eager longing felt by the soldier, suddenly wrenched from all the dearly-cherished associations of former years, for some expression of kindly interest from the loved ones left be-hind. On this hint, please write to   " MORLAND."

The reply to the above ran as follows:

" ST. MARC'S, *Jan.* 26, 1862.

" MY DEAR MORLAND :—I received your most fer-vently welcomed letter late last evening, and should have done myself the pleasure of replying at once, only I sat up until midnight making for you this havelock, which, if it but give you in the receiving a tithe of the pleasure it has given me in the making—thinking con-stantly for whom I wrought—will prove, humble as it is, one of the good gifts, blessing alike donor and reci-pient.

" Of that part of your letter which most deeply moved me I will first speak. Do not be depressed, Morland, because those less deserving of promotion than yourself are preferred over you. Biography teaches us that few indeed of the really wise and de-serving enter, during this life, into the full joy of their labors. We can do our very best in the way of effort, but, best beloved, we cannot control results. The country, torn and bleeding through fiercely-contending factions, claims the best and noblest manhood of her sons in her defence ; and yours, I am sure, she will not claim in vain, whether you labor with or without the appreciation so dear to every generous heart. The army must have men as well as officers ; commanded as well as commanders. What would a building be good for that was made of turret and tower, of belfry and spire, of peak and pinnacle, without a substructure

134 THE RIVAL VOLUNTEERS; OR

adequate to the support of its top-heavy petensions. Better a true soldier, by all odds, with garments soiled and frayed in obedience to duty's call, than the titled craven who keeps his velvet facings spotless, and his glittering blade stainless in its scabbard, while richly earning a coward's fate.

"You speak of winning laurels to lay at my feet, rather crown with laurels of noble, persistent endeavor the country's thorn-pressed brow, that we may the sooner rejoice in her restoration to peace and ours to each other. Come back to me with integrity unimpeached, unimpeachable, and I ask no more. I speak strongly on this point, because when I was all adrift on the surging sea of doubt and uncertainty, when through one man's deceit I grew skeptical of others' truth and others' sincerity, it was you who gave me back the blessed boon of renewed trust in human goodness; a boon of which no hand save yours can deprive me—which calamity, Heaven in its mercy avert.

"I cannot write more, as the clock is striking five, and duties claim every instant of my time throughout the day.

"Whatever neglect you may experience from other sources, rest assured that you will have none to complain of from   "Yours evermore,
                                        "MINNIE."

With a lighter heart than she had known for weeks, the writer of the above set about the performance of her daily tasks, and more than one brow, corrugated with tense lines of pain, smoothed beneath her speaking glance of earnest sympathy. Now that her betrothed had reached a comparatively permanent place of destination, whence she could obtain frequent intelligence of his movements, her apprehensions on his account had greatly subsided.

"In a week, at farthest, I shall hear from him again," she said to herself, counting the intervening days as they, one by one, slipped past, bringing nearer the period terminating this fond anticipation—fond but fallacious, as ten days went by without bringing her a line from one whose prolonged silence began to excite her keenest anxiety. On the fourteenth day from the date of her last epistle, she partially relieved her intolerable suspense by penning and dispatching the subjoined :

"My dear Morland:—Do, I entreat of you, from motives of compassion, if none other, find some means of conveying to me the assurance that you still remain unharmed ; and, if this be not so, pray let me know the worst I have to fear for you. Are you wounded ? then you must have some comrade near who will mercifully tell me to what extent, thus giving me something tangible on which to wreak my ceaseless apprehensions, and relieving me from these terrible phantoms imagination keeps conjuring up. Can it be possible that fancy is playing me a trick?—that my nerves have lost tone and impose on my credulity but false presentments of what seems so real?—or, is this pale, indistinct vision, that forever haunts me, waking or sleeping, of one stricken down in life's early flush, sorrowing, suffering, deserted, something of graver import than the baseless fabric of a dream? Am I clairvoyant, and, through some subtle spiritual intercommunion, has your misery, in reflex form, become my own ?

"Away, idle terrors ! You told me, Morland, that your powers of endurance were overtaxed ; and they have failed at last—nothing worse. You are worn out, and need rest ; that is all. You have so exhausted your best energies in patriotic service that your nerveless hand has not strength to respond to friendly call. To the comrade who gives you kindly tendance you will

not delegate the task you will soon be able to undertake
yourself. You can no more write me by proxy than I,
thus circumstanced, could thus write you. I will moderate my request; you are not to write me a letter, if it
would cost you wearisome effort, but just write my name
on this envelope I inclose and return it to me by
mail. The mere sight of the familiar characters, traced
by your own pen, would restore me to fresh life and
happiness.

"Do not delay, Morland, for you know not the
wretchedness your unexplained silence costs—

"MINNIE."

———•••———

CHAPTER IX.

NEWS.

THE faint glimmer of hope with which Minnie awaited
a reply to her letter was doomed to fade in disappointment, as no reply ever came. With a feverish restlessness, she hurried from one task to another, striving to
bury recollection in a ceaseless round of employment.
Never had her fingers been more deftly nimble, or her
step more light, than now when her heart was like lead
in her bosom.

One final resort, an appeal for information to the
captain of the company in which Morland had enlisted,
remained unto her; and to this she had recourse, writing
the word "urgent," in conspicuous capitals on the envelope inclosing her missive.

To this, after a tedious period of expectancy, she received the following brief reply:

"Captain Briscom was killed at the late severe engagement at Rover's Landing, forty miles south of this place. "Respectfully,

"A. L. CLYDE,
"*Secretary of Division.*"

This announcement Minnie read with blurred vision. If the captain had taken part in the conflict, his company, of course, had shared its dangers. After protracted and painful deliberation, she addressed a few concisely worded inquiries to the secretary who had already obliged her by intelligence conveyed in the above note, regarding the losses sustained by Company B. In reply, she was informed that it had suffered severely, only thirty-three of its members being fit for active service. The field, unfortunately, had been left in possession of the enemy, our wounded being brought off next day under a flag of truce. Morland Ellsmead's name was not amongst these, neither was it to be found in any official report.

This communication, furnishing particulars so scant yet so cruelly suggestive, fell from the reader's trembling hand, while her features hardened into a look of rigid despair. She did not think or reason, remaining dumb, in attitude bent and motionless, beneath the blow that had stricken her.

"Has anything gone wrong with you?" asked Mrs. Stanton, crossing to the corner of the kitchen where Minnie sat.

For answer, she picked up the letter she had dropped and handed it to her questioner.

"It seems from this that none but the dead were left on the battle-field," remarked Mrs. Stanton, as she finished the perusal of the note, in what, to her companion, seemed a cold, unfeeling tone; "and it naturally follows that"——

"Pray, do not go on," Minnie tremulously implored, "do not frame it into words; it may not be so bad as our fears make it."

"Can I do anything for you?"

"Yes; let me go away where I can be quite by myself—away up to the closet in the attic, where I can be alone—all, sole alone."

"But, my poor child, you know how much, with all these fresh arrivals, we need your help."

"I know it, Mrs. Stanton; but you must give me a little time to still this heavy pain in my head—this heavier ache at my heart. Heaven forgive me! how shall I again learn to labor with zeal in a cause trebly dear because *he* was with it, heart and soul?"

In using the past tense, the speaker had unwittingly framed into words the burden of her grief. Does not the woe-fraught cry, "He was, and is no-more!" form sad, *sad* refrain to all our national lyrics now!

"Take your own time; we will get along without you until you have a little recovered from the shock of this sudden news. Go; and come back as soon as you are able."

As Minnie crept up the front staircase, the light, laughing tones of a couple of visitors, relatives to a convalescing patient, floated down to her from the landing. What had she to do with mirth? The sounds smote on her ear like those of cruel mockery. She retraced her steps, gaining her haven of refuge by a back stairway. Closing the door behind her, she turned the large wooden button barring outer entrance. Her chosen place of retreat might have been six feet square; on one side were piled promiscuously together rolls of bandage, splints, flannel wrappers, and loose quilted slippers. Making for herself a place to sit down amongst all this sick-room paraphernalia, and crossing her arms over a package of old linen, she bent her throbbing head thereupon. If she thought at all, it was in disjointed, desultory fashion, expressing itself in broken, ejaculatory phrase, as thus—

"Has all the cream of my life gone so soon? and is the rest to be duty—only duty? I can bear it, or it would not be sent; but life seems long to look forward to—wearily, drearily long. You were always true, Morland; you are true still. Better even this than to know you false; better to lose you for this life than to lose you forever. If you are not mine for this present time, you are mine for all time to come. You have earned your release; I will be patient in well-doing until mine is also earned."

The sun went down on her grief, and still she sat motionless, her head bowed on her arms. There was a tap at the door.

"Who is it?" she asked.

"It is I, Mrs. Stanton. Aren't you coming down?"

"Not now. Give me until to-morrow morning, please."

"But you are not going to sleep in this uncomfortable place?"

"Not to sleep. I only wish to remain where I am sure of being undisturbed."

"Shall I send you up a cup of tea?"

"You are very kind; but I wish for nothing."

"Not even for a light?"

"Not even for that, I thank you."

Mrs. Stanton went softly away. On the stairs she met her brother, and stopped him to say:

"Minnie Brandon has received news of the probable death of the young man to whom she was engaged. She takes it so deeply to heart that I fear she will make herself ill, and we cannot spare her just now."

"Of course we can't: she can turn her hand to anything, and is never tired or out of sorts; I will attend to her case in the morning. Send me the poppy-leaf cataplasm as soon as it is prepared."

The hour of midnight found Minnie sitting upright on her unique couch, her eyes gazing blankly into space, not even noting the pitchy darkness of her little cell, which was lighted only by a pane of glass over the door.

"His name has been mentioned in no official report," she said to herself; "and no news is not necessarily bad news. There are a thousand chances in his favor. I did but jump at a rash conclusion when I so hastily gave him up as lost. He may have fallen into the hands of the enemy, and there is the hope of his being released on parole, if he would accept release on such terms, or of his being exchanged. He may have been wounded, and have crawled away to some safe place of shelter. If I could but go to him, and give him the kindly tendance he needs; it may not be. It is enough for me to know that he still lives. My consciousness cannot thus mock me with vain longings. This sweet, consoling presence comes as precious solace in my hour of sore trial—came of itself; I did not seek it, and it is only good gifts that come freely, like heaven's descending dews. No, Morland; it is not as of one gone to his long, last rest, that I think of you, but as of one suffering ills I am powerless to avert. You must endure; I must labor and strive in the way wherein it is appointed unto me to walk. I will not sit me down in idle repining over what I cannot alleviate. I will seek, through rest, to gain strength for the morrow's duties."

Contrary to her anticipations, sleep steeped her senses in balmy repose, and she rose calm and refreshed at her usual hour. There was a large accession of inmates to the hospital; and in incessant occupation with lancet and trephine, splint and band, Dr. Waldo forgot the ase which no longer needed his care. She was a little

absent-minded, at times, with the air of one searching
vainly for the unseen and the unreal—the impalpable
something which just escaped her vision; but aside
from this, she went bravely on, with unfaltering step,
in the course she had marked out for herself. No smile
ever came to her lips, but she was blessed with that
calm peace and self-approval which is the best substitute for happiness. It was only at the hour for the post-
boy's arrival that she became uneasy and restless. It
was hard to receive, as repeated reply to her eager inquiries, "Nothing to-day for you, Miss." Her spirit
almost fainted within her as she occasionally reflected
that the most dearly cherished hope of her life had no
foundation more stable than that afforded by her own
settled convictions.

Early springtime came, spreading carpet of living
green on prairie slope and sunny vale, and garlanding
with delicate bloom the nectarine and the pink rareripe.
Bees hummed in the shrubs, birds sang on the trees, but
to Minnie came sound more welcome, sight more joyous
than rarest tone or sweetest flower. It was with a cry
of rapturous delight that she recognized the handwriting
on the package handed her by the post-boy. In that instant's joy was obliterated every trace of the long hours
of tedious waiting that had preceded it.

She felt no immediate desire to ascertain the contents
of the little package that, like an enchanted wand, had,
by one wave, brushed away the lowering clouds that
threatened to darken all her future. It was enough for
her to know that he was alive and well; yes, well, for no
feeble, nerveless hand ever traced those bold, firm slopes
and curves on which she gazed.

A one-armed soldier waited for her to write a letter
at his dictation. He was a sturdy backwoodsman, rough
but honest. She sat down at the small table beside his
cot and arranged pen, ink and paper.

"Now, Mr. Hobson, I am ready to commence. What shall I write?"

"Wal, I reckon, you may as well tote in my love and respects strong; a whole grist on 'em won't do no harm."

"But wouldn't it be better to let that come in toward the close of the letter?"

"Mebbe so; I don't care where you bring it in, if you only do it up brown, and enough of it. Now I'll begin again. You tell Polly that taint no use grumbling at the ways o' Providence—she's kind o' riled up when things get into a snarl, is Polly; and flies into raving, distracted hy-ster-ics, which ain't to be wondered at, se-in' a woman ain't a reasonin' creetur, though as good-hearted as ever drew the breath o' life, and no more accountable for a fit of the tantrums than a nanny-goat for butting at a brier-bush and gnawing the bark off my best garden sweetin', for natur' made 'em so—and it's what I tole 'er an' tole 'er again, line upon line, and precept upon precept, that fall that the murrain got afoul of the sheep, and the cattle distemper was lively, and kicking Bill backed down the trap-door *that* shiftless Dave had left open at the back of his stall, into the pig-pen, and hung himself by the neck till he was stone dead; and little Cyrus got a bean up his nose; and baby crawled into the sink-spout and nigh about got choked to death; an', to cap the apex, mumps, measles and shakes lit on all the young ones at once, and turned our log shanty into a regular hospital. You can't blame Polly, can you now? for thinking that bedlam had broke loose and was bent on raising Cain about our clearin'."

"Your good wife seems to have been subjected to heavy trials; but you surely do not wish me to repeat to her what must already be familiar to her recollection."

"Jerusalem! I should hope not. Just tell the dear soul not to be down in the mouth and work herself into

an awful stew, but to keep a stiff upper lip, for we ain't
in so bad a kittle of fish as many a likely chap has fell
into—things might be worse, a master sight worse."

"May I ask to what things you specially refer?"

"I shouldn't think a body need to ask that, when it's
plain to see that I have got to wear one empty frock-
sleeve all the rest of my days."

"Has Mrs. Hobson been informed of this misfortune?"

"It stands to reason that she haint when I have to
make my mark every time I sign my name, and don't
know one letter from t'other. This is the very first time
I've got a chance to send a word home, though it's many
I should have liked to send."

"No doubt of it. I think I can send the word you
wish spoken now."

She bent over the table, wrote for a few minutes
rapidly, then read aloud to him what she had written.

On finishing the perusal, she failed of the approving
look she had thought to win.

"You are not pleased with my way of stating the
case," she said, questioningly.

"Oh, it isn't that; but you have worded it so cruel
genteel that, I reckon, Polly won't never know what you
are drivin' at. You see, we are plain, homespun folks;
and she likes my homely words, because she is used to
'em, an' never had 'em used to hurt her, better than the
newfangledest ones you could scare up, no matter how
'cute they was."

"She shall have your very words, Mr. Hobson.
What next do you wish said?"

"Tell her it was my left arm that was shot away, and
my right is as sound as a drum; and don't forget to
mention that though I got an ugly wipe across the face,
not one of the pesky varmints can boast of havin' hit
Silas Hobson in the back. Matters ain't so bad as they

might be, by a long chalk; I'm worth a dozen dead
men yet; for my eyesight is tip-top yet, an' I can bite
off a cartridge with the best on 'em. Ask her what
signifies the loss of an arm, when our next-door neighbor, Rolf Karl, had his head blew off with a howitzer,
and poor Gretschen will never get a hearty grip from
his strong hand agin."

" Wait until I finish what you have already told me,"
said Minnie, her hand gliding over the paper; adding
in a few minutes, " Now I am ready for what you have
to say."

" Perhaps you would think it sounded flat if I was to
say right out what was in my thoughts."

" Never mind what I think; it is to those who will
be thankful to have your real thoughts that you are
writing, not to me."

" That is so ; and here goes. Tell Polly I've forded
no end of water-courses sence I've been a-sogering, but
I'd give more for one look at Pinfish brook with the
water-wheel I whittled out for our Cy. than for all the
mill privileges on the whole of 'em. I'd ruther see one
of the stuntedest of our witch-hazels than a whole woods
full of the tallest kind of hawthorn, hickory and yellow-
wood tree. And come to women, I've seen 'em in their
silks and satins that would coax a man's secrets out of
him, like Delilah of old, and give him up to the Philis-
tines without no more ado. . If handsome is as handsome does, then my homespun Polly is the best of the
lot : and you tell her so, with my lovin' duty and ever-
lastin' respects. You ain't laughin' at me, be you,
young woman ?"

" Did you think I could be so heartless, sir, when I
am writing what your dear ones at home will be proud
and glad to know, that, in absence, you hold them in
constant and steadfast remembrance ?"

" That's the talk; I shouldn't mind a touch or two

of that kind o' sweetnin', jest to top off. with, when you've stowed away all the hearty victuals."

The missive was completed, at last, entirely to the satisfaction of its projector.

It was late when Minnie retired to the closet she had, through claim of prior occupancy, appropriated as dormitory, by transferring thereto the husk mattress which had been hers in the crowded sleeping-ward hitherto shared with her companions. It was late, as I said, but even had night merged in the " wee sma' hours beyant the twal," she would not longer have delayed an examination of the precious package whose receipt had given a fresh tinge to her cheek, fresh impulse to languid motive, and renewed vigor to her entire being. The removal of the outer wrapping disclosed to her view one of those little, closely-ruled books, in water-proof binding, and provided with rubber pencil-case, soldiers sometimes use in keeping their accounts. Well filled was the diminutive volume—a manuscript duodecimo written for no eye save hers. She read, or rather devoured, the pages.

"LAURENSTEIN HEIGHTS, Mar. 6.

" ABSENT YET EVER WITH ME :—Now that I can raise my head from the pillow, which is a luxury I once feared it would never again be mine to enjoy, I will expend any extra strength I can spare, in recounting to one who lives in my dreams, waking and sleeping, at morn and noon and even, the means which brought me to this comfortable retreat.

" You may remember my telling you, the last time I wrote, that I was almost worn out with using pick and spade, a kind of labor to which I was wholly unaccustomed. First my hands were blistered, then raw, and after taking cold in them, painfully inflamed. I did well enough till my appetite gave out, and then work

7

was a weariness to body and spirit, using up the tissues
which a prudent soldier, beyond all other men, should
hold back as reserve, in case of sudden onslaught from
that ever-vigilant foe of camp life, disease, or to repair
any unexpected drain on the vital energies, liable at
any moment to occur.   However, I toiled on with right
good will, cheering myself with the thought that the
moat was nearly completed and then I could rest, for it
would only be a case of emergency that would compel
me to shoulder arms with my swollen and bandaged
hands.   That emergency came.   We were supplied with
two days' rations and marched over the rear bridge of
the fort at midnight, that the villagers might not suspect our departure.   Of our place of destination I was
profoundly ignorant; a soldier obeys orders, but asks no
questions.

"My musket I slung over my shoulders, by permission, as I could not grasp its stock with my sore and
stiffened fingers.   Had it not been for our frequent halts,
I must have sunk from exhaustion.   As it was, flashes
of heat darted through my veins, succeeded by cold,
shivering chills.   An irritability for which I could not
account took possession of me; a parching thirst that
would not be quenched, though I filled and emptied my
canteen at every brook we crossed, tormented me.

"When the sun came out, I was ready to drop beneath its scorching rays that made me feel like a wilted
weed.   All day long, save during brief periods of rest,
we marched on.   I longed for the going down of the
sun that I might throw off the grievous burden of gun
and haversack, while the others ate their hard bread for
supper.   Nature, at last, would endure no longer; the
way was uneven, I lost my footing and fell to the
ground unable to rise again.   A mist was before my
eyes for a few minutes, and when it cleared away, one
of my comrades, who had dragged me to a tree and

leaned me against it, was pouring water on my head.
He handed me a ticket on which was written:

"'The bearer has my permission to fall out of the
ranks, he being unable to proceed with the regiment.
    "'E. H. GILMAN, *Captain of Company B.*'

"So I was left alone, at the edge of a dark pine
forest, where I couldn't help thinking there was much
probability that my bones might bleach. I crawled into
the shade of a clump of chinquapin, whose dry rustling
leaves would, in a measure, screen me from the observation of passers-by. There I lay, helpless and still, not
sleeping, but in a dull, heavy stupor from which nothing
aroused me. That protracted lethargy, during which I
scarcely felt or thought, was a mercy, I am sure; for it
prevented my dwelling on the deplorable condition in
which I found myself. My feet were in as bad a state
as my hands, owing to my long march in boots whose
inner soles were made of an apology for leather, worked
up from odds and ends of the same reduced to pulp and
passed between rollers, being thus pressed into sheets,
fit companions for the shoddy sometimes imposed upon
unwary contractors. With hands inflamed, feet ulcer-
ated, and fever raging in my veins, you will see that my
prospects of escape were not flattering. Fortunately I
was blessed with a plentiful supply of cold water from
a spring in the rocks. For a time, I needed nothing
more.

"In a few days the fever exhausted itself; and then
I needed those little acts of care and kindness so indis-
pensable to the recovery of the sick. In the full strength
of vigorous health, one may be self-reliant, self-sus-
tained; but when prostrate by weakness, one craves
kindly tendance from other hands, friendly tones from
other lips, and gentle looks from other eyes. It was a
burdensome effort for me to fill my canteen from the

spring, and soak in a tin cup the bit of hard bread which was all the food I took, or had to take.

" Do you remember how little Paul Dombey used to try and make out what the waters were saying as they glided out from the shadows of the dead past, and hurried along, with many-voiced murmur, to the shadows of the unknown future? Something of that sort I experienced as I lay on my couch of leaves in the sombre shade of that dim old wood. My brain, as matter of course, shared the general prostration of my entire system, and if it conveyed to my spiritual being impressions vague, shadowy and unreal, was hardly to be held accountable, as it would have been under more normal influences. It was the voice of the wind in the solitary pines to which I hearkened, in changeful mood, as its tones soothed me to rest or moved me to sadness. I strained my ears to catch the breezy whisper, at times, and again it swelled into accents of piteous entreaty, of sad and hopeless longing. One night, during which I never once closed my eyes, rose on the air the shriek of the blast, torn and rent by the coming tempest. I rolled myself beneath a shelving rock to escape the violence of the threatening storm. I was driven almost to frenzy by the howling of the elements, which subsided toward morning into those mournful, dirge-like tones we chant at the graves of those we love. If it seem strange to you that I could have been thus deeply moved by cause so inadequate, you must remember that I was weak as a child, and correspondingly childish. Besides, I was quite alone ; and have not solitary prisoners been known to lavish their regards on a weed, a mouse, a mole or a beetle, as a last desperate resort for companionship?

" When my two days' rations were exhausted, I was strong enough to bind up my feet with rags, and hobble along by aid of a stout cudgel, a short distance at a time. I thought it my safest course to keep the shelter of the wood, for I knew that if I should fall in with the guerillas, I should be shot down with as little compunction as though I were a dog.

"My prospects of forage were of the scantiest; as the few nuts of last year's growth I picked up under an occasional hickory or chinquapin formed my main dependence.

"I will write you more to-morrow, as I am unable to proceed at present, my pencil flying from my fingers when I strive to grasp it firmly."

CHAPTER X.

PRISONER'S DIARY.

Mar. 7.—It was but a short distance I could drag myself along at a time, wearily trailing my musket after me, so I followed the course of a narrow stream leading northwardly, that I might not be forced to encroach on my small remnant of strength in searching for water. On its bank, I came across a sort of wild thorn-apple tree, to whose leafless branches still clung a considerable quantity of the fruit, which, though softened by frost, was not to be despised by one whose commissary stores were in such a state of depletion as mine. As I could neither climb the tree nor fell it, I had recourse to a forked stick in pulling down its branches, from which I partly filled my empty haversack. A silver-grey squirrel bounced out of a hole in the trunk and was off in a twinkling. To the little creature's provident foresight I owed a timely supply of shell-barks, acorns, wild oats, and corn, which I appropriated without scruple, and proceeded on my way rejoicing in the proud consciousness of being a man of means once more.

The longer I followed the windings of the stream the farther it seemed to lead me into the depths of the forest, until I became convinced that, if nearing the fort at all, it was by a most circuitous route. At last, I approached an opening, and my eyes were gladdened at sight of human habitation, a humble dwelling of a single story, with cow-stable attached. I resolved to reconnoitre the position during the night, and to be governed by the result.

The near discharge of a gun gave me a violent start. I made off, through a copse of ground laurel, as fast as hands and feet would carry me ; and was just congratulating myself on escape from imminent peril, when crack went a second shot, which brought an involuntary cry to my lips, for I was hit. Another instant, and a man whose name I could not, and cannot now recall, although I recognized him as belonging to one of the regiments of our brigade, was bending over me, muttering with a look of consternation and horror, "Too confounded bad, by Jove! Who would have thought to find one of our fellows here?"

Through the slit he cut in the leg of my pantaloons, the blood spirted up in jets, showing that an artery had been sundered. Tearing his red silk handkerchief into strips, he bound the same as ligature above and below the wound, tightening the higher bandage by running his bayonet beneath it, and giving the blade a double turn, after which he dressed the hurt as well as the means at his disposal would allow. Gathering a pile of leaves for my pillow, and folding about me the blanket he had worn strapped across his shoulders, I was, aside from the fiery tingling of the deep flesh-wound throbbing through my injured limb, more comfortably

circumstanced than I had been since taking up with
forest-lodgings. Opening his haversack, my hospitable
host tempted me with its delicacies—parched corn,
boiled chestnuts, and freshly-baked oat-cake. "A gift
of reconciliation," said he; "pray partake. You know
I would not purposely have harmed a hair of your
head. On all fours as you were, I mistook you in the
laurel shrubs for a villainous wolf-hound which sprang
upon and would have throttled me, if I had not
clubbed my musket and fended off the brute. •See how
he tore my sleeve and lacerated my arm. You need
nothing I can get for you now, unless it be a draught
of fresh water, which I will bring from the well I
saw near the house below."

He started, taking his gun, but leaving his haversack
with contents temptingly displayed beside me. I was
roused to a sense of anxious foreboding by the sound of
a pistol-shot soon after his departure, and waited long
for his return; waiting in vain. He never came back
to me; and I have heard nothing of him from that day
to this.

I thought my trials had already been tolerably
severe; but they sank into insignificance in comparison
with what followed. Next day, my wound was much
more painful, and I couldn't move even a toe without
hurting the tense and swollen muscles. For food I had
not the least desire, but the claims of thirst became,
each hour, more importunate. Swarms of gnats clus-
tered about me, and drove me half frantic with their
stings. Winged bugs from some rhododendrons near
seemed sociably inclined, and one audacious ear-wig
really frightened me by repeated attempts to carry
auricular portcullis by a bold dash.

Toward nightfall, my craving for water became so
urgent that I determined to see how far locomotion was
possible to me; but only succeeded in raising myself on

my elbow, when I was forced to lie down again, half fainting with pain. The dew gathered on the tender laurel shoots, and the cool drops were grateful to my parched tongue.

A rain soft and continuous commenced at dawn. In one sense, this was a relief, for I caught the descending moisture in my mouth, absorbed it through my pores, and thus, in some slight measure, alleviated the feverish thirst that was fast degenerating into a burning scald from throat to stomach. But as every benefit in this woe-worn world of ours has its corresponding drawback, this steadily-pouring rain soon chilled me to the very marrow, and added greatly to my sufferings. In all my joints were such wringing pains that they made me writhe, which only irritated my wound; but worst of all to bear, was a sharp, darting ache that took its rise in the temples, coursed with various turnings and branchings down both sides of the face, and brought up in the teeth with such a sharp turn, that they seemed bent on quitting altogether, and were so nearly wrenched out of their sockets, that I couldn't shut my mouth.

Two days went by in this way, and then the sun came out once more—came out with a perfect blaze of brightness that penetrated like sharp blades through my weak eyes into my weaker brain. Again my poor throat throbbed and burned with a dry heat that filled me with a maddening longing for a cooling-draught. I think my senses must have slightly wandered at times, as I more than once started from an attack of drowsy lethargy to implore a cup of cold water from an imaginary bystander, who, tantalizingly placed the refreshing beverage just beyond my reach. I have heard persons complain of being light-headed; if that was the feeling I experienced, pray Heaven I never be called upon to endure it again. It was as though the

earth was solid and enduring, while I was so light and
visionary, that there were no sufficient ties to bind me
to its friendly hold—a hold to which I clung with the
tenacity of a drowning man to a straw.

I could not keep my eyes off a tree, a locust, I believe,
which stood a short distance from where I lay. Its
flexile, willowy branches, as they bent toward me,
swayed by the wind, seemed about to raise me from the
ground, and waft me away to realms viewless and afar.
With the strength of desperation, I strove with all the
might of my being to retain my hold on this mortal
sphere, by withstanding the allurements tempting me to
soar upward in untried flight, and grasping the laurels
so firmly rooted to earth.

There was a footstep, a soft, velvety, treacherous step
on the dry leaves about me; it drew stealthily nearer,
but yet inspired me with no fear. The sharp pointed
muzzle, the lean, hungry jaws, armed with deadly in-
cisors, approaching so dangerously near my unguarded
throat, yet awoke in me no terror. Full in the eyes of
the savage beast that had lacerated the arm to which I
owed my then helpless condition I looked without
blenching. Dr. Livingstone, the celebrated African
explorer, tells us, if I am not mistaken, that, on being
seized upon by a lion, he felt, after the first rough shake
by the formidable monster, neither pain nor apprehension of what was to follow. This, it seems to me, is
easily accounted for. The wolf-hound had not laid a
fang on me, and yet I was as indifferent to his talons'
gripe as though I had not been fully exposed to their
powerful grasp. Through physical suffering, added to
the dread that my spiritual being might become a wreck
before its release from material organism, I had so
nearly reached the acme of human endurance that an
additional pang would have driven me to insensibility
or insanity. In mercy the final blow was withheld.

7*

The hound suddenly sniffed the air, and betook himself to the forest depths.

A heavy step drew near, and a stalwart negro stood before me. Scarcely deigning me a look, he critically examined my musket, and leaned it against the trunk of a tree. Next he lunched composedly from the haversack; but started up in a fluster, emptying his mouth hurriedly, and stuffing his pockets with the remnants of his repast, as the sound of approaching hoofs caught his ear.

A call, like the clear note of a flute, vibrated on the air.

"Here I am, Missis; comin'," responded my sable visitor.

A lady, who, at first sight, made me think of Scot's Die Vernon, she managed her spirited steed with such an easy, off-hand grace, rode up. If you would know what she was like in feature, look at the Maid of Saragoza. in colored crayons, over your mantel—the same oval face, raven-black hair, almond-shaped eyes, slightly depressed at their inner corners, full of seeming languor, but veiling a latent fire that tells you the dagger at her girdle may be worn for other purposes than mere ornament.

"Why are you not at your hoeing, Grumbo?" she asked with severity.

"I'se jest gwine, Missis; I'se only dun ben snarin' a coon for that bressed Rose."

The lady reined her horse up beside me.

"How long have you been lying here?" she asked, with that compassion which is the birth-right of your sex.

I strove to answer; but, to my surprise, found that I could not articulate a single syllable. Springing lightly to the ground, she unfastened a small wicker flask from the ring attaching it to her belt, and pouring some wine into the tin cup beside me, held it to my lips. My throat was so sore and swollen that I could not swallow a drop, and came near strangulation in making the attempt.

"Here, Grumbo, go for a couple of servants, and see that they bring cushions and whatever is needful for carrying a sick man ; Aunt Winifred will direct you."

She remained beside me, her bridle rein thrown carelessly over her arm, while her behests were carried into effect. I was thankful for the protection of her presence, although her manner was marked by that air of haughty disdain so often acquired through constant association with flatterers or inferiors. The servants arrived promptly, and she sprang to her seat in the saddle, scarcely pressing, with her slenderly arched foot, the broad, ebon palm aiding her as step in mounting.

In passing the small dwelling of a single story I have already mentioned, I noticed that it had been burned to the ground.

Through a broad gateway my carriers bore me, up an ascending carriage-sweep, bordered on either side by double rows of the golden-belled cycanthea. Rounding an acclivity, studded with magnolia and cottonwood, we came in sight of a large stone villa, with a highly ornate tower, balconies, arcades, verandas, and all the modern pretensions to elegance and symmetry of architectural design. At the carriage-porch my benefactress met us, and, at a sign from her, I was borne through hall and corridor up the velvet-piled staircase, whose panelled mirrors showed me a face I at first mistook for that of a stranger—a face haggard and worn, with untrimmed beard and matted hair, with bloodshot eyes and furrowed brow—my own.

No one who has not suffered as I had, untended and alone, with the earth for a couch and the sky for a covering, can conceive the depth of my gratitude and my content at finding myself kindly provided for beneath the shelter of a comfortable roof. The chamber assigned me was a large airy apartment commanding a fine view of the grounds. The windows were barred and grated—but what of that? Disease, in my case, was more potent jailer than any other to whose watch and ward I could have been subjected.

A surgeon was summoned to my aid, and, for the first time, my wound was properly dressed. For three days I lay in a sort of stupor, partially induced by soothing drugs that lulled the pain and granted me rest. Then came that depressing faintness resulting from a sickly, fitful craving for nutriment which the system has no power to digest or assimilate. I didn't know this, however, and prayed for food with the pertinacity of a street beggar who wishes to get the servant away from the door that petty pilferings may be safely ventured on.

In a feeble whisper I assured the doctor that I was actually starving, and tried to put the case pathetically by telling him that when shipwrecked mariners, or Arctic voyagers, beleaguered by frost and snow, narrated their struggles for subsistence, everybody listened with the deepest commiseration, but when it was only a poor wretch of a patient who was famishing scientifically, under lawful medical ban, he was welcome to do so at his leisure, while Levite, Pharisee, Samaritan and all passed by on the other side.

" My dear fellow," said the doctor, with blandest goodhumor, "I must really congratulate you on your improved prospects. Your symptoms are more favorable than I had reason to anticipate."

" What symptoms?" I asked, sulkily.

" This excessive irritability, for one," he returned, " is, almost invariably, one of the earliest precursors of convalescence. Then your complaints of hunger are just what I could have wished—highly encouraging."

My indignation and disgust I had no words to express.
To think of the creature's prating of irritability when I
had only uttered the calmest protest against slow murder
by famine, and sitting calmly by expressing gratification at the pangs of hunger he was forcing me to
undergo. If I had told him what I thought of this
heartless persecution of one helpless to resist the tyranny
of professional dictum, it would have been in language
far from complimentary; but I had sense enough to
restrain all expression of resentment, and to ask with a
show of outward calmness how soon I was to be allowed
something to eat.

"Your appetite is naturally fastidious, at present," said
he, whisking a speck of dust from his faultless patent-
leathers; "we must allow it to become a trifle more normal in its importunities before it will be safe to yield to
its demands. I will look at your tongue. Better, decidedly; clearing at the edges, with less irritation of
the œsophagus. Can you think now of a thimbleful of
any sort of conserve you could relish?"

"Hang conserves," I answered, crossly; "I don't care
a straw for anything by way of relish; but I should be
thankful for a scrap of wholesome, nourishing food, if it
were nothing better than a bit of corn-dodger, to stop
this dying faintness which is as hard as pain to bear."

"I know it," he admitted, with pretended sympathy,
"and it is what we cannot at once alleviate. How would
the wing of a canvas-back, if boiled until very tender,
with macaroni, and a morsel of lettuce, suit you?"

"To a charm. How soon can I have them?"

"We will decide that point next time I call. If I have
succeeded in rousing your torpid digestives to a state of
more normal activity than they have hitherto evinced,
I have accomplished all, and more than all, I proposed
effecting at this visit. Amuse your fancy by conjuring
up all the dainty dishes Miss Winifred will have the

pleasure of preparing for you as soon as you take off
your ears—from the unruly member, I mean.   If you
can work off any of this surplus spleen by hard thoughts
of the doctor, so much the better for you, and none the
worse for him—he is used to it."

I thought this adding insult to injury, and scowled at
him, as, with urbane sauvity, he wished me "a very
good day."

I must close my record for to-day, as giddiness already
warns me that I have exceeded the limits of my slowly-
returning strength.   To-morrow, if possible, I shall resume the pencil which affords me, at once, employment
and recreation.

Mar. 10.—I can write but a few lines for your contemplated perusal to-day, Minnie; for Dr. Bolus, *né*
Saltonstall, has put an injunction on paper and pencil,
in order to restrain within bounds what he terms my
irregular mode of procedure therewith.   The fact is,
that I so exhausted myself by over-exertion on Friday
that I have scarcely been able to open my eyes or raise
my head from the pillow since, and have gone back to
hyoscyamus and lupuline as quietants.   I bear the in-
terdiction with the greater equanimity that it will be
all the same to you whether I write now or a week
hence ; as, owing to interruptions and irregularities in
postal service, I have no means of communicating with
you by letter or otherwise.

I have not as yet told you anything about the inmates
of this luxurious abode, because I have had very little
to tell.   The jauntily-dressed man-servant who looped a
cord about my wrist, and fastened it to the bell-spring
that was beyond my reach, that I might ring for him
when needful, never fails to obey my summons promptly,
and serves me with ready civility, but evidently looks
upon me as no friend to the house, and never wastes on
me a single superfluous word.

Miss Holmes—Aunt Winifred, as they call her—is a kind-hearted, elderly maiden, who makes me lotions and herb-drinks, and is the only living being about the place who ever condescends to enter into conversation with me. Through her I learn that the name of the lady who rescued me from a lingering death is Elanwood; that she is only child of Judge Carroll, a man of considerable local celebrity, and wife of a rebel officer to whom she has been less than a year wedded. Energetic, self-reliant, rather educated than accomplished, gifted with rare personal charms, and an heiress in her own right, no wonder that she exerts an influence not usually accorded a woman, not only throughout her own plantation, but over the community at large. These fearless, spirited southern women, when their fathers, husbands, and brothers are serving in the army, dauntlessly brave many a peril, and follow many a masculine avocation in a way that shocks our stricter sense of propriety; but it cannot be denied, after all, that this fervor of feminine partisanship, encouraged rather than repressed by the chivalry, is a source of strength to their cause. Pray Heaven that the trying necessities of the hour never force you to cast aside the delicate mantle of feminine reserve screening you from rude or vulgar gaze, and to brave the rough gales your form is too slight to withstand ; grasping the heavy brand never meant for such tender hands. If my hopes might but be index to your happiness. rest assured all would be well with you.

Wednesday, Mar. 12.—Yesterday was the first time that, by aid of a crutch and the doctor's arm, I was able to get across the room, and to sit for a couple of hours at the window. It was very painful to straighten out the contracted muscles of my wounded leg, but I was amply repaid for the suffering by the pleasure of looking forth on a scene so fair as the one greeting my sight. A cold grapery, with its white and purple clusters of luscious fruit, first caught my eye on a southern slope. The shrubs dotting the hillside lawn were already draped in cool spring robes of tender green, sometimes efiloretted with gold and silver, ruby, garnet and amethystine tint. A triple row of budding maples screened the huts of the negroes from observation. Farther on, I watched their leisurely labors in the hemp and tobacco fields.

As I thus indolently watched others toil, Mrs. Elanwood, whom I had scarcely seen since the day of my arrival, emerged from a side-door, followed by a couple of servants bearing a large heavy carpet, which they commenced beating, after carrying it to the rear of the premises. Her horse was led to the entrance-door, and from step to saddle she sprang without aid, and gallopped away to the field where her laborers were employed. Not a hoe or spade but moved more quickly at her approach. She seemed possessed of an exuberant vitality that inspired others with something of her own energy.

Was the woman ubiquitous? Scarcely five minutes had elapsed since I saw her picking her way along the ridges and furrows of the open fields, and there she was a mile away, throwing her bridle-rein to a colored youth, and entering a saw-mill on the stream.

My door opened, and Miss Holmes softly entered. After congratulating me on my improved appearance, she drew a chair for herself to the opposite window.

" Dear me," she sighed, " that irrepressible Adrienne will give us no rest. Up with the dawn, she seems incapable of fatigue, and we lag after her with tired steps, trying to second her plans. Is that Achmed, her saddle-horse, at the saw-mill yonder ?"

" If Adrienne be Mrs. Elanwood, she dismounted but a moment previous to your entrance."

" Pardon me—the same. She has received orders for lumber from the commandant at ' Brentford Barracks,' which she chooses to see filled, as she prides herself on having the entire estate as well managed during the General's absence as when he was here to superintend affairs. So absurd for a lady of refined and elegant culture to bother her head with sorting timber and planks, rafters and joists, boarding and flooring, as she does. Do you see that carpet she has had dragged up from the drawing-room floor this morning?"

"I have been looking at it; a splendid piece of weaving and coloring."

"I thought so when I applauded its selection at Nashville. The idea of cutting up a medallion like that for soldiers' bunks and floor-cloths! but she will have it so. When I remonstrated that a three-ply, or bocking even, would do just as well for the rough wear and tear to which it would be exposed, she shut me up with—'Bocking for the poor fellows who are blanketless, and you so please; but for the master of Laurenstein there is nothing at Laurenstein too good. He shall have soft carpets, and snowy linen, and palatable viands so long as there is strength in this poor hand to prepare them, and skill in this poor head to cunningly devise methods for conveying them to him.' I do believe she would screen the opening to his tent with the canopied curtains of lace and brocatelle if he would but express a half wish to that effect. As though, with all his cares, he would stop to notice whether he trod on straw or velvet, looked through lace or tatters; he might, though, if it was her hand that bestowed the gift.

"Why, we used to call him the confirmed bachelor— he used to dance with me, and has twice the age of my niece—he was so unimpressionable, in his lordly independence, scarcely glancing long enough at a woman to see if she were a crow or a swan. That's the sort of man, so secure as he deems himself in his trebly-barred mail of haughty indifference, to be enthralled beyond all

hope of release, if suddenly taken off his guard. He
went often to discuss questions of state with the judge;
and when he waxed eloquent over our sectional wrongs
from those who, reaping the full benefit of our prosperity, which puts bread in the mouths of northern me-
chanic and manufacturer, in return for which they seek
by all means to embarrass our progress and cast a bone
of contention in our path—one which they will gnaw to
their cost if they do not drop it soon—Adrienne, who
was present with me at these interviews, and gets hold
of burning words when her enthusiasm is roused, elec-
trified him by the zeal with which she echoed and
sustained his opinions.   It was through the head she
reached his heart, which she holds none the less securely,
perhaps, on that account.   I always thought him singularly unobservant of trivial events, but in all matters
pertaining to Adrienne his eyes are of the keenest ; not
a bud in her braids, not the fall of a fold, not the float
of a frill escapes him ; singular, isn't it?"

"It does not seem so to me," I replied.   Do you
know of whom I was thinking?—Minnie.

"See, she resumed, they are tearing down the beautiful iron fence that was so lately put up ; that goes
with the chairs in the veranda and the railings of the
balconies, for cannon-balls, I suppose.   I wouldn't be
surprised if the safe, with all its plate, went next.   How
I chatter to a stranger.   I hope I have given you something to think of and help pass away the hours which
must go slowly with so much pain, and so few objects
to fill them.   Have you sat up long enough? and shall
I send Meldrone to your assistance?"

I was not quite ready to forego my freshly acquired
privilege of sight-seeing ; and she left me to enjoy it unin-
terruptedly.   The carpet was freed from dust and carried into the house, Mrs. Elanwood disappearing along
with it.   I was thinking of pulling the cord at my wrist

for help to aid me in returning to bed, when she re-
appeared in velvet cap and closely-fitting jacket, and
commenced firing at a target—a rude wooden figure of
a man—aiming mostly at the heart, and proving herself
quite an accomplished markswoman in that direction;
though I couldn't help thinking there were more agreeable ways in which a lovely woman might approach
a man's heart, than through the agency of a pistol-
shot.

Monday, Mar. 24.—It is more than a week since I
have touched paper or pencil, for the weather has been
so delightfully bland and summer-like, that I have, per
order of Dr. Saltonstall, devoted my whole vitality to
the process of recuperating in the open air. First, Meldrone dragged me about in an old garden-chair he
rummaged the attic to find ; but now I stroll about the
grounds with only the drawback of a not very noticeable
limp.

When Mrs. Elanwood found that I was well enough
to walk, she exacted my word of honor that I would not
step outside certain prescribed limits; this move on her
part precluding all chance of escape, had it been otherwise practicable.

I must tell you of a little occurrence happening yesterday, which I shouldn't deem worth recounting at
another time ; but now that we are unhappily at variance with this people, any candid expression of their
opinion ought to be of interest to us, as it never does
any harm to look on both sides of a case, however
firmly we may be grounded in the faith that our own
side is wholly right, the opposing one wholly wrong.

You must know that the negro chapel, a rough
structure of pine boards near their quarters, although
not within sight of the villa, was plainly within hearing of the same. I was roused from a reverie, in the
summer-house where I was lounging, by a succession

of the most discordant yells and shrieks that ever burst on astounded mortal's ear. Fire or insurrection was the least I could suppose those direful sounds to portend. Creeping along in the shade of the shrubbery, I cautiously made my way to the rear of the chapel whence all this din proceeded. The position I was enabled to gain in the shadow of a shelving rock, afforded me, through an unglazed window with open shutter, an unobstructed view of the proceedings within, while I remained myself invisible.

It verily seemed to me that the whole congregation, judging from the writhings and contortions of men, women and children, had been suddenly smitten with St. Vitus's dance ; while no exhibition-room short of Bedlam could have poured forth such a harrowing concatenation of discordant sounds. While one shouted "Glory, hallelujah!" a second bellowed at the top of his voice, "With cherubim and seraphim, O speak thy praises forth ;" a third besought in excruciating falsetto, "Cry out and shout, O daughter of Zion ;" and in shrill treble came cries of, "Bress de Lord, Amen ;" with a variety of kindred invocations. I must confess that I was deeply shocked at this seeming parody on the sacred rites of divine service.

The door opposite my post of observance was pushed slowly open, and Mrs. Elanwood, holding up her cloth riding-skirt (she had just been to visit a sick child of the miller) in one daintily gauntleted hand, while in the other she carried a scarlet-handled riding-whip, banded with gold, looked with aspect of severe reproval about the shrieking assemblage. As one after another caught her look, so resolute, so replete with wordless censure, their voices died gradually away, until only an occasional subdued adjuration gave trace of the deafening uproar her entrance had hushed.

Then she spoke :

" When your master was at home, we had no such unseemly tumult as this to quell; and it is thus you make good your promises to conduct yourselves with all decency and propriety while he is away, fighting the hardly-contested battles that insure our safety. Is it seemly, think you, to desecrate these quiet hours of Sabbath rest by yellings and hootings that remind one of a disgraceful street brawl? Parson Cole, what excuse have you to offer in palliation of the pernicious example you were setting your flock?"

This question was addressed to the chosen expounder of Holy Writ, occupying the rude pinewood desk he had been vigorously belaboring by way of emphasis to his soaring elocutionary flights. Thus appealed to, the embarrassed parson winked at the obese deacon who, after much fumbling in a leathern pouch, from which plugs of tobacco, broken pipes, fish-hooks and willow whistles persistently obtruded themselves on his unwilling notice, drew forth a rusty key, and fitting the same to the lock of the desk door, thereby granted the clerical culprit release. Hanging his head with an air technically termed sheepish, the reverend transgressor approached his fair accuser.

" 'Taint none o' my fault, Missis; all dis yere screechin' an hollerin'; it was all trou' Brudder Broadfoot dat de rumpus was brewed. What business hab he to git up on dat bench an' go to spoundin, when he no preacher, no notin, when I holdin' forth in de desk to all dese yere hardened worshippers of dere trespasses and sins? Right in de midst of my peroration, dis stiff-necked brudder bust right out a prayin' on his own hook, an' when all dese yere black sheep see dis one ole wether gwine ober de fence, ober dey all goes after him, each one a hollerin louder'n todder. Den what could I do, Missis, but push right straight on in de eben tenor ob my way? Wasn't I put here to break de bread of truf to dese yere vile

worms ob de dust, an' was I to be blowed off de track
by de vile bref of such a scum as dat Broadfoot? I
spects not. When he roared like a mighty bull o'
Bashan, what could I do but put in all de louder to
drown him out? Didn't I hab a duty to perform to de
congregation, which was mine, not his'n?"

"A strange way you took of performing it. What
good did it do your congregation your outroaring it and
him?"

"Bress your heart, Missis, you no see dat? How de
sheep gwine to hear de voice ob de shepherd, 'less he cry
out an' shout louder dan all de rest ob 'em? More'n
dat, how de good God to hear me widout I pitch my
pipes louder'n all de oders?"

"He can hear the faintest whisper; even a thought
that is not breathed in words; never forget that."

"What! Massa God hear dis misable sinner, when all
his flock liftin' up dere voices like de mighty rushin'
waters dat carries all afore 'em?"

"Even so, Parson Cole; through the thunder's roll
and the hurricane's crash, the faintest breath from a
praying soul mounts upward to the great white throne.
Remember, God is not deaf to the prayers of his chosen;
that he is not to be mocked with vain repetitions of idle
sound; and remembering this, let me hear of no more noisy
disturbances like the present."

She turned to leave, and more than one voice cried in
tone of penitent fondness: "God bless you, Missis; you
no hab to speak again."

I, too, hastened to make good my retreat; but as I
turned a corner of the chapel, I came face to face with
the mistress of the Heights.

"*You* here!" she ejaculated, with a look of startled
surprise, which quickly gave place to a crimson flush of
indignation on her cheek, an angry blaze in her eye, as
she said in the low tones of suppressed resentment:

"You have broken your parole, sir; you are outside the prescribed bounds; I will take good care that you find no opportunity for a repetition of the offence."

I endeavored to explain to her that it was through purest inadvertence, when thrown off my guard by sounds which I feared portended evil to her household, that I had overstepped the limits assigned me.

"You anticipated nothing short of the rising of the negroes, an anticipation in which the wish was father to the thought," she returned, with a contemptuous curl of the lip. "Do not flatter yourself, sir, that any such rare spectacular entertainment awaits you. My people are too good a set to be tampered with—not an evil, base-hearted ingrate amongst them; for every irreclaimable knave or vagabond is relentlessly weeded out, to avoid contamination for the rest, and sent to our penal colonies—our Siberia, our Van Dieman's Land—the rice plantations South. It is you, and the like of you, who steal amongst us under cover of friendly guise, dog our footsteps, prowl about our servants' quarters, and—but this is no place for words like these. Come with me to the magnolia walk."

I followed as requested, until we were beyond hearing of any of the congregation disposed to become eavesdroppers.

I feared even to parry her reproaches, so much as attempt refuting her arguments, lest I should be drawn into an altercation that might prove strongly prejudicial to my own interests. Thus it was she who resumed:

"It is your demoniac philanthropy that prevents our teaching and training our dependents as many of us would gladly do. We cannot permit the unlettered hinds to learn the alphabet, in peace, from fear of incendiary pamphlets wherein most noble and Christian gentlemen do most Christianly proclaim doctrines which, if carried to strict logical result, would place the dagger of the assassin, the weapon of the malefactor, in hands now true to their trust. Yes; it is you, and such as you, who would turn to curses the blessings they now shower upon us—who would teach them to tear the hand that feeds them, and to render not unto Cæsar the things that are Cæsar's due."

I protested that she wronged me foully by her groundless suspicions; but she was too much under the sway of their influence to heed my protest, which she cut short by her own vehement flow of speech.

"I have been a quixotic fool," she cried, impulsively, "to extend the rites of friendly hospitality to one whose very garb—the cannon cross on whose cap front proclaims him foe to all my heart holds dear. Are these hewers of wood and drawers of water—these untutored children of a semi-barbaric race, who are but half brought under the yoke of civilization as yet—fit subjects for freedom and self-government, think you?

'Who would be free, himself must strike the blow.'

So far from being ready to do this, our colored laborers have thus far shown no disposition to improve to the utmost the blow others have struck in their supposed behalf. It is for us they still have delved and trenched; and, drive us too far to the wall, sir, and we will show you for whom they will fight. If you don't find your contrabands more ready to tax your charities than to render you diligent service, set me down as one who prognosticates falsely of these trying times. By my troth, but it would be a most edifying spectacle—oh, a most rare and suggestive spectacle—to see these faithful bondmen defending their rightful masters against the assaults of their would-be liberators; and this is what it would come to unless you find an opportunity (Heaven avert the same) for imposing on the ignorant credulity of the blacks some fanciful tale of possible or supposable wrong, and so turn to gall and wormwood the love they bear us. This is what you will find no second chance of accomplishing on *this* plantation."

" I have neither sought, nor do I wish to seek, the accomplishment of any such purpose as that to which you refer," I firmly but quietly assured her.

"Then why are you in armed league with those who would either subjugate or exterminate us root and branch?"

" When a traitor is shot, he is neither subjugated nor exterminated; he simply receives the just penalty for his crime ; put the singular noun in the plural, and the principle remains still the same. When one or many rebel against a government which has been true to its constitutional obligations, one or many, if persisting in rebellion, must reap the penalty to the hard and bitter end."

" You do but play upon words, and split straws of lingual nicety. What is it you do seek in this murderous conflict?"

" To maintain, in its full integrity, at all hazards of blood and treasure, this great and growing empire, marked, by nature herself, one and indivisible, through its great arteries of noble waters, its many-veined streams, and its mountain vertebræ of rocky ridge and low-browed hill."

" And it is this glorious empire whose disruption you have precipitated through rash, ill-considered attempts to raise the social status of a race not yet fitted for such elevation—it is not the violent who take the kingdom of Heaven by storm. 'God's mills grind slow,' and when short-sighted man, in his puny might, piles on crude theory and utopian nostrum, as infallible specific for all the evil wherewith the great Physician sees fit to medicine this sick world, ten to one but he gets entangled in

8

the machinery he strives to accelerate in speed—that is, if he be not one of those who bind heavy burdens for other men's shoulders, which he touches not with so much as a little finger—dragging thousands of his deluded followers to their doom, instead of hastening the millennium. For my part, I am content to take the world as I find it; walking, day by day, with steps as little faltering as may be, in the path of duty, so far as it is made plain unto me, and never pinning my faith to the skirts of those sanguinary reformers whose specious schemes grasp consequences too vast to be comprehended by any finite mind. I will see you again to-morrow morning, until which time keep your personal liberty and make the most of it."

Bending her head slightly, in haughty salute, she passed on.

What could she mean, I asked myself, by bidding me make the most of my liberty until next I saw her? Had I offended her beyond forgiveness by inadvertently infringing the strict letter of my parole? I surely had refrained, sorely against my will from exasperating her by opposing argument; and was I to be subjected to close imprisonment, or some worse penance, in expiation of the offence? I could but wait and see.

Last night, I need hardly tell you, I was restless and wakeful with apprehensions of what the day might bring forth. Early this morning I was summoned to the lady's presence. She bade me a frigid " good morning," as I entered the sewing-room, scarcely raising her eyes from the breadths of linen she was tearing into strips and passing to her female attendant to be pieced into bandages.

" I am engaged just this moment," said she ; " oblige me by passing into the next apartment—that door to the right—where I will attend you presently."

She came quite soon enough, unfolding her purpose without circumlocution or delay.

"Your parole, given informally and only to a woman," she commenced, "can hardly be deemed a stringently binding obligation; and I have decided to submit a new proposal, or rather a series of them, to your consideration. It is at your option to join the other federal prisoners at Guard Barracks; to be liberated on parole registered by proper authorities; or, if you prefer remaining here until your health is more fully reëstablished, you can do so by consenting to have a ball and chain attached to your leg by an iron band, as material guaranty for your good faith and honesty of purpose."

I was not slow in deciding which of the three to choose. I had heard so much of the ferocities practised toward prisoners in southern jails that I was strongly disinclined to testing such dangers and hardships in my own person. If I were liberated on my word of honor, I was debarred the privilege of entering military service again during the present war, an exemption of which I was by no means disposed to avail myself; so I declared my preference for the ball and chain, hoping it might not prove a serious hindrance to my natural facilities for locomotion.

CHAPTER XI.

THE MIDNIGHT FLITTING.

WEDNESDAY, *April* 2.—I am so differently situated, my condition and prospects so diametrically changed, since last I jotted down, solely for your own perusal, my dear Minnie, some faint record of my daily experiences, that it is only by an effort of memory I am able to resume the broken thread of my narrative.

I found my new badge of imprisonment a much more serious encumbrance than I had anticipated. Think of an eight-pound cannon-ball and heavy iron anklet, fastened by a lock, whose key my captor retained, to be worn as constant ornament. Then the chain attaching ball and ring was so short that I could only take the ball in my hand by stooping so much that it made my gait resemble that of a horse with head tethered to fore foot by a short halter. If I got tired of stooping forward and limping like a cripple about the place, I had only to drag my pretty locket after me when straightway it caught at bush or shrub, stalk or vine, and sent me pitching headlong to earth. I became so disgusted with the scratches, bruises and bloody noses I gained through involuntary experiment in this species of ground and lofty tumbling, that I gave up my daily strolls, remaining mostly in my own chamber moodily discontent. A steady rain, of several days' continuance, but added to my gloom. Miss Holmes brought me books from the library, and, by many a kindly feminine wile, strove to lighten my hours of their weariness; but I was so perversely inclined toward wretchedness that I neither was, nor affected to be, grateful.

She told me that they were daily expecting a visit from the General, who had received promise of brief furlough, and I heard her as one who heareth not, devoutly—I had very nearly written, savagely—hoping that he might prove an accomplished Petruchio, and that I might catch some faint glimpse of his method for taming this modern Kate, who had shorn me of freedom by expedient at once irritating and effective.

It was late in the afternoon of Thursday last, when, as I sat hidden from prying eyes in the friendly shade of closely clipped thorn and liriodendron hedge, Mrs. Elanwood, in rustling silks and soft white lace, her hair agleam with scarlet salvia buds, flitted across the ve-

randa, down the steps, and out upon the lawn, to meet—
psha! *that* the General!—that stout, broad-chested man,
whose resolute bearing is attempered by an expression
of the most winning and genial humor; who looks the
very personation of Hail-fellow-well-met to any and all
he might deem worth the meeting—a practised shrew-
tamer!—never! unless—well—it *is* the sun that oftenest
disrobes the traveller of his cloak, and it is only on rare
occasions that surly Boreas successfully copes with his
more ardent rival.

The haughty mistress of Laurenstein bowed before her
liege lord with gently submissive grace—aye, bowed
until the scarlet salvia buds touched his shoulder-knot,
but she spoke not a word save, " At last! oh Guy!"

When she raised her head there were tears on her
cheek ; I did not think it had been in those proud eyes
to weep.

They passed so near the bench on which I sat that I
could accurately note every change in his aspect, every
turn of his voice.

" I had purposed spending a couple of days in going
over the plantation with you," said he; " but found it
impossible in the present condition of our forces to
make arrangements for so long an absence; I must
leave you in an hour."

" Only an hour, Guy, when you have been such an
age away !"

Homesick and heartsick, I hobbled back to my
chamber.

Only an hour ! O Minnie, what would I not give
for but five minutes' speech with you?—for one sight of
your face, one sound of your voice, if yielded in assurance of unswerving truth and constancy !

It was nearly midnight, and I had not slept. Sweet
strains of music floated in through the grated windows,
while the rich, deep tones of men's voices, mingled

with the lighter cadence of flute and viol. I arose and set my door ajar.

"Adrienne," called Miss Holmes at her niece's door, "some of the neighbors having come to pay their respects to the General, and finding him gone, have decided, it seems, to compliment you with a serenade. Will you go down and speak with them?"

"I will," was the prompt reply, "and that to some purpose, or I do much mistake myself."

Curious to hear what she would say, I dressed hastily; and crossing the landing, stepped out upon the balcony commanding a view of the arcade, where, as nearly as I could judge, some twenty men were assembled. Mrs. Elanwood glided amongst them with resolute step, demeanor firm and dignified, not a trace of color on her olive cheek, but her eyes brilliantly aglow with the fire of the eager impulse that hurried her on. She stood directly beneath the colored lantern suspended from an arch, so that I could distinctly perceive her robe's silken sheen, and the scarlet buds in her raven hair.

"It is on no grateful errand I come to you, gentlemen," she began, in those low, emotional tones which, carrying with them the conviction of earnest sincerity and deep feeling, go straight from the heart of the speaker to that of the listener. "In ordinary times I should welcome you to the best cheer Laurenstein has power to confer on the guests it holds in high esteem; but bear with me, I do beseech, kind friends, Laurenstein affords but cold comfort to its mistress now, and of such as I have not, of that can I not give unto thee.

"I have no heart to listen to the soft discourse of sweet music, thereby beguiling my wakeful hours of the deep depression that drives sleep from my pillow, when strains as sweet, but sad, *sad*, daily wail forth mournful dirge over the graves of the brave and early-fallen—when I cannot tell how soon such dirge may sound in parting honor of one whose life is as dear to me as is my own.

"I know that this must seem to you but churlish and ungracious return for the kindly purpose that brought you here; but can I permit myself recreation while those I love are enduring danger, privation, and death, in camp and field? Shall I sit in silken ease and luxury, while they toil day and night, with head, heart, and hand, in furtherance of our young nation's cause? Shall I give my hours to vain musings, to fond regrets, seeking in music delicious consolement for every anxious ill? Not so; still let my harp rest, as long it hath rested, in idle disuse against the wall, and spiders alone find pastime in the cobwebbed cover of my guitar.

"With my weak hand, and faint, timorous spirit, I cannot brave the dangers of gory battle-field, and snatch from Mars' grim front the immortal laurels which only heroes wear; not for cowardly woman's brow the victor's wreath, the conqueror's crown; but bear me witness, that what I could do by way of aid and comfort has been freely done; and of such as I had to bestow have I given with no niggard hand. No requisition on my time or toil have I deemed too burdensome for prompt and cheerful compliance. My choicest possessions, my ceaseless endeavors, my most untiring energies, have I freely rendered in promotion of the cause which is uppermost in all my thoughts. Of my poor best naught have I grudgingly withheld. You, gentlemen—of your superior ability, can you say as much?

"I know how gaily the troubadour, in days of old, sang roundelay to ladye-fayre, but it was on his *return* from the war, not while the heel of the oppressor was still pressed firmly on his country's neck. Come to me as triumphant conquerors of a vandal foe, and I will greet you in far other words than these. Conquer for us the peace that shall give us the right to sit secure in the shadow of vine and fig-tree, doing as we will with our own, no longer cursed by that pharisaical anathema, 'Stand aside, I am holier than thou,' and I will meet you with eager, grateful welcome, with goodly cheer, the harp's liquid, mellow-dropping tones, and all joyous demonstrations of festal mirth and gladness. Not so fast ; I spoke but now of goodly cheer, forgetting how rapidly our substance is melting away beneath war's consuming blaze. Nay; what matters it though I have but a dinner of herbs to set before you? better that and love therewith, than a stalled ox and this fierce sectional hatred withal.

"Bethink you, fellow-townsmen, that the world stands ready to note your every deed of lofty prowess and daring valor; and let your deeds come up to the high standard worthy to win a world-wide renown and vindicate your boasted chivalry. Never give our noble and magnanimous ally across the sea—an ally who permits no opportunity to pass for encouraging us by lavish panegyric while persistently vilifying our northern foes—cause to blush for the belligerent she has honored by substantial proof of her friendly sympathy. Let us deserve the invaluable moral support so unflinchingly accorded us by a people of kindred tongue and race, who have so faithfully upheld and justified our righteous cause. We all know with how much greater zeal and courage a work is undertaken and pursued when fanned by the breath of generous approval and applause, than when smothered by the wet blanket of obloquy and opprobrium. Why, an evil name will hang a dog; and if the North has not gained an ill name through dogged support of an evil cause, it is because dirt won't stick, for she has been pelted with all shades and varieties of abusive, infamous epithet.

"Think, too, of all the material as well as moral aid we have received from our grandly liberal, though unacknowledged ally. What loss of time and treasure has she not risked from the blockading fleet off our shores, in sending to us through tortuous, unfrequented channels, under the favoring veil of night, the means and munitions we could ill have spared, and could not otherwise have obtained? Our medicine chests testify to her bounty; our stands of arms as well; our heavy guns and many a deadly projectile that has sent myriads of meddlesome Yankees to unshriven graves.

"Countless the thanks we owe to this great and disinterested nation, which, generously overlooking our occasional reverses and partial defeats, suffers no success that crowns our efforts to go unchronicled or unpraised. With the glorious and invincible champion of civilization enlisted in our sacred cause, can you longer hesitate to enlist yourselves therein?

"Pardon me if my words seem scant of grace and courtesy; come to Laurenstein in happier times, and you shall have greeting befitting our improved condition; till then, farewell."

Without awaiting response of any kind, she abruptly reëntered the house, and I heard the rustle of her robes on the staircase. It was her own hands that closed and barred the window through which I had made egress, thus fastening me out upon the balcony. I remained quite still until the last visitor had departed, and Meldrone had extinguished the light in the archway lantern.

I was debating the chances of escape and probabilities of recapture. By making known my exclusion from the premises, I could easily return to the comfortable room, the luxurious bed from which I had recently risen. I

8*

admit the prospect of resuming my broken repose was tempting. I was still weak, my freshly-healed wound often irritable, at times painful, and needed the care and attention I was here sure of receiving. Yes, sure, but for how long a period? Just so long as suited the whim of Laurenstein's imperious mistress, not another hour. Should I hold my future destiny subject to a woman's caprice? the more especially one who looked upon me as a dangerous interloper, who might, if allowed the boon of untrammelled movement, throw incendiary torch amongst the inflammable material which her own safety damanded that she should take stringent precautions to sedulously guard against such malicious designs! Furthermore, she had plainly intimated to me that I was only to remain at the Heights until my health was fully reëstablished; and what then? A southern jail, with its pestilent odors, its undisguised filth, its disgusting vermin, its fever-breeding malaria of respired and rerespired human breath, and its ruffianly, brutal guards. Better heaven's pure air than the stifling fumes of such over-crowded dens; better nature's wholesome neglect than the tender mercies given with cruel purpose.

No tie of honor bound me to Laurenstein; I had been absolved from my parole; I would go. I rose fully resolved on carrying out my purpose. The clank of the chain I wore against the iron railing of the balcony aroused me to what I had half forgotten, a vivid sense of my own hampered condition. I sat down and carefully reconsidered the whole matter, ending by taking a mental inventory of my entire personal effects. Of a strong pair of serviceable shoes, with stockings to match, I was right glad to find myself the possessor. My nether integuments, also, thanks to the General's well-filled wardrobe, were beyond suspicion of rent or darn. In pockets to same I found a strong clasp knife and a couple of handkerchiefs, one of silk and one of linen. My under-clothing was unexceptionable; and in the pocket to my grey flannel was safely stowed this little book you are now reading, with interest I would fain hope. A coat of blue soldiers' cloth, with cap of the same material, completed my outfit—a scant one, you will admit, considering the forced marches I had resolved to undertake; for I had resolved to risk the chance of flight, and nothing remained for me save to employ to the best advantage the limited resources at my disposal.

To gain the terrace below, I had to descend fifteen feet, by an iron trellis, about which a prairie rose was closely entwined. To do this without the iron danglet at my ankle disturbing the inmates of the house by its noisy clatter, was clearly out of the question. Tearing in two my linen handkerchief, I covered the ball, and wound the chain in its soft folds. Next I fastened one corner of my bandanna to the chain, just below its attachment to the pretty bauble forced upon my wear, firmly securing the other to my belt.

My descent was more painful than perilous, as my hands were severely lacerated by the sharp thorns of the rose. I did not allow such a trifle as this to delay my departure for an instant. Shaping my course by the stars, I made all possible haste to increase the space between Laurenstein and my own fugitive self before the early dawn. A broad stream intercepted my way—a stream whose ordinary volume had been so much augmented by recent rains that it was no longer fordable. Swimming was not to be thought of; and I was obliged to seek the road and cross a bridge, where I was exposed to imminent danger of detection through the portions still retained of my military outfit. A rebel sentinel shouted at me from a distance, which call I received as signal for taking the double-quick, and gaining the shelter of a stony ridge.

In the course of the forenoon, I came across a herd of cows quietly browsing on a secluded hillside, and nothing loath, prepared to break my fast on fresh lacteal supply. Approaching a likely-looking quadruped, with the most amiable and insinuating demonstrations, I seated myself at her right in approved fashion, and was about to commence the milking process, when the vicious and unreliable bovine female left me sprawling on my back; and the last I saw of her, she was clearing a five-rail fence, with her hoofs in the air and her nose tending earthward.

The sun had nearly reached the zenith, and still I kept unwilling fast. I verily believe that there is no whet to appetite like lack of means wherewith to appease the same. A man in a fenced inclosure was setting out a bed of onions, of which he had a plentiful supply in reserve. I prophesied that on his return from dinner he would find his supply decreased. With impatience, for the goadings of hunger are not promotive of the milder virtues, I awaited his departure, which came in due time. He took his gun, but left my coveted fare. Not mine so soon as I thought. I was about venturing forth from cover, when the onion-planter drew a tin pail from a cypress clump, and seating himself on a knoll in full view of the prize on obtaining which I had so confidently reckoned, commenced munching his noontide meal. This untoward combination of opposing forces necessitated the adoption of a fresh system of tactics on my part. I waited the man's return to his labor, and then, by slow and cautious approach, made my way to the cypress clump, where I gained possession of the dinner-pail, and won a second prize, in the form of a flint he must have dropped, proving that it was an old-fashioned flint-lock shooting-iron he carried.

On bacon and bread I lunched with gusto, and, much refreshed, resumed my tramp, feeling the charm of the roving, vagrant life I led; lacking only the friend to whom I would fain have whispered, "How sweet is solitude!"

I walked nearly the whole of the ensuing night, only resting a couple of hours toward daybreak. As soon as it was sufficiently light to do so, I extracted, to the best of my ability, the rankling thorns from my hands.

The life of a vagrant did not seem quite so alluring, now that I was at my wits' ends to devise means for procuring a morsel of food.

I was about to turn aside from my course to avoid a small lonely hut, when its door opened and a large-framed, masculine looking woman, strode forth, hatchet in hand, and after proceeding a short distance to the rear of her humble abode, began chopping some dry brushwood and binding the same into fagots. She had left the door open behind her; and the opportunity for reconnoissance was too good to be lost. I made cautious advances and narrowly scanned the premises. Not a living creature within, save a purring tabby stretched before the fire upon the hearth. I entered without hesitation. A hoe-cake was baking on a shingle placed at a proper angle of declination before the glowing hardwood embers. Without one compunctious twinge for depriving an unoffending human female of her breakfast, into my tin pail I slid the hoe-cake, and looked about for any additional supplies that might be forthcoming. A bottle of goose oil I courteously declined; but lest I should seem insensible to the hospitality of mine involuntary hostess, I stuffed my coat pockets with a bountiful supply of cream cheese, and drained a bumper from the milk-pan. A bowl of yeast and basin of tallow drippings I also passed by without exacting contribution therefrom; but for this neglect I amply atoned by deluging my hoe-cake with the contents of the maple-sugar jug, and pocketing a handful of savory muriate from the salt-cellar.

I was startled by the sudden clatter of falling metal—
it was only the frightened cat, which had thrown down
shovel and tongs in the hurry of escape—and decamped
with my booty. Neither that day, nor the first half of
the next, was I under the disagreeable necessity of re-
newing my supplies. My last crumb of cheese disappeared for Sunday's breakfast; and as evening shades
drew on I grew desperate in my search for some means
of satiating the ravenous hunger gnawing at my vitals.

Little did I think, when I used to read in the daily
prints, with most lofty and unmitigated contempt, of
the depredations committed by paltry chicken-roost
thieves, that your most humble and most devoted would
ever be included in category so despicable. But even
so has it come to pass; and I have therefrom educed
this moral: Never look with pharisaical contempt upon
sinning publican, until you have been tried in the same
school of experience, and from such trial come out
scathless. I can do better than some of these needy
wretches who must beg, starve or steal—namely, plead
in exculpation of my offence.   •

If the world did not owe me a living, and I am not
prepared to assert or substantiate any special claims on
its bounty, Rebeldom did, in return for cheating me out
of a handsome salary, and reducing me to the condition
of a penniless wanderer on the face of the earth. If
they had cheated me, hadn't I as good a right to re-
taliate as they to transgress the common rules of honesty?
Now don't be hyperlogical, and ask how two wrongs
make a right, and knock my argumentative stilts from
under me. Assuredly, if it be an easy matter, as sages
admit, to set forth plausible arguments in support of
foregone conclusions, I can frame better vindication than
the above.

I see where my mistake has lain—in trusting to plain
and homely phrase rather than the varnish of elegant,

polished epithet. What man of high social standing likes to be termed a speculator in the fancies, while a heavy operator in the stock-jobbing line has about it the ring of the true coin of respectability? I will not stoop to the petty criminality of robbing a hen-roost; but a soldier in an enemy's territory must, as a simple matter of necessity, forage for his subsistence—a self-evident truth; I will not villainously poach upon, but I will most respectably forage, my neighbor's preserves. My theory thus satisfactorily disposed of, under the convenient rule of military necessity, I proceed with serene self-approval to record the practical workings of the same.

As I said, the deepening shades of twilight were curtaining the western skies. An unpretending farm-house was half concealed by tall cottonwood trees, while on a low-branched cypress roosted a score or so of domestic fowls. I waited until every light had disappeared from the windows before attempting the execution of my plan. A lusty chanticleer I singled out as my prize. Evidently the stupid bird was attached to his native soil, and did not relish the idea of having the Confiscation Act carried into effect on his own behoof, and was plainly inclined to show fight, giving me an ugly dig with his spur that roused my pluck and made me bent on securing him at any cost short of my own capture. Grasping him firmly by both legs I swung him off his perch.

As if from pure spite, he set up a series of the direst squawkings possible for a feathered throat to emit. I stopped that fun by a skilful turn of the wrist, but not until the mischief had been done according to the design of the defunct fowl.

The door of the house opened, a man's voice cried, "Speak to him, Growler," and an overgrown mongrel cur leaped upon my track.

Catching a bludgeon from the wood-pile, I started off on a run ; but an instant's reflection convinced me that it was folly to think of out-distancing such a pursuer ; I turned suddenly and faced the ferocious brute, which made a spring for my throat. Avoiding the same by a backward volt, I brought my club down on his skull to such good purpose that he dropped senseless for an instant, and then slunk howling away toward the house.

A musket-ball whizzing past showed that I was not yet safe from pursuit. Reaching the crest of a hill, I rolled down its opposite side, and on gaining the foot of the descent, crept along, veiling my progress by a young growth of cottonwood on the river bank. Not until I had put miles of space between myself and the pilfered hen-roost, did I dare to flatter myself that I should be permitted to enjoy the feast I had risked so much in purloining.

While the darkness lasted I dared make no attempt at lighting a fire, lest the smoke arising therefrom should betray my whereabouts to some lurking foe still dogging my steps. Daybreak found me traversing a precipitous bluff overhanging the river. From crag to crag I let myself down toward the water's edge. Beneath a beetling cliff projecting far over the stream, I safely crept, hugging myself with the sense of security its shelter afforded. Preparations for my morning repast were entered upon with a zest of which the dwellers in stated habitations can form but a feeble conception.

By the aid of my flint, punk-wood with which I had filled one pocket, and dry twigs and branches, I had soon a crackling fire, in front of which I suspended, by a twisted willow withe, the plucked fowl in readiness for the occasion. My tin-pail served as dripping-pan, the salt with which I had provided myself in case of contingency came not amiss ; and but brief time elapsed before my olfactories were greeted with gratefully appetizing odors.

Secure from molestation, with a supply of creature comforts sufficient for my immediate need, rest, peace and plenty, the blessings that crowned the hour, my heart expanded in deep thankfulness to the Giver of all these mercies. Do not make the mistake of supposing that I was perfectly, or even approximatively content with the condition in which I found myself, when I was only relatively so—thankful that things were no worse. In this transitional period of our being, where hope and aspiration are amongst our choicest pleasures; if, all our longings satisfied, we had no blessings to crave for the future, palled to satiety by the good gifts of this life, what greater boon than speedy release from the "fitful fever" which for us would be over? Pardon my sermonizing; it was morn of Sabbath rest to me; and in the restless onflow of the unquiet waters hurrying onward to meet the turbulent sea, in whose mighty embrace they are borne over mountain wave, in foam-capped crest to—calm haven of rest!—no; to be dashed, spent and helpless, upon a foreign shore, and by it be thrust back with the ebbing tide destined to lave the borders of another continent—I found my text.

I started to tell you one special reason for my lack of content. I was so lame that walking was a burdensome effort; and this fact weighed heavily on my spirits, forcibly reminding me of the severe and protracted sufferings I had undergone when languishing, untended and alone, beneath the whispering pines that seemed as sorrow-stricken as myself. The wounded leg had become painful through over-use, and against the other, just above the knee, the eight-pound ball had knocked, as I ran, until the flesh was black and blue, and the muscles so weak and strained as to be scarcely fit for active service. I racked my brain in attempts to devise some method for ridding myself of the encumbrance which proved such a serious clog to all my movements. With a stone I tried to break the lock of the iron band, and only succeeded in half breaking an ankle bone. With a piece of rough-edged quartz I rasped away with a will at the chain and produced not the slightest impression. Finding my efforts fruitless I desisted therefrom, philosophically determining to make the best of matters I could not mend.

After breakfasting luxuriously, I lay down on a couch of dry twigs, and lulled by the soothing sweep and plash of the dreamy waters, slept soundly. It lacked scarcely more than an hour of noon when I awoke. With renewed courage I climbed to the top of the bluff; and ignoring, as far as practicable, the awkward limp in my gait, resumed my forward tramp.

"Providence still holds me in its kindly keeping," I said to myself, as I heard the clink of a blacksmith's hammer, and caught sight of the sparks rising from his forge.

I had not long to wait before, casting aside his leather apron, he donned a decent coat, and started in the direction of the smoke-wreaths I saw curling upward through the trees at no great distance.

I hastened to improve the opportunity created by his absence. Minutes were precious, and I lost several searching vainly for the implement my purpose required; I was successful at last. Placing my foot beside the top of the anvil, with a few bold hammer-strokes I drove the cold chisel nearly through the chain, close to my ankle, and twisting off the remaining portion of the link, turned exulting in my freedom—turned to feel the grasp of brawny arms upon my shoulders; to be thrust summarily forward into a closet lighted only through the warped seams of its roughly-boarded walls, while its soot-smouched floor was littered with the nondescript odds and ends usually to be found in this sort of smithery.

A heavy bolt was turned in the lock; and plenty of time was given me to reflect on the nature of the new position in which I so unexpectedly found myself. The prospect was not encouraging; but I am naturally of sanguine temperament, and was by no means inclined to despair. Let the smith be called away from the shop, for ever so brief a period, and I would try the efficacy of sledge-hammer blows on the boarding, old and brittle, of this impromptu lock-up. The words of a speaker outside strengthened my resolve to improve to the utmost the first opportunity for escape. I jot down his remarks.

"I say, Daggett, where is the use, when provisions are so scarce and high, where is the use of wasting our substance on these northern locusts that are swarming all over our land. Where is the use of taking the bread out of our childrens' mouths to put into those of these bloody-minded Hessians! Our minister—let him preach mercy and good works, he is paid to, and can afford to cant for his hire—came to me with a paper and wanted me to put down something for the sick prisoners in jail. 'Not a red,' says I, 'do you get out of me. We don't want any prisoners; and the sooner they are under the ground the better.' What I said to him, I say to all. Not one that falls into my clutch shall ever escape to tell the tale. The malignants outnumber us, and we must outmanœuvre them until we are numerically their equals. Mercy to them, now, is cruelty to ourselves; and I'd slay my own son if I caught him offering so much as a cup of cold water for their aid and comfort."

You will readily perceive that vindictive expressions like the above were but ill calculated to add to my comfort. Comers and goers came and went; and steadily sounded the clink of the smith's hammer through the

long hours of that dreary afternoon. It was nearly
nightfall when the blast at the forge and the ring of the
anvil ceased. The lad who had been blowing the bel-
lows was dismissed. The heavy outer doors were swung
together and hasped inside. To what did all this preparation tend? Was I to meet foul end in that foul
den, and be put under ground with the least possible
delay? I would defend myself to the last extremity;
but the remembrance of the brawny figure that had so
easily overpowered and forced me into durance vile was
not a reassuring one. I am not ashamed to own that
my heart beat a little more quickly as I heard the heavy
step of my captor approaching my cell. The strong bolt
was turned back in its lock. I grasped a bar of iron,
determined to sell my life as dearly as possible. The door
swung open, and I saw for the first time, by the light
of the lantern he bore, the face of my captor—as open
and honest a face as one would care to look upon.

"I had to be a trifle rough, or it would have been all
over with you by this time," he said, with gruff hearti-
ness of tone and manner. "Throw down your weapon
—you see I am unarmed—and then we can treat on
equal terms."

Fearing treachery, and dreading to be taken unawares, I hesitated to comply with his request.

"You misdoubt me, which is a kind of treatment Eli
Buckwood isn't given to putting up with, from friend
or foe; but being a stranger, and not knowing that my
reputation for fair and honorable dealing is as good as
that of any other man, I don't care who he is, I'll let it
pass for what it's worth. Hold on to your knock-down
argument, if it eases your feelings, and come out to this
bench where we can have a talk."

Disarmed of suspicion by the candor of his bearing, I
abandoned the defensive, and took the seat to which he
pointed me.

"I have been shoeing horses all the afternoon," he explained, "for the Lone-star Rangers; and if they had once caught a sight of that frontlet on your cap, or that stamp on your buttons, salt wouldn't have saved you. It don't do to show Federal colors here, young man, though my heart warms toward the old flag whenever I see it. It is a long time since I have said as much as that, for I am the only Unionist in the neighborhood; my own sons, even, are in the rebel army, and their mother sides with them. Tell me how and why you are here, and I will do the best I can for you."

I related to him the occurrences that had brought me to so sorry a plight, in far fewer words than I have used in describing the same to you.

He soon removed the iron band from my ankle, and then led the way to a stable at the rear of his dwelling.

"I would offer you my spare bed with right good will," said he; "only I couldn't do so without Mrs. Buckwood's knowledge, and it is always safer not to take a woman into a man's counsels where life and death depend on keeping a secret. You had better get into this covered cart and make no noise until you hear from me again."

In less than an hour he brought me some supper and an old coverlet.

"Eat at your leisure," said he, "while I keep guard outside."

I waited no second bidding, but proceeded to discuss corn-bread and cold sausage with as keen an appetite as though I had not fared sumptuously during the earlier half of the day.

On the hay-mow, with a carriage cushion as pillow, I found a comfortable place for repose.

I must have slept but lightly, for I was fully aroused from my slumbers by a click of the barn-door latch.

"This way, Jim," said a cautious voice; "and don't

run afoul of the calf and set old Brindle a-lowing, or
we shall have all sorts of a, hullybaloo. Blast your picture, that is the cow's stanchion you are fumbling at ;
lead your ringboned nag into this stall, can't you ?"

There was a sound of horses' hoofs on the planked
floor, after which the speaker resumed :

" Give me the saddles, and I will put them into the
cart, as I know exactly where it stands. Now you litter down the horses—here is the straw on the barn-
floor—and, if I can find my way in the dark to the
grain-chest and the hay-mow, we need not disturb the
old folks till morning."

I began to feel an interest more absorbing than agreeable relative to the purposed movements of these new-
comers. Strongly disinclined to follow the course pro-
verbially attributed to misery, of making strange bed-
fellows, I preferred rather to resign my berth than to
share it with any.

Hastily depositing cushion and coverlet on top of the
cart cover, I pulled up the hay from the side of the
barn until I had hollowed out a space sufficiently large
to contain a single person, and having ensconced myself in the recess thus obtained, I drew the covering of
hay about me, defying the machinations of all midnight
disturbers of balmy rest. Up the ladder came the
unhallowed interloper, and I cringed involuntarily as
the tines of his fork sought undesirable propinquity with
the shrinking muscles of—yours truly. Added to this
cause of uneasiness was a second, quite as serious. The
finely powdered dust arising from the disturbed contents of the mow penetrated throat and nostrils to such
a degree that I had almost an irrepressible desire to
sneeze—an inclination, however, which yielded, as other
ideas supposed to be irrepressible have and will yield,
to the force of persistent repression. I firmly willed
the maintenance of silence, and silence I maintained.

The sound of receding steps on the ladder, I welcomed as one betokening release from impending danger.

"All right now, Jim," said the previous speaker; "the back window is always left unfastened; we will take a cold snack from the buttery, and I could find my way to the bed-room under the eaves if it were too dark to see my hand before me."

It was a relief to be left once more in undisputed possession of stable precincts. Throwing off my stifling herbal spread, I assumed posture as comfortable as circumstances would admit, and once more addressed myself to repose. Sleep was blandly poising itself with dreamy pinion on my eye-lids, when I was roused to sudden consciousness by the distinct utterance of a single whispered word—

"Ellsmead."

It must be my friend the smith, thought I, as to none other have I revealed my name. Thus it proved.

"I would have been glad," said he, "to have given you the advantage of a good night's rest; but it is not so ordained. My plans were well laid, but they were all brought to naught by the unexpected return—for how long a stay I have not learned—of my son and a young comrade of his. Unbeknown to them, I heard them slying in at the back window, rattling away at the knife-box and pickle-jar, and tip-toeing up the staircase. They are asleep now, for I passed the light across their eyes without their even blinking. You must be off before they wake, as I wouldn't be answerable for the consequences if they should detect me harboring a sworn enemy to the Confederacy. Here is one of the boys' caps, which you had better wear in place of that military tile, which might serve as death-warrant with one of our fire-eaters. Put on this jerkin of mine, too ; for, though I can't say much in praise of the fit, it may save you a closer one from hempen cravat. The lads sleep soundly after their long jaunt, I'll warrant you; but I'll run no risk for all that. Go out to the bars yonder and wait for me. If the trampling of the horses should disturb the youngsters they will find no one but me to deal with."

I obeyed without question or comment.

He soon joined me at the appointed rendezvous, riding one horse, and leading a second which he signed me to mount. A ride of ten or twelve miles brought us to a secluded stone cottage which gave few external tokens of occupancy. A sharp summons from a whip handle brought a middle-aged man to the door.

"Ah, Buckwood, it does me good to see you; come in, and let me make you welcome to a bachelor's fare."

"Thanks for your hospitality; but I must be home by daybreak or I shall be missed. I rode over to ask you to add another to the many good turns I owe you. This young man belongs to the Federal ranks, and is anxious to rejoin his regiment. Find out where it is (you see the papers), do what you can to further him on his way, and consider me freshly beholden to you."

This request was faithfully complied with.

I am sitting, now, in the Rainsford station house, waiting for the next downward train, which will leave me within twenty miles of the garrison where our division is at present posted.

I wish I could tell you how to direct a letter to me; for, aside from a sight of yourself, nothing would so gladden my eyes as a glimpse at that dainty caligraphy over which I have enacted such fondly foolish rhapsodies.

I will write you again at the earliest opportunity; but remember, my dear girl, that a soldier in the field has no will of his own, but is wholly at the command of his superior officers. Owing to the fatigue of marches and counter-marches, the restraints of strict military discipline, and the thousand vicissitudes to which we are exposed, with the best will in the world, I may be unable to convey to you one single word of intelligence. Do not forget this, if you should fail to hear from me regularly. Hope for the best; look not for clouds while the sky is bright; and strive to so live, as I, Heaven helping me, will also strive, that, though we should miss of happiness here, the immortal Hereafter should yet be ours. See how I linger over these parting words, loath to sever the last faint tie binding me to one in whom I have unshaken trust.

CHAPTER XII.

LOVE IN DISGUISE.

SOFT tears rained over Minnie's face as she concluded the perusal of the narrative penned, or rather pencilled, in her behoof.

" He would not place in me such unreserved confidence," she said to herself, " if he were not worthy a similar confidence in return ; and he has it—in life or death, he has my undivided trust. I never can lose Morland as I lost Mr. Caruthers ; for, even if he should fall, upholding a glorious cause, and take all earthly sunlight out of my skies—

' It is not all of life to live, nor all of death to die.' "

With the precious manuscript volume beneath her pillow, she slept soundly for a brief period ; and, buoyed up by sweet consciousness of unconfessed support, resumed, with renewed courage, the sober burden of daily duty it was hers to bear.

9

Days merged into weeks, and not an added line from Morland. The bitterness of hope deferred she partially assuaged by self-framed excuse for his prolonged silence. Postal arrangements were not always to be depended upon. He might have been unexpectedly ordered to a distant field of service, where he was cut off from all facilities for communication with friends. He might, as before, be keeping a diary, whose receipt would dissipate, on the instant, the shade of gloom darkening all her life. At all events he had bidden her hope for the best, and she strove to comply with his bidding, taking up her appointed tasks meekly and uncomplainingly, although with scant show of cheerfulness, endeavoring to inspire in others the peace and happiness which were strangers to her own breast. If a letter was to be written in the sick-wards, no one could express like her the unappeased yearnings of friendship, the protracted severance of tenderer ties; for, fresh from her own heart's bitterness, she drew the inspiration enabling her to divine another's grief.

Small wonder that she became a favorite attendant amongst the patients; for no voice was more gentle, no look more kindly, no hand more ready for any and every needful service than that of the pale sad-eyed girl who strove to forget her own sense of trial in ministering to that of others.

She was in the kitchen, following directions from the presiding matron, when word was brought the latter that callers were awaiting her in the small room set apart for the reception of transient visitors. As Mrs. Stanton was too deeply engaged to brook interruption from such a source, Minnie was deputed as bearer of explanations and apologies for the non-appearance of the former.

The young deputy was surprised, on entering the reception room, at finding herself face to face with Miss

Lucy Sears, who graciously accepted Mrs. Stanton's ex-cuses, adding, with persuasive mien. "I think I have already enjoyed the pleasure of making your acquain-tance—Miss Burr, if my memory serves me rightly."

"We met at Mrs. Thornton's," assented Minnie, shrinking from any correction of the speaker's mistake regarding her name, or, indeed, from any move calcu-lated to improve their acquaintance.

"Allow me, Miss Burr, to present my friend, Miss Lily Barton, and our obliging escort, Monsieur Meurice."

Minnie expressed a gratification not profoundly felt, and received appropriate response from a young lady alert of movement, of manner frank and unrestrained, and of speech fluent and outspoken, while a second acknowledgment was tendered by a young gentleman in glossy moustaches, atrociously perfumed locks, immacu-late primrose kids, and with a certain dainty accent of our home-bred idioms betraying his foreign extraction.

Profuse in compliments was Mons. Meurice; and, according but brief abstracted reply, Minnie turned in time to see Miss Sears touch the arm of her friend with her parasol, whereupon the two exchanged glances of smiling significance, and went so far as to titter aloud.

Surprised and indignant at this exhibition of imper-tinent ill-breeding, Minnie met the same by a look of cold inquiry addressed to whoever chose to answer the same. Miss Barton replied:

"We must seem very rude to you, Miss Burr; and, pardon us, we were rude. It seems so very odd to see one so young in a plain muslin cap such as thin-locked dowagers and antiquated spinsters wear, that we could but smile at the incongruity of the effect. It is like putting new wine in old bottles—a happy simile that, eh? Mons. Meurice? Let me have the advantage of your cultivated taste."

"Mademoiselle does me too much honor. I presume not to venture a word on such matters when the arbiters most gracious and most charmingly unapproachable through our less ethereal comprehensions do make themselves to stoop in elucidation of theories conflicting *nouvelles, ravissantes*."

"That is just your way, Mons. Meurice; we ask what you think, and you set us aside with a compliment, which is more easily bestowed than a reflection which you keep for those worthy the gift."

"Ah! Heaven! I am in despair. How have I so unfortunate been as one grand false step to make, and offend past the retrieve. Make me to see the way of amend that I do, contrite, seek it instantly to promenade."

"Don't distress yourself about her nonsense," interjected Miss Sears; "Lily is only trying to draw you out, she was so delighted with your discriminating admiration of those lovely coiffures at Madame Flancibel's."

Monsieur laid his hand upon his left waistcoat pocket, and professed himself enchanted at the prospect of being drawn and quartered, or by any other mode of excruciating torture, to be made to subserve the lightest caprice of the sex, whose frown was the shadow of Hades, and whose smile was the iris-hue of Paradise.

"That will do," smilingly responded Miss Lily. "Your protestations and abasement are so evidently sincere, that the offended goddess is thereby propitiated; the more readily since you displayed the most unexceptionable taste in selecting for me the head-dress of orange and jet which you pronounced the *chef-d'œuvre* of the establishment."

"Treason," cried Miss Sears, with mock-tragic air. "Faithless deceiver! did you not make oath that the rose-colored spangles on the silver-wound chenille was a perfect triumph of art, and the gem of the collection ?"

" For a delicate complexion, pearly white, only tinted with pink, in truth, yes. For a brunette, brilliant contrasts, gold and jet."

"Thank you. I am unusually particular about the ornaments I purchased to-day, as they are to be worn to the Lancers' charity ball, where I shall occupy a conspicuous position, as principal patroness of the entertainment, in which the claims of benevolence and of social festivity are delightfully harmonized. Mr. Caruthers has generously placed Montalbon Hall at our disposal. We have issued two hundred tickets, gentlemen only paying for admission, which, of course, they will be glad to prove their love of country by doing, as the net proceeds of the affair, after the music and refreshments are paid for, all go to the 'Gamble Addition Society.' Now that you have selected my head-dress, Arnaud, you must plan the remainder of my costume to match. Shall I wear my blue moire with bands of embossed velvet ?"

" Decidedly not; moires and velvets are too little ethereal for sylphs to float in through mazy dance. The rose-pink in Mademoiselle's cheek is enough for color, let it alone; heightening will not it improve, and lowering does but dim its native bloom. Coral for the lips, carnation for the cheeks, sapphire for the eyes, and not an added tint, say I."

" You are a sad flatterer, Arnaud," said Miss Lucy, with a blush and a smile. " You have not yet specified a single article for my toilette."

" A thousand pardons; but the wearer does furnish theme so much more attractive than costume the most recherché that I marvellously from my subject do find myself beguiled to stray. The robe, is it ? of which you would have me to speak. Something light and airy as

gossamer, I would advise, with puffings about the
shoulders no heavier than the breath of a song, or the
vibrations of ' El Zepateado.' "

" You are vague, not to say poetical, Monsieur."

" My theme, Mademoiselle; all the fault of my
theme. Am I to blame that there are some so essentially poetic of inspiration, that mortal may not approach them through conveyance of plain prose speech?"

" There, that will do, Monsieur; you have exerted
yourself quite sufficiently for the present. I will mercifully grant you a short respite. Shall I send you two
or three complimentary tickets for our ball, Miss Burr?
We are seriously embarrassed from lack of gentlemen,
so many have enlisted for the war; you may have
friends who would like to attend you."

" I am obliged by your kindness, of which it is impossible to avail myself."

" What a shame! I would not consent to be made a
fright of, with poky widows' weeds, and a high-necked
dress like a Quaker, for all the prim old hospital matrons
that ever breathed."

" You mistake; Mrs. Stanton places no irksome
restraint on my movements. I have become so accustomed to sights and sounds of suffering here, to descrip-
tions and apprehensions of it elsewhere, that it would
but sadden me the more to go where others are gay.
Here is my post of duty, and here will I remain, thankful to bear my poor part in the country's sorrow."

" We are as ready to do our part as anybody else,"
asserted Miss. Sears, bristling in defence of the patriotism she fancied had been impugned. " I am sure I
never worked so hard in my life as I have done lately,
crocheting caps, slippers, and mittens for the young
officers at Camp Bolivar. It is sad, I know, to see the
best men in the city going off to the battle-field; but
one can't be always sighing; though it is enough to

break one's heart to think how many of the poor fellows will come back maimed and disfigured for life. Dear me, I couldn't marry a man who returned with a frightfully scarred face, like young Selmore's, or one who was doomed to stump about for the rest of his days on a wooden leg. Could you, Miss Burr?"

Minnie's face paled perceptibly, and her eyes involuntarily filled.

" It is painful to think of such casualties for those dear to us ; but if I loved another as my own life, he would only be the dearer to me, the more he needed my care ; so long as his mortal garb was sufficient to clothe his spirit, so long should he be my very own, aye, longer yet—mine still in Heaven, if haply it should be mine."

" I *do* think, Miss Burr, that over confinement has somewhat unhinged your faculties, you talk in such a strained, impassioned way, for a person of your years. Do you mean to say that you would walk down one of our fashionable thoroughfares with a man whose face was black as a moor's from accidental gunpowder discharge; or who was such a wreck of humanity as to excite the pitying gaze of every passer by ?"

" In such case, I would care to frequent no fashionable thoroughfare. No eyes, save those of tenderest compassion should rest on disfigurement earned in cause so glorious. Not in crowded streets, but rather on grassy prairie slopes, would I strive to be unto him help meet in his endurance of stripes gained in support of justice and right."

" One would think she was in love, she makes the case so personal in application," smilingly remarked Miss Sears.

" Why not?" queried Mons. Meurice, with a look that brought the crimson to her cheek.

" We are wasting time, and forgetting our **errand**,"

suggested Miss Barton. " Will the hospital regulations
permit our seeing one of the patients, if we should ask
it ?"

" Put your application in the singular, if you please,"
hastily interposed Miss Sears, " I'll run no risk of con-
tagion by needlessly thrusting myself into unwholesome
wards where there is no knowing how many infectious
disorders are to be had without the asking. You have
robbed my flower-stand of its very choicest treasures—
exotics from Mr. Caruthers' conservatory—pray, let
that content you as my share of the contribution ; and
not give me a fit of low spirits, and expose me to the
chance of catching a fever, by dragging me where I
have no wish to go."

" She has reason," averred Monsieur, with a shrug.
" Why lacerate her nerves without force, and of chord
exquisite rare, by the sights most miserable excruciate ?
Go you both who have of adamant the brace, and con-
template, without one fracture of the sensibility acute,
such scenes as thrill with pangs the *spirituelle* superla-
tive, the incarnadine most rhapsodous of poet-fire and
music-tone."

Miss Barton gave the speaker a look of surprise, not
unmingled with annoyance.

" If you will have the goodness, sir, to come out of
your fine frenzy and condescend to ordinary modes of
speech, such as every-day mortals, not grossly ignorant
of the plainest rules of syntax and all that, generally
use, I will strive to make myself intelligible to your
transcendental perceptions."

Monsieur bowed with a slight air of pique. He had
a thorough detestation of a sharp woman or a sarcastic
woman, and, although finding amusement in laughing
at, and mystifying others, was by no means pleased at
having the tables turned and being laughed at himself,
especially by one of the sex which he had all his life

looked upon as composed of charming triflers, fit subjects for flattery and *persiflage*, when creation's imperious lords saw fit to unbend from serious employ and stoop to mirth and relaxation.

An awkward pause ensued, which Minnie broke by assuring the visitors that none but the nearest relatives of their occupants were allowed to visit the sick-wards.

"We may at least inquire after, and leave a bunch of flowers for, a friend, may we not?" asked Miss Lily.

"Certainly," replied Minnie; "I will see that any message or gift that you may intrust to my care is faithfully transmitted to whomsoever you may direct."

"Hear her talk of friends, when she never so much as changed words with Lieutenant Lonsdale," airily interpolated Miss Sears.

"I am better acquainted with him, for all that, than with many who pass as my intimates," stoutly insisted Miss Barton. "He lived next door to some New England friends of mine with whom I spent a week last fall. He enlisted then, but his widowed mother (he was the only son left at home with her) repented at the last moment, and procured a substitute to go in his stead, he obtaining a situation as clerk in one of our mercantile houses. An urgent requisition for troops induced him to join a battalion recruiting at Camp Bolivar. He was severely wounded, I hear; and being an almost entire stranger in the city, I have made bold to bring him this little floral offering, not daring to intrude on him any more serviceable gift."

"I am happy to be able to give you a good account of Mr. Lonsdale; he is out of danger, and is rapidly improving. I acted, yesterday, as his amanuensis; writing, at his dictation, a long letter to his mother."

"A very nice person; she will be overjoyed to hear that he is in a fair way of recovery. I will leave my bouquet in your charge; and please be careful not to

9*

drop this *carte de visite* held by the ribbon, as I think
he knows me by sight if not by name."

While handing the nosegay to Minnie, a spray of
delicately-scented florets fell to the floor.

" Ah! Heavens! what covert treason," cried Monsieur, with affected dismay. stooping to raise the fallen
spray. " Do you know, Mademoiselle, what fatal gift
you were about sending to this unfortunate young
man ?"

" What gift do you mean, Monsieur Meurice ?"

" Nothing less than love-in-disguise. an exotic of most
rare charm and subtlety, fair demoiselle."

Miss Lily reddened with resentment.

'. If you read me riddles, yourself must furnish solution ; I am not apt that way."

" Spare me the infliction unbearable of your displeasure. Is it possible that you did not know the
name of this harmless-looking blossom, which has,
nevertheless, its own appointed means of striking sharp
and under disguise. Examine, while to you I recount
its qualities recondite. Behold its petals of Tyrian purple, its scarlet filaments, its heart of gold. Then comes
the flower-cup which of it has for the description nothing ..
worthy of to note. But now of it note well all the mystery. In these bracts, as in a nutshell, it does lie in a
manner most admirable of nature for the purpose to
secern. That tiny row of leaflets at base of calyx, dost
observe ?"

'. Those are what you refer to, of course," said Miss
Sears, carelessly touching the calycle to which he pointed
and instantly drawing back her hand with a slight cry
of pain.

'. What do you mean, Monsieur, by serving me such
a shabby trick? I could not have thought it of you ;
I do not like practical jokes when they bring one to
harm. I am excessively angry with you."

"I am exalted into rapture and depressed into the misery the most poignant. I welcome the anger as better than the indifference; but how can I endure sight of the suffering that hand so sweet and *espiègle* unto itself hath drawn? Ah *Ciel!* rash descendant of an over-curious ancestress, had you but been content to await due course of explanation botanique, you of it should not have been brought to sudden grief. We here of it have not—how of him call you the name? one *guêpe*, thanks—yes, one vasp. These bracts have hidden nettle-stings; comprehend you the disguise?"

"As well as I care to comprehend anything to be learned at such cost. Pah, how my finger tingles. Throw the vile prickly weed out at the window, Monsieur, as I will throw the whole plant when I reach home—a much-to-be-dreaded and most villainously vile plant, with its false pretences and treacherous lures. I'll none of it; its very name brands it infamous. Love-in-disguise—why should love, if true, seek any disguise? why fear to express itself openly like any other honest emotion?"

"Ah me! Mademoiselle, why?"

She darted at the speaker a quick glance of startled surprise, toying uneasily with her fan.

"The question is of your own asking, Monsieur; answer it, if you think it worth your while."

"Then I have your sanction for speaking freely."

She changed color beneath his searching look, but replied with air of assumed indifference,

"Speak on, if you like; I place no hindrance in your way."

"Thank you from my heart," he said, bending low to her; "I am not prepared to take advantage, on the instant, of Mademoiselle's graciously accorded permission, which shall be remembered at season more propitious—do not fear but it shall be remembered and acted

on. Behold here of you the fan. The clasp of its san-
dal-wood supports, in your grasp agitated and unconscious, has snapped asunder. Suffer that I to smith of
silver do carry it for repair."

With graceful assurance, he took it from her unresist-
ing hand.

"I will return it to-morrow. Will that be soon
enough?"

"I am in no hurry; I have another, and have no
immediate use for this."

She spoke in an oddly fluttered way, which seemed
rather to augment than detract from Monsieur's equanimity. His superior coolness and self-possession gave
him incalculable advantage in every wary move.

"Delays are fatal," he declared, with a firm compression of his moustached lip. "I will to myself do the
honor to call when it has the hour of eight at the evening to-morrow."

"That will answer to a marvel, as I shall be away at
the naval exhibition with Mr. Caruthers at that time;
but you can leave the fan with my landlady, whose
memory may be trusted."

"Pardon; but I have not the honor of Madame's
acquaintance; besides, you forget the lecture botanique
I am to deliver by permission explicit and of condescension the most sweet and captivating. I will have
of the pleasure to pay of my respects when it has eleven
of the morning after the exhibition."

"Very well; I shall most likely be out for a promenade, as I generally am at that part of the forenoon."

"What sort of cross-purposes are you two sparring
with?" curiously queried Miss Barton.

"Too subtle ones to be trapped in words like silly
flies in amber," he returned with a shrug; "but—who
lives shall see."

"Well, you have contrived between you to hang

a tolerably weighty burden of discourse on a peg so light as a French nettle in bloom. Throw it aside, Monsieur, and take this pansy, which is pretty and harmless."

"I prefer my gorgeous floral queen, in its purple and gold; it is a souvenir."

"As you please. Let us go, for my poor nosegay is already beginning to wither in this warm room."

The three took their departure. Mons. Meurice all volubility and subservience; Miss Sears laboring under a sense of constraint and embarrassment she strove vainly to subdue; and Miss Barton keenly observant of her companions.

Minnie carried the bunch of flowers to the patient for whom it had been left; but as his eyes were closed, either in sleep or through disinclination for the effort of speech, she put the bouquet in a glass of water, and leaving it beside his cot, softly withdrew.

Down to the kitchen she ran, where Mrs. Stanton was still employed in hurrying forward the preparation of specified incarnatives. Minnie gave prompt and efficient aid, while her free thoughts roamed widely from the scene of her labors.

"Miss Sears wrote truly," thought she, "when she told me that we could never meet as friends. She takes all the earnestness out of my best purposes, with her talk of gems, and gauds, and adornings, when heads that are dearer to us than all Golconda's gems may be lying low; the hands we have held lovingly in our own stiffening on the dank sod, and the heart we would gladly shield with our own sending forth its last throb, far away from kindred and home. Oh me! who am I, that I should thus uncharitably judge another? It is not long, long as it seems, since I too wore costly brilliants —wore them not meekly either—gloating at thought of the envy I thereby inspired. Remembering my own follies, let me be lenient to those of others.

How foolish of me, when thrown off my guard by her suggestions of shattered limbs and maimed forms, to pour forth, as I did, the deepest feelings of my inner life—feelings I should have sacredly held in my most guarded consciousness, instead of exposing them to the derisive scorn of one who could never comprehend their fervor. Idiot! shall I ever learn better than to wear my heart on my sleeve when daws are by? At all events I stand a chance of rapidly attaining unto the Christian grace of humility, unless I reach a higher place in my own good opinion than any to which I am at present disposed to aspire.

CHAPTER XIII.

WARD FOR INCURABLES.

Minnie's busy hands and busier thoughts were suddenly suspended in action by a message from Dr. Waldo, requesting her to join him in the laboratory. Supposing that he wished to send his sister some directions requiring special accuracy of verbal transmission, Minnie hastened to obey the summons. The doctor, busy as he was with percolators, filters, crucibles and retorts, paused at once to hand her a scrap of soiled paper on which her own name had been scrawled with a pencil. Her eyes dilated over the paper, and her cheek blanched to a livid pallor.

For an instant she found speech impossible, and then with difficulty articulated:

" Where did you get this ?"

" I took it from the hand of a poor soldier but recently brought here, who has evidently but a few hours to live."

" His name—did you learn that?"

" Ellsmead, so the man said who left him here. Poor fellow, he has thrown away his last chance of life, it seems, by insisting, with a persistence that would brook no denial, on being conveyed to St. Marc's, when his recovery depended solely on his being kept perfectly quiet."

" Where is he now?"

" In the ward for incurables," was the calm reply.

In her own mind she accused the speaker of stony-hearted indifference in pronouncing words unmoved that wrung her very soul with anguish.

" I am bound to Morland Ellsmead by marriage engagement," she piteously acknowledged, " and entreat you to tell me his exact condition."

The doctor carefully adjusted the neck of a retort before replying.

" You must give me a minute's time; for I have listened, of late, to so many similar recountals, that I cannot, without some little consideration, recall the precise case to which you advert."

He hummed a tune abstractedly while watching an infusion of *ptelia trifoliata*, which he slowly stirred with a porcelain spoon.

" Please tell me, as soon as you can call to mind, what I am deeply anxious to hear," implored Minnie, in tone of urgent appeal.

The doctor hummed on, without raising his eyes from his employment. He was not the man to be hurried at another's beck. When he had taken due time for reflection, he, as if prompted by the occurrence of a sudden thought, drew a small memorandum-book from a side pocket and ran his eye down the pages as he turned the leaves.

" You see, Miss Brandon, that my memory is so over-
burdened that I have to adopt all practicable modes of
aid and relief; and I find one in jotting down some faint
indications of the treatment best adapted to each individual case. Here is what will help me to the diagnosis
in which you are particularly interested." He read
aloud :

"Ellsmead—imminently critical. Food, if any be
desired, simple, mucilaginous drinks. Medicine: alterative, nervine, mildly sedative. Outward application :
lobelia inflata, antispasmodic ; *viburnum oxycoccus*, same ;
capsicum baccatum, rubefacient."

"I have it now ; it is tetanus of whose effects we
are more immediately apprehensive. Do you comprehend ?"

" Lock-jaw," she returned, with quickened breath and
quivering lip.

'' That is it ; one of the most malignant forms a disease
can assume."

" You speak of it as a form assumed by disease—
what is the disease itself?"

" It springs from a complicated laceration of the tendons of the foot, which might have united, healed, and
left the epidermis to cicatrize, if he would but have
remained content where he was, instead of dragging
himself back here to die."

" Then it is only his foot that is injured ?"

" Bless you, that would have been a trifle but for su-
pervening effects, resulting from causes draining the
system of its vitality, and almost exhausting his recupe-
rative energy. He lay for two days on the battle-field,
faint and nearly unconscious, through loss of blood from
a wound inflicted by a sabre stroke, doubtless intended
for the neck, but luckily falling on the upper part of the

arm. Then a coward, who ought to be gibbeted for striking one too weak to return the blow, gave him a bayonet-lounge, probably meant for the heart, but fortunately failing of its mark, though completely perforating the left lung and breaking one of the ribs."

"That was the fatal wound, then, doctor?"

"No; a man may breathe as easily through one lung and a moiety of a second, as go through life on one leg. We might call him well, that is, pathologically speaking, free from disease, although, of course, not sound of life and limb, like one in full possession of every organ and function whose normal activity constitutes health in the highest sense of the term. The trouble with our patient was, that when he was at last borne from the field and placed in comparatively comfortable quarters, he wouldn't keep his mind at rest long enough to give nature, aided by art, time to effect needed renovations; nothing would do short of St. Marc's. It is a hard case, I admit; but we meet so many hard cases now, that one more or less can hardly be expected to call forth any special interest."

"But this case calls forth my most especial and absorbing interest. You will surely let me see Mr. Ellsmead. I may go with you to the ward for incurables?"

"No woman ever does go there; you will be content to return, after a brief look at the wounded soldier, if I will let you go?"

"Why may I not stay and smooth his way for him down to the very last?"

"Child, you do not know what you ask. You have not the nerve, no woman has, to endure the sights and sounds you would have to see there. Why, the cries and groans of the poor fellows when their wounds are being probed and dressed, accustomed as I am to such scenes, sometimes move me so deeply that I am long in shaking off their depressing effect."

"It would be strange if I could not bear expressions of pain which they must endure."

"Come with me; and when you have seen the reality, and calculated the cost of your undertaking, you will probably think better of it; but if you decide that you can bear it, I will do what I can to facilitate the performance of the arduous duties you take upon yourself."

"I am deeply grateful for this kindness; one must learn to bear what is of necessity to be borne."

Together they ascended the broad staircase.

"Why do you put those whose condition you regard as most hopeless in the top story of the building?" she asked as they reached an upper flight of stairs.

"Because their nervous systems are so overstrung, that their senses are sharpened to an almost preternatural acuteness, until we have amongst them those to whom a sight of the sun would be positive torture, and the sound of a footfall, overhead, actual misery. This highest ward is more readily darkened, more easily kept quiet than those below."

He opened the door as he spoke, motioning her to enter.

"Tread lightly; some of them may be sleeping. I am glad you wear felt slippers and skirts that do not rustle."

He closed the door softly behind him. Coming directly from a landing, bright from the sun's glare through a large skylight in the roof, to an apartment with closed shutters and drawn blinds, Minnie could at first but dimly discern the outlines of surrounding objects. Her heart fairly sank within her as she did trace the ghastly lineaments of more than one doomed occupant of the narrow pallets ranged in rows down the ward. Here was an emaciated unfortunate, having had his jaw shot away, who was taking, through a glass tube he had not sufficient strength to raise in his own behalf, the slight quantity of liquid nutriment wherewith was cked out the small remnant of his days; there another, with glazing eye and clammy brow, who grasped his attendant's hand, murmuring feebly:

" I can't see you; but don't go, it will soon be over."

Her face blanched, and a strong shudder shook her frame.

" Is it too much for you?" asked the surgeon.

" No;" she resolutely replied; "it is too much for them."

" It seems cruel to leave you here," he said, feelingly; " but perhaps it would be a greater cruelty to take you away."

At gesture from the speaker, she paused beside a cot whereon lay the worn, emaciate frame of a seeming stranger, whose very posture, one arm thrown over the head which was drawn painfully to one side, was indicative of exhaustion and unrest. Those lustreless, half-closed eyes, that forehead corrugated by premature wrinkles, the face pinched and worn, the lips pale, tight-drawn, the beard matted, the hair unshorn—what was there here to remind her of one upon whom she had last looked in the full strength and prime of early manhood—of the voice which had besought her love-troth—of the glance that had read and responded to her own—of the parting kiss that still in memory thrilled on her lips?

" That wreck Morland Ellsmead!" she ejaculated, doubtingly, and with an appealing look at her conductor, as if half desirous that he might be able to contradict her words.

" It is but rarely that a visitor to this ward is able to recognize a friend," the surgeon assured her. " Since you are bent upon it—I don't pretend to deny that it may soften your regrets in after years; I never pretend

to dictate in such affairs—why, even stay and smooth
his way, if you have the heart for it, through the few
hours, or days at farthest, that will put him beyond
reach of our soothing, if he be not already beyond such
reach."

"I cannot do my best for him if you bid me despair,"
she plaintively remonstrated.

"Do your best and I will do mine, prescribing as
faithfully as though I were more sanguine of the result.
Woman's tender and vigilant care, the thousand trifling
needs of the sick to which her fine intuitive sympathies
naturally fit her to minister, are sometimes of marvellous efficacy, as I have frequently. in the course of a
long and extensive practice, had occasion to observe.
I have but brief time to spare, as we are constantly in
receipt of fresh arrivals to-day, so I will explain to you,
as clearly as I can, the mode of treatment I propose
adopting in the present case, knowing that, with your
natural aptitude and the experience acquired below
stairs, you are capable of intelligently carrying out my
directions. First, I will endeavor to make your position as tenable as circumstances will allow.

"Here, Franz, catch hold of that foot-board and help
me lift this bedstead into this recess. That will do;
you are very handy. Now run into the splint-room and
bring me one of the largest screens you can find—you
understand, green glazed paper tacked to frames."

The messenger quickly returned with the portable
screen, which was placed before the recessed room.

"Now that I have done what I could in the way of
providing for your seclusion, Miss Brandon, give me
your closest attention while I explain the professional
dicta you are to vary as varying phases of the disease
require. The side and foot have been dressed for the
day—pass them by. This mixture, to be outwardly
applied to the lower part of the face and to the throat,

cannot be too frequently used. Here is a soft brush to facilitate its application. If the spasmodic muscular contraction should abate in severity, so that you could introduce between the patient's teeth this small, flattened cylinder, fill it with this *gelseminum*—ah, it's the powder I have; I'll leave it in liquid form—and administer it without delay. If he should still be restless, tossing about and moaning, don't let him waste his strength in that sort of useless effort. Opium is so obviously depressing to vitality, that I dare not prescribe it in cases of extreme prostration; but here are valerian, hyoscyamus, lupuline, scutellaria—directions for use accompanying each—with which I may safely trust you. In case of severe pain, moisten your handkerchief with ether, allowing him to inhale it at intervals, and sparingly. If, which I have not the remotest anticipation will occur, he should manifest the slightest desire for food, give a teaspoonful of this restorative cordial, followed by one, or more if he can take it, of elm-bark tea, which is both demulcent and nutritive."

The speaker left, at call of pressing duties demanding immediate attention, and she was in sole tendance of her all-engrossing charge. She laid her hand on the shrunken wrist whose feeble intermittent flutter but faintly betokened life. A sense of awe and isolation such as she could nowhere else have experienced, made her spirit quail within her. She had with her the one dearest object in earth's gift, and yet she had him not; for a dead blank wall of unconsciousness as effectually barred her from his presence as though floods of sea and mountains of space had intervened. Perhaps in the whole dull round of human sorrow none casts on the heart a more withering shadow of forlorn desolation than this of sitting beside the form of one beloved while the spirit it enshrines is withheld from our converse by the inexorable bonds of insensibility. She busied herself constantly about the sufferer, never permitting the liniment to dry on face or throat, while he knew nothing of the loving watchcare by which she unweariedly strove to win him back to life. Hour after hour went by, and still the faint flutter at his heart, the scarce perceptible pulse at his wrist, were the only assurances that he might still be classed amongst the living.

At last there came a change, a reddening of the skin beneath the liniment, a slight moisture on the heated brow, a stifled moan, and the hand that had lain motionless on the spread was slowly raised. The wan lips moved, pronouncing but a single word.

"Hark!"

She bent over him in an agony of solicitude

"What is it you hear, Morland? Speak to me, if it be but a word."

With a shudder he murmured: "The solemn tolling of a far-off bell."

Scalding tears gushed to her eyes; it is possible that, through power of anticipation, she realized, for the moment, the exceeding bitterness of bereavement.

Dr. Waldo looked in upon her in passing.

"You must not confine yourself too closely here, Miss Brandon; run down stairs, rinse out your mouth with vinegar, and take a turn in the yard for a breath of air."

"Never mind me, Doctor. What do you think of him?"

"Have you noticed any change in his symptoms?"

"He has spoken a few words."

"Intelligibly? and did he recognize you?"

She shook her head in sad denial.

"It is not of good omen, this protracted lethargy. I had supposed he would rally a little before the very last; but in these cases of extreme exhaustion we can predicate nothing with any approach to certainty. All I will venture to affirm is, that he can't hold out in this way long; and you may look for a change, either for better or worse, at any moment."

The speaker passed on, leaving her alone with the grief which was only less than despair. She knew not whether to wish the weary hours away, trusting that their flight might bring assuaging balm to the sufferer's relief, or to supplicate that their tardy progress might be yet further stayed; because she knew not whether the waning hours were to bring her consolation, or a corroboration of her worst fears.

A kindly attendant, in ministering to the needs of a patient on the opposite side of the screen, caught a glimpse of her deeply anxious face and came at once to her side.

"Poor fellow! he is dying, isn't he? How his fingers catch at the bed-clothes; that is a sign it is almost over."

"It is nervousness and exhaustion," returned Minnie, gulping down a sob; for she remembered well this identical movement in her dying sister's hand. Grasping that of her charge, she restrained its aimless wanderings in a clasp firm but gentle.

O, joyous revulsion from the numbing misery of despair to even the faintest glimmer of hope! His eyes opened, faint and bloodshot, but meeting hers with a glance of half-conscious recognition. The rigid muscular contraction so far relaxed that, with little difficulty, she succeeded in administering the *gelseminum* according to direction.

His lids slowly drooped over his weary eyes, and for a few minutes he remained perfectly quiet; then she perceived that his lips were moving, and bent to catch their whispered accents.

"I could bear the pain, Minnie, but my strength is gone."

She gave him a teaspoonful of restorative cordial,
which he swallowed with effort, and one of the tea as
well. The potion acting favorably was, at frequent intervals, repeated.

But, as his strength faintly revived. so also quickened
the pain in ratio so disproportionate that nature was
almost overpowered in its feeble attempt to rally. The
hand she held in her own felt as though it had been
dipped in iced water, so moist was it with a cold dew;
and every breath he exhaled terminated in a scarce
audible moan.

She bethought her, then, of that blessed anæsthetic
agent which, to suffering humanity, has proved boon so
beneficent. Pouring ether upon her handkerchief, she
so held it that he could inhale its stupefying fumes, and
soon had the satisfaction of noting that his breathing
grew more quiet and regular, after which he sank into
that fitful, unrefreshing sleep which is the best substitute for healthful, wholesome slumber artificial aids to
repose can superinduce. Brief the respite permitted by
even this poor apology for rest.

A sensation of deadly faintness swept through his entire system. He vainly clutched at her sleeve.

" Save me; I am sinking, sinking quite away. I think
this must be death,"

She crushed the tears beneath her lids; it was no
time to give way to weakness, so long as a forlorn hope
of saving him remained.

"Sal-volatile, quick," she cried to the nurse, still busy
with his charge on the other side of the screen.

The stimulant was brought, mixed with water. She
moistened the sick man's lips with the same, as he was
no longer able to swallow, bathing his forehead and
chafing his temples. Slow and lingering his return to
conscious life, if life, the mere fact of drawing his
breath in torture could be called.

Through the long night-watches she hung over him in unrelieved suspense, often bending her ear to catch the breath that assured her he still lived.

The morning brought with it Dr. Waldo, his sister, and an accompanying surgeon.

"Come with me while the patient's wounds are dressed," proposed Mrs. Stanton, leading away the worn-out watcher.

"What sort of pencil-case was that the doctor held in his hand?" asked Minnie of her conductress, as they descended the stairs.

"The pencil is of lunar caustic, the case of aluminum, I think, the only metal the nitrate will not corrode."

"Why did he have it with him?"

"To try and eat out the morbid growth in the patient's foot, which would not heal otherwise."

"It must be a painful process."

"It would be if its object were not unconscious, which is the condition most favorable for its performance."

Just one hour Minnie allowed herself for rest and refreshment, before returning to her post. For days, her helpless charge seemed hovering on the very brink of eternity; deadly attacks of faintness alternating with those of fierce wringing pain that strung his flaccid nerves to their highest point of tension. Through it all, love faithful and untiring, fanned with gentlest breath the feeble spark of vitality that, but for such unwearied tendance, must, in all human probability, have gone out forever.

The wound in his side forced him to a single constrained posture, whose continued observance became an unspeakable weariness.

"If some one would but raise my shoulders a trifle, it would be an indescribable relief," he imploringly suggested.

"I can do that by passing my arm beneath your pillow, so as to bring your head a little higher. There; are you easier now?"

"Very much so; the change is such a rest."

In the more comfortable position thus afforded, he soon fell into a calm and tranquil sleep. As hour after hour went by, her own position became one of painful constraint; but this might be his saving sleep, and she was by no means disposed to cavil at its length.

Mrs. Stanton stepped behind the screen.

"I have come, at my brother's request, to take your place for a half hour or so."

"It is very kind of you both, busy as you are, to think of me; but this is the first time, since he came here, that he has slept without some sort of anodyne, and it would be cruelty to disturb him now."

"It is not to be thought of; I will run up again when I find time. Is there nothing I can do for you now?"

"My throat is so dry and parched that I am in constant dread of coughing, which would awaken him in an instant; a swallow of the elm-water in that cup might remedy this."

The cup was handed to her.

As Mrs. Stanton pushed aside the screen in passing out, Minnie caught a glimpse of a plain pine coffin, which two men were passing through a side entrance still farther down the ward. She was thankful that her precious charge was not awake to behold a sight so startlingly suggestive to one in his enfeebled condition—more thankful still that his ear was not cognizant to the sound of the hoarse rattling breath of a fellow-sufferer whose last earthly conflict was almost over. These were not sights and sounds calculated to promote the recovery of one whose overstrung nerves quivered and thrilled at a tone or a look as only sick nerves can quiver and thrill at cause so apparently trivial.

THE BLACK PLUME RIFLES.

No such sight, however, met Morland's gaze as his
eyes opened upon the tenderly watchful face, expressive
only of gladness at his improved prospect of recovery.
Without demur, he took quietly from the spoon she
held to his lips the broth that at her request had been
brought by an attendant.

By various feminine artifices, she strove to divert his
attention from the trying incertitude of action occasioned
by the efforts of long inert digestives to resume the
functions which, through protracted disuse, had become
irksome and almost beyond power of attempt.

When I say that she made it her first aim to distract
his attention from his own personal ills, I do not mean
to convey the idea that she beguiled the hours of their
tedium by conversing with him ; on the contrary, she
refrained from more than an occasional word of address,
well knowing that the exertion of replying, or even of
listening, to her, would be a heavy drain on the scanty
strength he held in reserve.

Taking a needle-book and thimble from the pocket of
her muslin apron, she commenced darning the rents in
a bed-gown she found thrown across the foot of the cot.
The term amusement was not one appreciable by a person in his languishing condition ; but the sight of the
cheerful face, now and then bestowing on him a gracious
nod and smile ; of the deft fingers so thriftily busy with
the defaced garment he had cast aside as worthless, bore
with it a certain indefinable charm which was not
wholly that of novelty. Altogether, he was in as delectable a frame of mind as a man with lacerated cellular
tissues and cauterized tendons could reasonably aspire
to attain unto. A few days more, and he was able to
talk, for a little while at a time, without danger of sub-
sequent exhaustion.

"That man's voice sounds familiar to me," he more
than once remarked, as the patient on the opposite side

of the screen gave orders to a nurse in attendance. "I have it," he said at last; "he is the soldier I met in the woods, near Laurenstein. Please, Minnie, now that he is once more left to himself, to ask him if he would like to renew the acquaintance of the man he shot in mistake for a hound."

The reply that she brought back in answer to this message was an eager affirmative.

The screen was drawn a little aside that the wounded patriots might obtain a sight of each other. Each uttered an exclamation of surprise at the worn and haggard face of the other.

" I never yet knew the name of the man whose death I feared to have caused," said the stranger; "permit me to ask it now."

" Private Ellsmead, they called me in the ranks."

" And this young lady ?"

" Is Miss Minnie Brandon."

The querist started at sound of her name.

" Pardon my seeming rudeness. Is she a relative ?"

" She is not," replied Morland, somewhat stiffly.

Minnie reddened, but said with quiet, womanly dignity :

" He is more than a friend ; I have his pledged word to that effect."

" Thank you, I understand," returned the stranger, in courteous acknowledgment. " As I am strongly desirous of improving the acquaintance so casually commenced, I should give you my name; but I have a whim for passing myself off under a false one ; so call me Ashby ; I can answer to that as easily as to a more high-sounding cognomen. What did you think of my not returning that day I left you half dead in the forest ?"

" I feared some fatal mischance had befallen you."

" And so there had. I got my death-wound that day.

I had to go near the house you will remember to have seen, in order to obtain the water for which you were thirsting. I had just risen from filling the canteen at the brook, when a pistol-shot struck me in the right side of the chest, passing through the lung and fracturing the shoulder-blade. As I recoiled a few steps before falling, I caught just a glimpse of a white lace sleeve, and a woman's hand, holding a pistol, drawn inside an open window of the house I reminded you of. There I lay bleeding internally and externally, as miserable a wretch as was to be found on the footstool. The thought that another lay not far away in case quite as deplorable, and through my means, was far enough from giving me consolement. It is the misery that finds no company, no safety-valve in speech, that is heaviest to bear.

"I was so weak and faint, that I could hardly raise my heavy eyelids; but for all that, I was aware of the light step that stole to my side. I heard the rustle of a silken gown, and, without seeing her, knew that a woman was bending over me. I waited for some word of sympathy, some tenderly pitying tone to assuage the intensity of my anguish, for it seemed to me that I could not endure more and live; and that no human being without a heart harder than the nether millstone, could look unmoved on pangs that almost stopped my pulse, and took my breath away.

"'Die, dastard,' hissed the low tones of malignant female venom; 'now, Gorham, have I begun to execute my vow of vengeance for the foul murder that left me childless.'

"I raised my look to the cold, stern face so vindictively bent on my own, and begged for a drink of water.

"She glared on me in a way that I cannot better describe than by saying that it reminded me of a wild

beast gloating over its prey. Save through her glance,
she did not speak. As she went away, I noticed that
she bore a respectable appearance, clad in a narrow-
skirted black silk, with a decent cap covering her grey
locks. She entered the house, but soon came back with
a tin basin in her hand.

"'Her words and looks belie her,' I said to myself;
'she has some spark of humanity left in her yet; she is
bringing some freshly-made tea to quench my thirst.'

"She raised the basin and dashed its contents full in
my face—some sort of alkaline preparation it must have
held, judging from the caustic smart it caused in my
eyes and nostrils. No tongue can describe the unutter-
able rage that boiled in my veins at this unprovoked
and barbarous assault on one whose sufferings were
already well nigh past endurance.

"I never had a sister; my mother died when I was
so young, that she has always held a saint's place in my
memory: and this accounts, in some degree, for the
exalted place woman has always held in my estimation
as the incarnation of all mild and gentle virtues, one to
shield, to toil for, to protect to the very death; but
when, instead of the benign ministrant I had loved to
picture her, she stood forth a stealthy and treacherous
assassin, my feelings underwent a sudden and violent
revulsion, the intensity of my hate being proportionate
to the chivalric regard it had displaced. When she out-
raged all the diviner instincts of womanhood, by forcing
herself into the arena of strife and bloodshed, from
which man and nature had conspired to shut her out,
she was no longer a creature privileged with defence,
but an enemy to be attacked and disarmed. I swore
that no brother officer should ever receive his death-blow
from the same hand that had dealt mine. From the
necessity of the case, I combined in my own person the
triple function of victim, judge and jury. What say

you, Ellsmead, ought I to have left this fiend in female form to go at large and repeat the crime of murder?"

Morland raised quickly his glance to Minnie's face, as though loath to pronounce judgment against any member of the sex toward which he was tolerant for her sake.

" She was a dangerous and hardened criminal, and death but her just desert," slowly faltered Minnie.

Mr. Ashby started.

" You have avoided the only difficulty in the case, Miss Brandon ; she undoubtedly deserved a criminal's doom ; but was it right to mete out to her such doom without the benefit of law or clergy? I asked myself no such question at the time. I held it to be a sacred obligation I owed to the innocent, to punish one guilty of so dark a crime, and greatly feared that my last hour might come, and the earth not be rid of her. Had my strength been equal to my will, brief the time she should have had wherein to shrive herself; as it was, I had to wait and watch my opportunity, husbanding well my resources, not wasting, by so much as a groan, one single particle of that waning strength, every iota of which I should need in carrying out my purpose.

" As evening drew on, I kept a close watch on the house that no one might enter it unbeknown to me, as I wished to make sure that she was quite by herself on the premises. I satisfied myself that such was the case. I thought the hours would never go by; but, at last, heard a clock striking ten. She came out with a lighted lantern in her hand, and passed it slowly, several times, back and forth across my eyes. I had noticed, as she approached, the glitter of a sharp blade ; and, not knowing for what purpose it might be intended, I discreetly composed my features to the most rigid immobility they were capable of assuming. Evidently convinced that I was beyond the need of any further assiduities, she left me without speaking.

" I waited an hour after she had fastened the windows and blown out her light, before proceeding to put my plan into execution. No one who has not gone through the same can form any conception of the torture I underwent in writhing myself over the ground from the spot where I had been lying to a window directly beneath the stairs by which she had gone up to her bed-room. At every move the blood gushed from my wound, and the pain was like that of a shovelful of live coals heaped across my chest.

" It was a work of time and patience to tear off a portion of my muslin shirt-sleeve, which I placed carefully beneath the wooden sill, and, adding a few dead twigs from an ailing shrub, lit the pile with a match from the little metallic box I never go without, and the deed was done. The house was soon in flames, and I dragged myself away from the fatal spot.

" The dry timbers roared and crackled with awful distinctness on the still night air ; but that was not the sound I was listening for. The cry of a frightened bird came up from the woods ; but not for that was I harkening with strained and eager expectancy. The distant baying of a hound came from afar ; but that was not the one sound I waited to hear. It came—wild with fear, shrill with terror—a woman's shriek, sharp, sudden, as suddenly stifled by the densely rising smoke.

" The single staircase leading to the upper story was all ablaze—no hope of escape by that. A white face appeared at the window, weak, trembling hands tried to throw up the sash which resisted their efforts.

" Did her eyes and nostrils smart as, thanks to her barbarous malignity, my own had done not many hours before? A man is half dehumanized when maddened by rage or any other blind, ungovernable passion. I could have looked with composure on her last throes, even though knowing my own were likely soon to follow.

" Let me not dwell on such a theme. The roof fell in, and all was over.

"I looked for death, and even hoped for it, as my only chance of relief.

" Next morning, a farmer, driving with a load of corn to the Laurenstein grist-mill, got off his wagon and came to look at the scene of the fire. He discovered me, of course. I offered him my watch if he would place me in charge of any stanch Union man he might happen to know. My offer would probably have been of but little avail, as he could easily have appropriated any valuables in my possession, had he not proved to be himself a firm Unionist. He took me home with him, and gave me the kindest care until I found means of travelling north to join my friends ; I might have spared myself the trouble, as the relatives I sought had fallen victims to guerilla outrage. I came here in preference to testing the accommodations of a crowded hotel. Now, Ellsmead, let me hear how you escaped from the fearful position in which I left you."

" I will tell you all—it exhausts him to talk more than - a few minutes at a time—when he is sufficiently rested to set me right on any points I might accidentally mistake. You can see, by this cold dew on his forehead and the tremor of his hands, that even listening would weary him just at present. You shall hear all, but not now."

CHAPTER XIV.

HOME.

PLEASANT sights, and perfumes no less pleasing, were in the airy, cheery room where lay the sufferer but recently removed thither from crowded hospital ward. Let me describe the room, and you will see that I have not over-estimated its attractiveness. A cool straw matting is on the floor; in the corners are tasteful triangular book-shelves, suspended by a framework of varnished pine-cones; on the walls are prints etched from paintings by masters celebrated in the old world, in home-made frames of variegated leaves from the new.

The windows contribute to the room its best of charm. Through climbing rose-sprays fall fleckered rays of softened light—creeps in the fragrant breath of unobtrusive mignonette, and odor more pronounced from the brilliant sydonia, showy of petal and of perfume alluringly subtle. Of all these alleviatives to the sharp ills that descend as time-honored heirlooms, from one generation to another of the human family, the sole occupant of the room, a man young in years but with the furrows of stern endurance on his brow, was keenly sensible.

The door opened, and a sunny faced young woman, dressed in plain and cheap material, but with that perfect adaptation of shade and contour to the style of the wearer that constitutes true elegance of attire, stole quietly to his bedside.

" How is my patient, this morning ?"

" Better, Minnie ; the songs of birds are not like the sounds to which one became accustomed at St. Marc's, and the scent of these roses brings with it no unpleasant reminder like that of tinctures and drugs. It was for-

tunate for us that your father lost his voice in that last
severe bronchial attack which forced him to quit his post
at the Institute. A god-send to us this ill-wind to our
host. Eh, Ashby? There, that is the second time I
have spoken to him and received no answer. Do see if
anything has gone amiss with the poor fellow."

Noiselessly she crossed the room, looking in upon the
bed-ridden occupant of the adjoining apartment.

"He is sleeping, Morland ; speak low or we shall disturb him. He is so much afraid of putting us to the
slightest trouble on his account, that the least we can do
in return for his kindly consideration is to repay it with
consideration as kind. How much more happy he seems
here than he was at St. Marc's. How strongly he insisted on coming here with us, and wouldn't take 'No'
for an answer."

"That is where he was right ; hospital accommodations are very different from the tender cares of home ;
and, if Mr. Ashby were with his own relatives, he
couldn't be more faithfully tended than he is here. A
precious pair of incurables that spring-wagon, with its
mattress and cushions, and its horse upon the full walk,
brought you as recruits, didn't it ?"

"You are no longer to class yourself amongst the incurables ; on the list of convalescents we have you,
remember. Think how light are your sufferings in
comparison with those you bore in the dreary, bitter
past."

"I do think of it, and with thankfulness, dear con-
soler ; but let me tell you one thing. I had hope of
ultimate recovery to buoy me up then ; now that has
gone, and with it half my courage."

"Why will you talk in this dispiriting way? Only
yesterday, the doctor told me you were out of danger
and improving daily."

"Did he tell you that the sundered tendons in my

foot are dead?—that the whole foot will probably wither, quite likely as high as the knee?—that I shall never walk again without the help of crutches?—that, young as I am, I have outlived my usefulness? Oh, Minnie! that is the hardest of all to bear—not a creature in all this weary world the better for my being alive in it."

"Morland, my own, you are not to talk to me in that despondent tone; it is not right; it is not true; you are not wont to distress me with phrase so ill applied. Not a creature in the world the better for your living in it! Do I not rejoice at every gleam of comfort that comes to you? Do you ever sorrow that my sorrow is not incalculably greater than if it rose from source purely personal to myself? Your gladness is mine, with tenfold increase; in your grief, too, I proclaim myself rightful participant; and if you deny my claim you wrong yourself as deeply as you wrong me."

"You are looking at the case from a standpoint entirely opposed to the one I occupy. The very fact that my ills come doubly barbed to you does but strengthen my resolve not to selfishly inflict upon you such burden doubly weighted. I would have devoted my life gladly to the pleasing task of making yours happy; but as this is not to be, let me explain to you, calmly and candidly, the process of reasoning by which I arrived at the conclusion that it is better for us to part."

"I will listen to what you have to say in vindication of the course you have decided on pursuing; but I give you fair warning that I shall do my very best to upset the reasoning you deem so conclusive."

"Fully appreciating the friendly malice of this threat, I have, first, to request that you will give me full particulars concerning the destruction of the powder mill in which the whole of your father's available funds were invested."

"Certainly, if that will interest you. The mill was built, as I think you have already been told, of limestone and iron, to prevent the possibility of its being set on fire. In addition to this precaution, a sufficient guard to defend it against assault was left in the building every night. There was a great scarcity of workmen, so many had enlisted, and the agent for the Company engaged one, who, as it has since been discovered, was in the rebels' interest. It takes but a spark, as you are aware, to blow up a powder mill; that spark was thrown by a traitor's hand, and the whole structure left a mass of ruins."

"And your father's fortune in ruins beside. Do not look startled; we will talk the matter over calmly. Broken in health, weighed down by increasing infirmities, he will have quite enough to do in obtaining his own livelihood, without taking the burden of my support upon his heavily-laden shoulders. As I have lost the power to earn my living in serving my country, surely the country ought to provide some sort of asylum, however humble, for those who served it faithfully while strength held out. I shall make inquiries, and ascertain if there is not some such place of refuge for disabled cripples like me. Of course I have long considered the engagement null and void, binding you to such a stranded wreck as I."

"My 'stranded wreck' I refuse, point blank, to leave to the mercy of the waves. What! you would solicit aid from the country; but that lordly arrogance, which is the most easily besetting sin of your imperious sex, will not let you stoop to accept help from one who would work for you with pleasure and alacrity a thousandfold greater than for herself. Were you my superior in strength, I would lean on you gladly; but while I am the stronger of the two, you must bow that proud spirit, and even learn to lean on me. You are going to no asylum save such as I can provide for you."

"But, Minnie, what does a delicately-reared little woman like you know about earning a living? What could slender hands like those do toward providing for our maintenance?"

"Do not speak too slightingly of my abilities for gaining a livelihood until they have been thoroughly tested. I know I cannot scour and scrub like our hard-palmed Chloe; but if I cannot put these hands, whose capabilities for useful employment you are pleased to doubt, to occupation as respectable and remunerative as many a mode of labor others profitably pursue, it will then be time to write me down an imbecile, and incapable. Music has always been to me a recreation; I can make of it something better. I was last year offered a situation as soprano singer in a quartette city choir; I had not the courage to accept the offer then; I have found the courage to do so now. Then, I could give lessons on the piano, or teach a juvenile singing school. Miss Caruthers would, I am sure, aid me in procuring pupils, and that is a sort of favor I could ask of her without any diminution of my own self-respect. Some one spoke; was it you?"

"Not a word."

"Then it must have been Mr. Ashby."

She crossed to the open door of his room.

"You called to me, I think,"

"Yes; I wish you would bring me writing materials; there are a few friends in the city I wish to see, while I have strength to converse."

She brought him paper, pencil, and the little book whose cover he proposed using as writing-desk. He was not even able to raise his head without her assistance, which she freely rendered, propping it up with pillows. He strove to grasp the pencil, but it slipped from his nerveless fingers, the little book sliding from his hand.

"Let me write for you, Mr. Ashby; it is over-taxing your strength to make the attempt."

"No; this is the last labor of love I shall ever undertake, and if I can but accomplish it, it will remain unto me a sweet memory to my very latest breath."

By dint of persevering effort he succeeded in tracing a few irregular lines. Folding and directing his brief missive, he requested that it might at once be sent to the office, and sank back in a state of complete exhaustion.

Next morning, a vehicle containing three persons made its appearance at the garden gate, fronting the cottage. One of the three alighted and ran up the walk. Minnie met him at the outer door.

"Good morning, Miss Brandon. I am in great haste, but sit down in this hall chair a minute, as I have news for your special delectation, if the proverbial curiosity of your sex has not been grossly exaggerated. Think of tidings direct from Mr. Caruthers! Isn't that a tempting bait?"

"Not particularly so, Mr. Auverne; although I am still glad to be assured of his welfare."

"Tell that to some one who has had less chance than I for studying poor human nature in its phases mutable and perverse. If I had nothing but his welfare to inform you of, I'd not waste breath in telling what you wouldn't care one snap of your finger to hear. Poor Caruthers is in no end of trouble; so call up your choicest feminine malice in delighted anticipation of revenge for past slights."

"I have no such malignant feeling to gratify, I do most earnestly assure you. There was a mutual mistake between us, that was all; and as it was discovered in season to admit of effectual remedy, there was no lasting harm done. He misunderstood me as completely as I misunderstood him ; I bear him no grudge on that account, as I hope and trust he bears none toward me."

" I can never quite make you out, Miss Brandon ; you certainly are not destitute of quick feeling, the result of the vivid, emotional nature incidental to your temperament ; it must be that you have unusual power of self-command."

" I perceive that you suspect me of some sort of reserve or equivocation, it matters the less what, that your suspicion is groundless. I have seen so much of suffering in those long months last gone by, that I have learned to look on life with a sadder eye than most persons of my years. It seems to me that there is already enough of human sorrow in the world ; if I can do nothing toward assuaging the same, I can, at least, refrain from adding by word or thought to the misery of any fellow-mortal. Believe it or not, I should be glad to receive assurance of Mr. Caruthers' welfare ; and if any evil has befallen him, no one will regret it more sincerely than myself."

" You heard, of course, that he went off as captain of the Black Plume Rifles, who were ordered south more than a month ago."

" I heard nothing of the kind ; a hospital is no place for news excepting for those sick and disabled ; and here, with three invalids to be cared for, we have lived in the most rigid seclusion."

" It was in strong opposition to his own will that Mr. Caruthers was forced into military service. He was captain of the Black Plumes a dozen years back or so, when they were only called upon to do escort duty or meet on public parade, and as his name still remained on the roster of the legion, he was called upon to head his company, and leave with them at twenty-four hours' notice. Not that he was actually compelled to go ; but if he had deserted his post in the country's present strait, public opinion, not a pleasant thing to brave, would have set in strongly against him. It was with a rueful countenance he started ; for his wedding day had been agreed upon, and a trip to Europe planned in honor of the occasion."

How vividly these words of the lawyer recalled to Minnie's recollection the time when she had thought to look with Mr. Caruthers on sculptured fountain, carved arch, storied wall, and all the monuments through which old-world Art has proclaimed itself immortal. With a little sigh she returned to memory's crypt the dead illu sion erstwhile so vital, so fondly cherished.

" I am sorry for his disappointment," she said, gently; " it must have been hard to bear."

" He found it so. I do not believe there was as heavy a heart in the company as its commander bore away with him. Good cause he had, too, for not a trump has turned up for him in the game of life since. Not-withstanding my earnest expostulations against the adoption of a course so unwise, he persisted in present-ing Miss Sears with a warranted deed of that superb new mansion of his. I told him repeatedly, that it would be far safer not to place in her unlimited trust, but rather to so arrange matters as to foster in her a whole-some sense of dependence on his generosity. To the policy of keeping her dependent on himself he was not in the least opposed ; but it seems that he had a presen-timent of coming evil, and was not inclined to leave his bride elect to the tender charities of his mother and sisters, who detest her most cordially. I think that by this time he rues the folly that led him to set my counsel at naught."

" Why, has Miss Sears abused his confidence ?"

" Of course she has ; exactly as I predicted she would

do. Not that she is in the least wicked or malicious
of intent—it would take a deeper style of woman—no
offence intended, I beg leave to protest; for that—but
she is just the sort of person that I would no more trust
with the unrestricted control of a fortune than a mis-
chievous urchin in dangerous proximity with match-box
and shavings. Last week I heard that Mr. Caruthers
had had an arm shot off, and was otherwise frightfully
mutilated; three days later Miss Sears was married,
and she is now on her way to Paris."

"You surprise me: Mr. Caruthers could not have
been fit to travel so soon after receiving such severe injuries."

"You are quite right; Mr. Caruthers is in a southern
hospital, and Lucy Sears has been guilty of the unpar-
donable folly of marrying a Frenchman, a quondam
music-master of hers, who, if I am not far out in my
reckoning, will lead her a sorrier life than any she ever
began to dream of. What possessed her to absolutely
throw away her chances for happiness I can't begin to
imagine. The worst aspect of the affair is, that the marriage ceremonial was conducted under very suspicious
auspices; and, if I am right in my conjecture, that the
observance was not conducted in strict conformity with
legal usage. She has sown the wind, and must reap
its natural product in due course of time. She seemed
very much out of spirits when she came to me, not a
week since, requesting my advice with regard to letting her house, ready furnished, for three years. She
obtained a tenant for the time specified, at twenty-five
hundred per annum (rents have fallen, as you are aware),
and on that amount, in a number of the continental
cities, they can live in luxurious style, hiring an apartment in an antique palace, with a chariot and four, and
lackeys to correspond, if bent on ostentatious display.
Poor Caruthers!"

"Poor Miss Sears rather, if you have any reason to believe that her marriage has not been legally solemnized."

"It may be nothing more than a suspicion on my part, strengthened by the unprincipled character of the groom, of which I became convinced through conflicting evidence he once gave in a case where I was employed as counsel. I will tell you the flaws I see cause to suspect in the preliminaries to this marriage, if not in its actual solemnization. So far as I have been able to discover, there were no published bands. Another circumstance that would bear inquiry is, that Monsieur Meurice is a Catholic, and it was not according to Catholic ritual, if indeed it was in accordance with any established form of church ceremonial, for such occasions made and provided, that this wedding was conducted. In my opinion, it is only her fortune that Monsieur is after; let him once get that into his possession, and, in my belief, her hold on him would be greatly weakened, if not wholly destroyed. The day she called on me for advice, she consulted me as to the expediency of selling her house—a measure I strenuously opposed, as it would place her entirely at his mercy. I will tell you how it chanced that I was the first one, aside from the bogus clergyman officiating at the rite, to get an inkling of the game that was being played. I was walking in great haste, down an avenue, when a woman, closely veiled and in a grey travelling suit, started to come down the broad flight of stone steps leading from the covered porch of the Gresham boarding-house. The heels of her boots being too high and tapering for secure foothold, she made a misstep and would have fallen if I had not lent her a helping hand. I recognized and spoke to her, addressing her as Miss Sears. 'Allow me —Madame Meurice'—corrected a man, got up in the highest style of art, and overpoweringly perfumed with

'lily-dew' and 'breath of balm perennial.' She introduced me to her husband, and he made me acquainted
with the Rev. Abednego Witherspoon, who, it seems,
had just united them in the holy bonds of wedlock. An
odd spoon, I must say, the parson looked, with a long
cigar in his mouth, a knowing leer of the eye, a hat set
jauntily on one side, a flashy waistcoat, and a stunning
neck-tie. I jumped at once to the conclusion that the
swaggering Witherspoon was much more likely to have
received the hand of fellowship from some sporting
brother of the turf than from any of the regularly
ordained sacerdotal authorities. Those superstitiously
inclined might have found a bad omen, also, in the
fact, that the sun did not shine on the bride. The first
drops of a thunder-shower sprinkled her dress as she
stepped across the sidewalk to the carriage in waiting,
as if the skies wept—did you know I could be poetical,
Miss Brandon?—at the poor child's sad fate. The truth
is, that she is such an impulsive, warm-hearted, foolish,
confiding, shallow creature, that she interests me by her
very need of such interest; and I would a thousand
times quicker do her a good turn than one of your strong-
minded females, who demand a favor at the sword's
point, never of grace or courtesy, and ask of you no better concession than to keep out of their sunshine.

" Who is this Mr. Ashby that has written me to come
to him at my earliest possible convenience ?"

" I supposed you was a friend of his when I saw, yesterday, that his letter was directed to you, as he said
he wished to see some friends from the city before his
strength failed ; and I supposed it was in answer to that
summons you came."

" I have no recollection of ever having seen a man of
that name; but let me go to him and I will soon find
out what he wants."

Minnie, having ascertained that the sick man was

awake, and eagerly desirous of an immediate interview with the lawyer, communicated this fact to the latter, who proceeded at once to the invalid's room.

Nearly an hour elapsed before the legal gentleman came hurriedly out of the apartment to which he had been shown, and the two men who had remained outside in the carriage were beckoned in, accompanying him to the room he had just quitted. A minute later, Mr. Auverne once more made his appearance, this time motioning Minnie to follow him.

"The effort of directing a disposition of his effects has quite overcome him," explained the lawyer in a subdued tone. "He has asked for you; prepare yourself to see a great change in him."

Mr. Ashby held out his hand to her as she approached his bedside.

"Quick!" he adjured her.

Springing forward, she grasped his ice-cold palm.

"Air!" he entreated, gasping for breath.

Mr. Auverne threw open the window near the head of the bed. Minnie raised the head of the sufferer on her arm, that he might be the sooner revived by the entering breeze.

In vain for him, the breath of the wind that fanned his cheek. For the last time has his hand been clasped; for it is his no longer. Never again will that head be pillowed on friendly arm; for the mysterious intelligence that made it human and precious has fled. One more struggling mortal has been swept from life's narrow strand by the resistless waves of that viewless, boundless sea that will, full soon, wash also our shallow footprints from the sandy shores of time.

Morland Ellsmead, for the first time in many weeks, had been able to don dressing-gown and slippers, and sat in an easy-chair, enjoying with the zest of a novel experience, the roses and their foliage of vivid green draping the window of his room. About him were grouped the members of the little household.

Mr. Auverne had been reading aloud the will he had recently drawn up for the deceased. It was not a lengthy document; but its verbose technical repetitions there is no occasion to chronicle. The brief conversation I am about to record will sufficiently explain itself.

"He kept his secret well," remarked the lawyer; "not one of you having ever suspected that the prospective benefactor you were entertaining unawares was none other than Falkland Courcelle."

"If I had but known he was my mother's nearest surviving relative," Minnie regretfully subjoined, "I should have felt more at liberty than I did to offer the constant attentions his condition required, but which he was so slow to claim."

"I am sure you have nothing to reproach yourself with on the score of neglect," Morland warmly interposed. "If he had been your own brother you could not have been more kind."

"He had the satisfaction of knowing," added Mr. Auverne, "that your kindness proceeded from purely disinterested motives—a rarity in this self-seeking generation. His incognito also gave him the opportunity of thoroughly convincing himself that you were worthy of the fine inheritance he has bequeathed to you, or rather to Mr. Ellsmead, which is a different means of reaching the same result. Only a single restriction, and that not difficult of compliance, clogging his acceptance of the estate: that he shall assume the name of Courcelle on the day of his marriage with Miss Brandon, when the title deeds of Pré-Fleuri are to be placed in his possession. A highly valuable piece of property it is, too, with its rich alluvial soil adapted to every species of culture, ample tenements for all the laborers it may require to carry it on, and the roomy brick mansion-house, spacious if old-fashioned and ill-contrived, built by the grandfather of the present testator. To be sure, the place looks, with its untilled fields, and unpruned fruit-trees, a little forlorn and deserted, just now; but occupancy and anything like tolerable husbandry will remedy this temporary neglect, and make it the garden it used to be. Exact to the verge of punctiliousness, this Mr. Courcelle has been in carrying out the wishes of his deceased aunts. He not only stipulates for the enfranchisement of their colored dependents, but has, in addition to this liberality, made suitable provision for their support in case of sickness or destitution. Wishing you many years enjoyment of your newly-acquired fortune, I may also wish you a very 'Good day.'"

Minnie watched the lawyer as he drove away, and then drawing a low stool near the chair in which Morland reclined, sat down beside him.

"You see," she said, in a tone of subdued thankfulness, "that, after all the impatience you have felt at the helpless condition to which wounds nobly earned have reduced you, Providence has marked out for you a path of usefulness. You will soon, we have good ground for hoping, be strong enough to oversee the laborers on your estate, and then you will once more have it in your power to aid the cause you have so zealously upheld, and to make your life a blessing to others in the many ways your own generous heart will dictate."

"I put in my claim for the first guerdon to be dispensed," interposed Mr. Brandon—"namely, a quiet nook for book-cases and book-worm in the new home."

"It would not be home without the dear father he has been to me, the true friend and sage adviser he has always proved himself to you, would it, Morland?"

"I have not yet become accustomed to my new honors, Minnie. I have become so used to being the object of Mr. Brandon's bounty, that I can hardly persuade myself that the privilege of returning, in part, the heavy obligations I owe him is really mine to enjoy; for whatever I give to one so near to you will be scarcely a gift, as the means for giving came through your relative, and solely on your account."

———•♦•———

CHAPTER XV.

REAPING THE WHIRLWIND.

CHILL moaned the autumn winds about the corners and casements of a small, plain dwelling; but the little parlor inside was bright and cosey, and beside the grate with its glowing jets of flickering flame sat two women —their conversation will tell who.

" I did not know, Mrs. Thornton, that so much wretchedness could be crowded into so short a time as that which has passed since I left you. I look ten years older than when I went away from here, you must have noticed that."

" You certainly are looking pale and worn; but you have only yourself to thank for it. It would have been better for you to have heeded my warning when I repeatedly told you that whoever trangressed the plain rules of right must pay the bitter penalty to the uttermost farthing."

" I suppose what you say is true, but it is none the more consoling on that account. Will this wind never have done with its dismal wail about the corner? Has every pleasant sound gone out of the world, or is it that my ear will take in nothing but broken and jangled chords? I tried the piano to-day, and it must be sadly out of tune. for everything I undertook to play was as dismal as this howling wind. Nothing that I undertake prospers. Since I have gone wrong everything goes wrong with me. How could I have been so infatuated as to take the course I did? It is too late to talk of that; I have cause enough for present worriment. A woman isn't fit to have the care of renting and repairing an elegantly furnished house like mine; it was a gift from Pandora's box, and has brought nothing but heart-burnings and misery in its train; while I keep it I never expect to know a moment's peace, and shall certainly never be safe from the pursuit of Monsieur Meurice. I am in deadly terror of that man, he has such treacherous, wily ways of gaining any purpose on which he has fairly set his heart. I deprive myself of every pleasant out-of-door sight from fear of seeing him. I sit in my chamber with locked door, and window-shades closely drawn, lest by some sly underhanded device he should gain access to the lower part of the house, and so find his way to me. When I go out for a walk it is with a double veil over my face and by the least frequented streets. It is a horribly unnatural life to lead, this skulking round and shrinking from the light of day, from the eye of all human kind, as I have done since I escaped the toils in which nobody but a shallow witling like me would have been caught."

"Why, Lucy, you are in worse spirits than you were yesterday. Has anything new happened to distress you? Now I think of it, you have been gloomier than before ever since you went to see Lawyer Anverne."

"I have had good reason for being so. He went with me to look at my house, and such a state as we found it in! The carved walnut of the furniture and baluster scrolls all scratched up with pins by the children; the

11

canvas carpets of the basement story riddled like a sieve
with the sharp points of their tops; frescoes soiled and
defaced by hard usuage, damasks and canopies full of
moths, and gildings tarnished and peeling from their
frames for the want of drying and airing. I could have
cried at sight of that lovely statuette of Lurline, en-
chantress of the lyre, who harped so sweetly on the shore
that the fishes gambolled at her feet to listen—there she
was with her nose broken off and stuck on with vile,
colored cement. Who would buy a sea-nymph with a
patched up nose like that? I could not have been more
unfortunate in the selection of a tenant. A quarter's
rent due, but not a cent of it forthcoming. Worse than
that, I am almost sure they have exchanged those rich
brocatelle curtains in the large drawing-room for others
of the same color, but made of some sort of cheap cotton
and worsted stuff."

"I should think you would prefer having your house
stand empty to seeing it injured in this way."

"So I would, if I had any other source of income;
and even as it is, I would rather run the risk of finding
another tenant than keep the one I have; but Mr.
Auverne says it is impossible to summarily eject them.
There is another thing that troubles me; I have received
a reply to the letter I wrote Mr. Caruthers, deprecating
his anger and entreating his forgiveness. I do not know
what to make of his answer. As nearly as I can find
out, he doesn't seem disposed to overlook or pardon the
past, letting bygones be bygones. Here is what he
writes, or rather somebody for him, the writing is not in
his hand:

"'Come to me. I will hear the story from you own
lips or not at all.'

"What shall I do? I can't go."

"Certainly you can go; the entire route between this
place and the town where he is lying wounded is entirely
—_____"

" O, it is not any danger on the journey that I dread."

" What then ?"

" I dread to meet the man whom I have given good cause to overwhelm me with upbraiding and reproach."

" It is very generous of him, I think, to be willing to hear you in your own vindication."

" But I cannot vindicate myself—there's the sting. Whatever should I say to him ?"

" Tell him the whole story as he requests—tell it without the slightest concealment or prevarication, as you told it to me on your first return."

" O, Mrs. Thornton, he would never listen with the indulgent forbearance you showed me. How shall I ever confess to him the ungrateful return I have made for all the benefits he has showered upon me ?"

" It is the only wise and safe course left you to pursue."

" But, supposing he should be stern and severe, reproving me harshly for my misdoings—I have been through so much that I never could endure it."

" Do you merit anything better at his hands ?"

" Perhaps not ; but my deserving it doesn't make it any the easier for me to bear. He will say that I left him because he was maimed and disfigured for life ; but, I am sure, it wasn't that, though I did once declare that I never could marry a cripple, or be seen promenading Grand Avenue with such a one ; but I have learned, since then, to value a kind and feeling heart as I never valued one before."

" Say this to Mr. Caruthers rather than to me, Lucy, and I am convinced you will have no cause to regret your openness and candor. I earnestly recommend you to go to him, at once, in compliance with his express desire."

" Well, what must be, must. If I stop to think it over, I shall never find courage to start, so I will not

take time for reflection, but go straight to Mr. Auverne
for some papers and directions I shall need on my
journey."

A most dreary, drizzly and comfortless journey it
proved, but one not marked by any mishap worthy of
note. The hack she had taken at the station-house
drew up in front of a handsome and commodious stone
mansion.

" This is the street and number to which you directed
me to drive," announced the hackman, lowering the
steps for her to descend.

" There must be some mistake," she objected, drawing back with a look of hesitation and mistrust ; " this
splendid structure never could have been intended for
a hospital."

" Certingly not ; they don't have them dandy curtains
and marble cuttings and curvings to hospittles. The fact
is, this structur has come to a better use, by all odds,
than its owner ever meant it for. The man as built it—
a powerful rich man, too—has gone off a rebeleering ;
and, to come up with him, they have confiscated his
house, which is full of sick soldiers, and peace be to their
ashes, and all whom it may concern. Shall I take your
portmanteau, or whatever you call it ?"

" Thank you ; I can take it myself, it is quite light."

" Shall I give a pull at the door-bell ?"

" I need not put you to any farther trouble; here is
your fare. Can I see Mr. Caruthers ?" she asked of the
servant who answered her summons at the door.

" I don't know of anything to prevent," was the stolid
reply ; " but perhaps you had better ask himself. That
is his room, the third on the first landing ; ' green-room,'
it says on the label tied to the key, so you can't miss it."

With slow, reluctant step, Lucy followed the directions thus given, pausing before the open door of the
room she sought, thus gaining an unobstructed view of

its occupant. How different the reality from the scene
her fancy had pictured. She had expected to find Mr.
Caruthers surrounded by all the discomforts of the
roughly constructed hospital barracks she had seen at
Camp Bolivar; but there he sat in a luxuriously furnished apartment, a little paler and thinner than formerly, whereby he was in personal appearance much
improved. A slight discoloration of cheek and forehead,
a deep scar on the left temple, and the right arm suspended in a sling, were the only visible effects of the
wounds he had received. Not an item in his surround-
ings escaped her penetrating gaze.

In a capacious arm-chair upholstered in green plush,
he comfortably lounged. A newspaper he had apparently been reading was held carelessly in his left hand.
The dressing-robe of Chinese fabric he wore was faced
at cuff and collar with crimson satin, curiously picked
out with elaborate stitching. Little threads of gold
glistened in the maroon-colored velvet of his slippers.
His eyes complacently rested on a slender-necked
Bohemian jar filled with choicest flowers; he always
had a weakness for lovely colors and sweet odors.

For the first time his intended visitor, herself as yet
unperceived, bethought her of her own haggard, forlorn
appearance, and travel-stained attire. Creeping to the
head of the staircase, she consulted the mirror which,
from the back of an alcove, reflected a group of Nereids
in alabaster. Disconsolate enough the living image
reflected by the glass. A pale, sad face, with heavy
eyes of rueful look; a grey bonnet of flabby cap crown
and unbecoming scoop; the strings creased and crumpled, ruches disconsolately drooping, and flowers so
limp that threads of the tinted muslin whence they
derived their origin, all too distinctly revealed themselves.

"I am looking and feeling my very worst," she said

to herself; "but it is too late to mend matters now; a bold dash is all that remains to me, and the quicker it is made the sooner it will be over."

She made an attempt to smooth her hair, rubbed some blotches of mud from her travelling dress, pulled out the bow at her chin, and tapped at Mr. Caruthers' door. He turned with listless, languid air, and without the least appearance of surprise, looked her calmly in the face.

"Is it possible," he composedly inquired, "that I have the pleasure of addressing Madame Meurice? Pray be seated, Madame."

The little conciliatory speech deprecatory of his anger, and begging that he would not wholly condemn her until he had given her an opportunity for stating all the circumstances palliative of her offence fled her memory on the instant. She had been prepared to meet his reproaches with free and contrite confession, with humiliatory and abject acknowledgment even; but this immovable indifference from one who had never before hesitated in manifesting, both by word and deed, the warmest interest in her welfare, overcame her entirely, and she sank into the first seat that came in her way, wholly oblivious of the fact that she had been guilty of the rudeness of leaving his question unanswered.

"You sent for me, and I have come," she said, with a dreary sigh.

"It was more than I had a right to expect; it was not of a piece with your ordinary conduct of late," he moodily rejoined; adding, with scant courtesy, "your appearance shows that you have had a stormy and tiresome journey, Madame Meurice."

"I wish you would not call me by that name; I lay no claim to it now."

"You had better lay claim to it; I can tell you that.

Of your treatment of me I have nothing to say; don't
flatter yourself that you have hurt me too seriously for
recovery; I shall get over it. False as you have
proved, I have no desire to see you go from bad to
worse. You have made your choice, and must abide
by it. You can't be so entirely devoid of common
sense as to suppose that, in a miff, you can throw off
your husband's name and take another; such a suicidal
step leaves you—nowhere. I talk with you as Madame
Meurice, or I talk with you not at all."

His listener colored deeply with indecision, bewilder-
ment, and distress. An embarrassing silence ensued,
which she broke as soon as she could trust her voice to
speak, by saying,

" I am rejoiced to find your injuries so much less
serious than I had feared. We heard that your arm
was shot off, and your skull most probably fractured."

" The wild way in which unofficial army reports usually fly. It was my horse that was shot under me. I
procured another which turned out as vicious a brute as
ever yielded to curb and spur; not that he ever did yield
to them, or showed himself in the slightest degree inclined that way. His worst trick was stopping suddenly,
at the top of his speed, and pitching his rider over his
head. That was the way he served me, sending me headlong over a stone wall, breaking my arm in two places;
and, I really thought, at first, crushing in my forehead
like a bandbox. You thought so too—thought I was
fairly shelved, and so hastened to secure the first eligible
offer that turned up, by way of consolation for my loss."

" Do show some mercy; I have suffered so much,"
Lucy piteously implored.

He was not mercifully disposed, and went on.

" Dolt that I was to dream of faith and constancy
from a creature who finds her aptest type in the shifting
winds that blow as they list. The return you have

made for the trust I placed in you; for all the efforts I
have made to secure your happiness and well-being;
for all the pains I took to provide for your comfortable
maintenance, in case I should fall in battle—for all
this kindness and forethought, I say that your return
has been that of a base and thankless ingrate. Can you
deny it ?"

"I cannot deny it," she faltered, with bitter, burning
tears in her eyes.

"How long," he asked, with gathering wrath, "since
you became infatuated with this moustached exquisite
of a foreigner ?"

"I never was infatuated with him," she earnestly protested.

"Well, then, since you beg the plainer question, how
long is it since you were married?"

"I never was really married."

Mr. Caruthers' brow grew black as night, and his
whole face stern to the verge of austerity.

"Never really married!" he enunciated with withering accent; "then you had better have died than have
gone off with that man, as you did, with no wedding
symbol on your finger, no solemnly pledged vow on your
lip. It is true, then, that you have no rightful claim
to any name other than that you have always borne."

"It is true," she hesitatingly admitted, averting her
glance, and cowering beneath his look.

"That I should live to hear you confess to accusation
that no one but yourself could have made me deem
credible of belief; to learn that the woman who sat as
a petted child on my knee, and beguiled me of my time
with her innocent prattle, has given just cause to any
for mocking gibe and scoff. Know, Lucy Sears, that it
is hard enough for a man to face the scorn of the world;
but to a woman, it is blight, infamy, ruin. As well
might a lily attempt to withstand the hurricane's rush,

as a woman think to brave the blasting breath of public scandal."

At first she had been shocked and bewildered by his words, and deeply pained by his manner of speaking them; but it was not until she noted the scornful flash of his eye, the contemptuous curl of his lip, that the full significance of the withering rebuke he had uttered burst upon her amazed comprehension.

Then the scalding tears in her eyes were quenched in the burning gleam of anger; and through her entire being seethed a sense of wrong and outrage as concentrated and intense as it was in her nature to know.

Tossing back the hair from her heated brow, and unconsciously crushing the artificial flowers wreathed across her head, she impetuously made reply:

"I have been weak and imprudent, quite likely; I have been duped and deceived, very surely; but a God-forsaken creature for woman to shun and man to sneer at, *never*. I did not know you could be so hard and cruel. I did not know that you could with only words—words?—daggers! so strike me to the heart. Let me go. No one has scoffed at me but you; and I will put such space between us that you shall not wound me by a second blow like this."

She groped her way blindly toward the door; but unable to proceed more than a few steps, sank half fainting upon a lounge, crushing her bonnet against the cushions supporting her head.

Mr. Caruthers was seriously alarmed at the unlooked-for effect his words had produced.

"Do not agitate yourself in this way," he soothingly entreated. "I must have drawn a wrong inference from your admission; don't think of it again; there is no harm done."

She neither moved nor spoke.

11*

He crossed hastily to her side, and with his left arm turned her head so that he could see the face.

Her eyes were closed, her pearly teeth just visible between the white and parted lips.

His sudden alarm deepened into the gravest apprehension, betrayed by the assertion through which he sought to reassure himself: " It cannot be that a woman is so easily killed."

Removing her bonnet so awkwardly as greatly to add to its defacement, he tossed it upon the floor; and dipping his handkerchief in water, laid it wet and dripping on her head.

She opened her eyes, closing them with an involuntary frown as they met his own.

" I hope you are better, my dear."

" Better," was all she said.

He fidgeted uneasily about, stepping on that unfortunate bonnet, not at all to the improvement of its already dilapidated condition. A brilliant idea occurred to him.

" Let me give you a glass of wine, Lucy, it will revive you."

" Not any ; a physician prescribed it for me when I was ill at Paris and it has ever since been unpalatable to me from unpalatable associations."

She sighed heavily; his kindly intended proffer had awakened a train of thought full of pain and humiliation.

He pressed a glass of water upon her acceptance, and the draught revived her.

" Don't mind what I said, Lucy ; if I took your words in a wrong sense, it was nothing worse than a mistake, and a very natural one, all things considered. I have not yet heard your story, recollect ; tell it me now ; it shall have my undivided attention, and every circumstance shall be most carefully weighed and sifted."

"A sifting and weighing of my very life! It is more than I could bear. How can you ask it of me?—to submit a second time to the dagger thrust that has struck me to the earth? Isn't one blow enough? Aren't you satisfied? Do you want to kill me?"

"You are very unreasonable; I do not wish even to grieve you. If I misinterpreted your admission, say that it was owing to my own obtuseness, and let it pass. We will talk the matter over together, kindly and candidly, as soon as you are a little more composed."

"I shall leave, then; this air stifles me. There is but one subject I wish to speak of before I go; that is your house, which is in a sad condition, owing to the abuse and neglect it has received at the hands of its present tenant."

"Your house, you mean."

"Mine no longer. I never could consent to be heavily indebted to one who holds me in such light esteem as your words imply."

"Will you never forget that?"

"Is your own memory so little retentive that you think mine like a sieve that holds no water? I do not say that I shall never forget; I shall try to put this msierable meeting out of my thoughts, but the time for forgetfulness has not come yet. I shall consult Lawyer Auverne, as soon as possible, as to the proper steps to be taken for restoring to you the property that is yours."

"But what will you do? Where will you go?"

"It matters little what or where, so I do but get far enough away from—from—my friends. Speaking of Mr. Auverne reminds me that he gave me a paper, just before I started, which he said would explain to you much better than I could—the law phrases he used were so hard for me to remember—all the causes that had operated to set me free from any future control on the part of Monsieur Meurice."

"By all means let me have the paper, which should have been handed me at your earliest arrival. You will at least do me the favor to remain while I examine its contents."

"I will stay since you ask it; but you will please make my detention as brief as may be."

He bowed acquiescence.

Not yet wholly relieved from the giddiness that oppressed her, she leaned her head upon a small inlaid table, which she drew beside the lounge.

Mr. Caruthers had not finished reading the first page of the paper she had presented him, when a thin, studious-looking man entered the room without even the formality of a rap at the door. The former received the new-comer with easy courtesy.

"I need nothing more to-day in the way of professional aid, my dear doctor; but I should be greatly obliged to you if you would receive this young lady, a ward of mine—Miss Sears, Dr. Cairnes—as your guest for the night. Thinking me much more seriously wounded than I am, she has made great efforts to reach me, is sadly fatigued, and beneath your hospitable roof will find the rest she needs, that is if you accede to my request."

"I would accede to one far more serious for the sake of obliging you, sir. Your ward does, indeed, look as though she needed rest; and Mrs. Cairnes and my daughters will be happy to show her every attention in their power."

Both speakers turned toward Lucy for some expression of assent or acknowledgment, but she neither noticed nor replied to their questioning looks. Her eyes were fixed on the floor, her brow contracted, and her lips firmly compressed. Across her forehead was a deep purple indentation, caused by the sharp edge of the table against which it had rested.

For the second time since her arrival, Mr. Caruthers
went to her side, bending on her a glance of compassion
wholly thrown away on its object, as she had not even
observed his approach.

" Lucy," he gently inquired, "have you heard what we
have been saying ?"

She started, colored, and impulsively withdrew the
hand he had taken.

" What is it you are asking of me, sir ?"

" Only that you will go home with my good friend,
Dr. Cairnes, and find the rest you need after the fatigue
of your hurried journey."

" Can I have a room quite to myself where you propose sending me ?"

" That, or anything else you may require to make
you comfortable," the doctor hastened to assure her.

" How soon can we start ?"

" Directly, if you wish it."

The alacrity with which she rose, bent her bonnet into
presentable shape, tied it on, and announced her readiness for immediate departure, sufficiently attested the
sincerity of her desire to be gone.

A shade of mortification crept to Mr. Caruthers' face.

" I shall see you again, before you leave town,
Lucy?"

Her eyes flashed forth a prompt and indignant denial.

" I insist on seeing you," he peremptorily subjoined,
" to return to you papers I hold in my possession, if for
no other reason. You will come to me to-morrow ?"

" I will come since you exact it," she coldly responded,
avoiding his glance, and not even taking the hand he
held out to her at parting.

" When your son goes to school in the morning, doctor, will you let him walk round this way with Miss
Sears?"

"I will do better than that, by leaving her here on my earliest round of calls."

"I am greatly indebted to you; command me, if there is any favor I can bestow in return."

CHAPTER XVI.

THE REBOUND.

Dr. CAIRNES, knowing his companion to be a stranger to the locality, pointed out to her such objects of note as would be likely to reward the attention of an unaccustomed observer; but she paid so little heed to his remarks that he soon desisted therefrom.

Declining to join the cheerful home circle in the physician's parlor, she was shown directly to her own sleeping-room, where, unrestrained by curious eyes, she could indulge in wretchedness to the top of her bent. Ignoring the summons to the tea-table, she paced her room with rapid, restless step until she was completely exhausted, when, retiring for the night, she cried herself asleep, and slept soundly until morning. When she awoke, clouds and mist had disappeared, and the cheery sunshine flooded her room with its bright and gladsome presence. Her spirits rebounded from their deep depression at sight of the genial sunny aspect nature had once more assumed.

A bell rang below stairs. Some one rapped at her door, and a silvery girlish voice called out:

"The dressing-bell; breakfast will be served in half an hour."

She joined the family at their morning meal, and

scarcely a trace of gloom marked her demeanor as she listened to the lively, playful chat of the younger members of the domestic group. Far more light and elastic the step with which she returned to her room than the one by which she had entered it on the previous afternoon.

Seating herself on a cushioned stool, and burying her face in her hands, she pondered long on the ever accumulating difficulties of her position; and strove, to the best of her ability, to ascertain the method most available for extricating herself from her embarrassments.

" I told him he had struck me to the earth," she said to herself, with a gleam almost vindictive in her eye; " let him make the most of the triumph in his power to strike so heavily which that admission gave him ; he will never wring such another weak cry from my lips. Am I so abject and spiritless a creature as to allow myself to be crushed by the weight of a mere opinion—and a false one at that! It was because the blow came so unexpectedly that it stunned me for a time. Now that I am on my guard, I cannot be stricken down unawares in that way again.

" I humbled myself to entreat his forgiveness, and in return he humbled me to the very dust; I will never again abase myself thus, only to gain additional abasement.

" I sued for pardon, he denied it ; and the hour for such suit is past. Oh, Monsieur Meurice! see to what a pass your arts and wiles and guile have brought their victim. Would to Heaven I had never seen your fair face or listened to your false vows. But for you, I should never have gained the hatred which has replaced the love that once was mine. Hatred! Mr. Caruthers does not think me worth it ; he despises me, and cuts me to the soul with taunts the most unbearable that could be levelled at a woman. Well, that is all over now ; for the short time that I must be with him, once more, I will steel myself against any thrust he may attempt to aim at me.

"Why did he so strongly insist on seeing me again before I left town? Perhaps to make arrangements for my restoring the house he gave me; but why should I restore it? He will think no worse of me if I keep it than he thinks of me now. I have already forfeited his good opinion, and cannot lose it over again. To be sure, I promised to return his gift; but then I was so beside myself with rage and resentment when the promise was given that it could scarcely be considered as binding. Now I think of it, it was no promise, but simply an offer, on my part, which he failed to accept when it was made. I have a right to change my mind, and change it I will. What could I do by way of earning my own support? Make soldiers' shirts at ninepence a day? I never could endure the confinement and privation incident to such a life; and I am not going to endure it. A poor needlewoman I need not and I will not become.

"On the whole, I might be a great deal worse off than I am. An heiress in my own right, with full liberty to come and go as I choose, many might deem mine a most enviable lot. I may think so myself in time, if I can only sunder all associations with the past, and move to some place where there will be nothing to remind me of these last few wretched months. Mr. Auverne is right; it is better, far better, for me to retain my property in my own keeping than to resign it to that of any living person. The lawyer is the safest counsellor, and the best friend I have—so long as he is sure of his fees.

"If Mr. Caruthers had been inconsolable at my desertion of him, he would be less taken up than he is with all those little luxuries he has gathered about him. Men don't die of broken hearts, nor women neither; and

I'm the last person to be guilty of such a folly. I have not hurt him, did he say? Neither has he hurt me. Is he fastidious and particular to a nicety in matters of dress? so am I. Does he affect rich silks, lovely colors, and costly embroideries? so do I. Is his mind so much at ease that he can devote his attention to all sorts of elegant apparelling? so is mine. I will not go to him a second time looking like the forlorn, forsaken outcast I did yesterday; he shall not again have the advantage over me in that respect. I never can satisfactorily acquit myself when weighed down by the painful consciousness of a dowdy bonnet and crumpled face trimmings."

She started up with an alacrity indicative of her newly-formed resolve. Robing herself in bonnet and cape, she went down to the breakfast-room in search of Jenny Cairnes, a lively, spirited miss of sixteen.

"I wish to make a few trifling purchases," Lucy confided to Miss Jenny; "is it quite safe for me to traverse your streets alone?"

"Perfectly safe; but please take me with you. A shopping expedition! I have not enjoyed such a felicity for an age. Do let me tell mamma you require my services as chaperone; I should fill the office admirably, I am of austerity so formidable, and of dignity so unapproachable."

"Then you must be quickly ready, as I have no time to lose."

"In a trice."

They were soon on their way. Exhilarated by the clear, bracing air, brisk movement, and sight of the stir and bustle in the thronged streets, Lucy listened to the playful rattle of her companion with an interest she had not accorded to the valuable information imparted by the doctor on the previous day.

A dapper young gentleman from an opposite sidewalk doffed his beaver to Miss Jenny.

"Young Lieutenant Gauer, at home on furlough," she exclaimed; "very agreeable; did you ever know a music-master—he was mine before his enlistment—who was not?"

Lucy's gaiety fled on the instant; she turned pale, and gave her companion a searching look, vaguely suspicious that she might in some way have gained an inkling of her own private personal history.

The young girl met her look with one of perfect openness and cordiality; and, ashamed of her suspicion, Lucy strove to atone for it by resuming her former demeanor; in this she succeeded, but the dull aching sense of misery so unintentionally aroused was not easily subdued.

"One of the most delightful of mimics, was Franz Gauer," Jenny rattled on; "the way in which he imitated the leading stars at the opera, tenor and baritone, hitting off the peculiarities of each, was irresistibly comic. He would go down into the thorough-bass till his voice was lost in a hoarse growl, and then he would soar up a couple of octaves, note by note, until he wound up with a diminuendo of excruciating wire-drawn squeak. What could I do but laugh? Papa heard me, one day, and sent for me to come to his study when my lesson was over. If there is anything I do dread, it is to be summoned to that study; for, though he doesn't scold, like mamma, he isn't to be coaxed like her, either; and his word, once given, is never retracted. He only said to me, that I might practice my old pieces, for the present, and consider my lessons suspended. I understood the reproof as well as though it had been set forth in plainer terms. I wonder if most girls find it easy to put on dignity with their first long dresses; it did not come easy to me. Before that dreadful assumption of womanly paraphernalia, I could be as jolly as I liked, without check or hindrance; but since then, I can't bound a ball, or climb a tree by way of calisthenics, or drive a donkey cart, or get up a bit of masquerade in burglar costume to frighten the maids, and so squeeze a little fun out of this dry rind of life, than straight comes the reproof: ' You had much better be storing your mind with useful knowledge than playing this sort of childish prank.' They are talking, now, of sending me to a boarding-school; I wish I knew what it was like. Were you ever at such an institution ?"

" I was a pupil in one for several years."

" How nice; you can tell me so much I wish to know. Was the discipline very stringent ?"

"The rules seemed strict to me ; but I presume they were not more so than they ought to have been to secure the confidence of the seminary's patrons."

" But what if the rules were transgressed ? was there a penalty in such a case ?"

" Of course there was, or where would have been the use of the regulations ?"

" How barbarous ! What! actual punishment in an establishment fitted up solely for young ladies ?"

" Certainly ; actual enough of its kind."

" What kind was it ?"

" O ! there were various modes of correction, according to the circumstances of the offence."

" Don't put me off so, please ; if you would not think me impertinently curious, I would like to ask you a plain question—may I ?"

" As many as you like."

" Did you ever break a boarding-school rule ?"

" Yes ; a number of them."

" Do tell me what they were, and all about it."

" I will, as clearly as I can. In the large dining-hall a number of tables were laid, and, at a side one, the teachers of foreign languages always took their meals ; and their pupils, sometimes one class and sometimes another, breakfasted and dined with them. Now, it was

a rule at this table that not a word should be spoken
excepting in French, that the speakers might learn to
converse in that language with facility.

" One day we had for dinner mock turtle soup ; and,
as I couldn't for the life of me remember the French
name for it, I awkwardly enough had to go without.
Then a clam-chowder was brought on, and there was no
such dish set down in Chouquet, or any of the printed
lists of viands I had in my pocket. Monsieur Lancens,
a brother of Mademoiselle, who presided that day,
understood my dilemma, but would not help me to the
chowder unless I sent a special request for it through
Fifitte, who couldn't speak a word of English. I whispered Mademoiselle, who sat next me, merely asking her
to pronounce the term I wanted, in her own language.

" All she said was ' You have been guilty of breaking
a rule, Miss Sears, if the offence is repeated I shall deem
it my duty to report you.' "

" Why did you not catch the word from some of the
other pupils ?"

" Their orders were given to the table-maid in so low
a tone that it escaped me. Tired of the quizzical looks
meeting me on all sides, I asked to be excused, and left
the hall. Instead of going to my chamber, I thought I
would go out to one of the music-rooms in a building
detached from the main body of the seminary. In
crossing a passage, I saw the cook with a large tray full
of pies going into the pantry. On coming out, she left
the door open behind her, while she went to refill her
tray. I had lost my dinner sorely against my will ; and
without stopping to think of consequences, I darted into
the pantry, seized a pie, and, prize in hand, ran up to
my room. I lost some time in looking for my fruit-
knife that had been mislaid, and by the time I found it
dinner was over and the girls trooping up-stairs. That
sound did not disturb me, but another one did. This is

what a person was saying in the hall below: 'This is not the first time pilferers have found their way to the pantry. The real culprit shall be exposed. Let every pupil's room be thoroughly searched. Close your doors, young ladies, and remain where you are.' I learned from my room-mate that not one of the teachers had come up-stairs, and tucking my pilfered trophy under my cape, I darted down the first flight and safely deposited my unfortunate prize in Mademoiselle's band-box, under her Sunday bonnet."

"So you turned the laugh on her; good."

" Not so good as one would think; for Mademoiselle Lancens owed me a grudge, and she was not the woman to forget that sort of debt. She only waited her opportunity to pay me with interest."

" And did she get what she waited for ?"

" You shall hear. Emma Ford, my room-mate, and I always went to church with Mademoiselle. In the same pew with us sat a tolerably prepossessing stranger, whom we called Master Slender, he was so slight of figure. I noticed that Emma always contrived to occupy the seat next to him, and I strongly suspected that the notes they took of the sermons would scarcely have tallied with the heads of the discourses preached by the clergyman. Mademoiselle seemed to see nothing amiss, indeed was wonderfully unobservant for one usually so sharp-sighted.

"One day when we were out, under charge of a teacher, buying a few articles we needed, I noticed Emma sliding a tiny fish-hook into a clasped division of her porte-monnaie. I was curious to know the purpose to which this odd purchase was to be applied; but as she did not seem disposed to be communicative, my curiosity remained ungratified for the time. Somehow Emma lost all relish for her studies, and was more than once repremanded for ill-prepared lessons. As a gene-

ral rule, I was an excellent sleeper, never once waking
through the night; but I was foolish enough to buy a
cosmetic of a street vender, who assured me that it
would not only remove all tan and freckles, but would
also marvellously heighten and beautify the complexion;
it heightened mine with a vengeance, smarting like fire,
and eating the skin half off my face. That was why I.
couldn't sleep, and that was how I happened to find out
the mystery of the fish-hook. We were to be in bed,
with lights all out, at ten; that was the rule, strictly en-
forced. My face pained me so that I could not close my
eyes; but as I had nothing but my own credulous folly
to blame for it, I held my peace and made no complaint.
The clock was striking eleven when Emma got up, put
on slippers and wrapper, and softly raised the window.
The moon was at the full, and I could see distinctly
every movement she made. Taking the hook, to which
a folded paper was attached, she let it down from the
casement by means of a cord, and then hauled in her
line, having hooked a missive superior in size as in
quality, I presume, from the look of edification with
which she read it, to the one she had thrown out.

"Her next venture in this novel species of angling
was less successful. She had thrown out her line, baited
as before; but suddenly lost hold of it with a stifled cry
of affright. Forgetting that she was unaware of my
knowledge of her indiscretion, I was at her side in an
instant, looking from the window to find out the cause
of her agitation and dismay. It was easily accounted for.
There were two men, the husband of our principal and
a porter, holding Master Slender by the arms; and
there, at the casement of the window below ours, was
Mademoiselle Lancens, drawing in the cord, with its
baited hook. Next morning we were both sent for to
enter the presence of teachers and scholars in state assembled. I thought poor Emma, who hadn't slept a

wink all night, and who was naturally proud, shy, and keenly sensitive to disgrace, would have sunk into the ground at the prospect before her. I got off with only a reprimand for my complicity in the affair; but Emma's note—a most sweet and delectable billet-doux, they called it—was read aloud, as a warning to all the pupils then and there assembled. She half cried her eyes out with regret and mortification, and scarcely held her head up for a week; but she learned a lesson she will never forget, and one learned all the more easily for having been learned while she was young."

"I think she was most severely punished for an offence no more serious than a mere harmless flirtation," decisively affirmed Miss Jenny.

"Harmless flirtation! there is no such thing," asserted her companion, with emphasis. "Where one person trifles with the feelings of another, it may be sport to the trifler, but to the one trifled with it is almost worse "——

She paused abruptly, her voice unsteady and her sight obscured by gathering tears.

An arch look was in Jenny's bright eyes, a mirthful sally just ready to escape her lips; but something in Lucy's face checked her purpose of playful raillery, and they walked on in silence until they reached a milliner's shop, which they entered together.

Numerous were the parcels borne by the shop-boy, who followed them on their return.

The doctor sent word to his guest that in half an hour he would be ready to start on his first round of professional calls. This time was quite short enough for making a toilette she had determined should be unexceptionable as to style and material. First her curled tresses were smoothly brushed and looped back by the jewelled comb, partially restraining their luxuriance. A violet-colored jacket, of Lyons velvet, was worn over a dress of plain royal purple silk; both bonnet and cape being of similar material in shade and texture, the former decorated with flowers of rose sublime, powdered with pearl dust, and falls of lace worth scores of times its weight in gold; Paris boots, of irreproachable form and finish, and snowy kids, of fit exact, completed her costume.

"What a lovely outfit!" exclaimed Miss Jenny, as Lucy presented herself in the breakfast-room to take leave of her kindly entertainers; "I did not know you were so bonny."

The young girl's compliment was, under the circumstances calling it forth, appreciated at more than its full value. Dr. Cairnes had also a remark to offer in regard to the improved appearance of their transient visitor.

"Nothing like a brisk shopping expedition for feminine ailments," he good-humoredly asserted—"nothing in the whole pharmacopœia to rival it in efficacy."

---•••---

CHAPTER XVII.

CHARITY.

VERY different the calm, self-possessed, elegantly attired woman who now sought Mr. Caruthers' presence from the timid, shrinking penitent, who, in travel-stained garments, and with hesitating, reluctant step came to him on the previous day. Then she had come to confess a wrong; now she had one she deemed far deeper, to resent. Then it was as a humble suppliant she had presented herself; now it was as one determined to surrender no right, no matter what the inducement to forego such determination. Anticipating an interview painful as well as profitless, she was fully resolved to avail herself of the first tolerable excuse that might arise,.for abridging it.

Mr. Caruthers rose to receive her ; a courtesy he had not extended on the occasion of her previous visit, and drew a chair for her near his own. After a mutual exchange of the ordinary forms of greeting, a silence ensued which seemed to embarrass him ; but to which she submitted with immovable composure, furtively consulting her watch, as though calculating the time of her departure.

" You are looking much refreshed by your night's rest," he ventured at random.

Vigilant, alert, watchfully on guard against any manœuvres threatening the outposts of firm resolve defending the stronghold of dignified reserve she deemed impregnable, her reply was warily and cautiously worded.

" Quite recovered, I thank you, from the fatigue of having travelled forty-eight hours without sleep. To be broken of my rest, even for one night, always makes me stupid next day ; but doubling the infliction really gives me the appearance of having been through a severe fit of illness. I dread my return unspeakably, and shall be too happy when it is over with. How soon does the next up-train start, and how shall I manage to procure a hack to take me to the depot ?"

" The next train starts in an hour ; but you surely do not think of leaving so soon as that."

" I must, positively *must*, I have decided to make my permanent home in one of the Eastern States ; the exact locality I can more readily select after the tour of inspection I am eagerly desirous to undertake, as soon as I can arrange with Mr. Auverne for ejecting the present tenant and obtaining a new one for my house."

12

Mr. Caruthers was so far discomposed by this assumption of cool self-reliance on the part of one who had long yielded to his most lightly-expressed opinion with boundless deference, that he betrayed his uneasiness, both by his perturbed look and by the restless way in which he trifled with the tasselled cord of his dressing-gown.

"I wish to have a candid talk with you, Lucy; and you really put me out of all patience by falling back upon your dignity in this way, and being so frigidly unapproachable."

"Better, a thousand times better, reproaches for frigidity and reserve, than scoffs and sneers for inconsiderate levity or imprudent concessions."

"Why will you so disagreeably harp upon that unfortunate expression of mine? If I could unsay the words I would; but as that is impossible, I can do no more than to wish them unsaid, which I do from the bottom of my heart. If this is not a full and ample apology for a hasty, ill-considered remark, I do not know how to make one. Is it accepted?"

"Certainly; after humbling myself to sue for your forgiveness, and receiving from you contemptuous scorn in return, I could not have dreamed of being beholden to you for a condescension like this; accept my warmest thanks for the same. Now that this little difficulty is happily adjusted, will you allow me to wish you a very good morning, and to seek a conveyance for "——

"Adjusted! nothing of the sort. The legal bearings of the case I have from Mr. Auverne, but your own version of the affair is what I now want, to make the chain of evidence complete in my own mind. I agree with him that, Monsieur Meurice is an accomplished chevalier, with principles conveniently elastic; and that in the eye of the law you are blameless in act and intent; but admitting all this, I am still strongly desirous of hearing from yourself the many particulars you alone can give, and to which I am prepared to listen with the lenient indulgence of a long-tried friend."

Lucy's look evinced a decided disinclination for the fulfillment of this intimation.

"That is the way in which I thought you would listen when I came to you yesterday; but I soon found out my mistake. Since I am free from blame, why should you wish to know more? If you really have such a wish, I will make full confession to Lawyer Auverne, and he can write it down for you, or repeat it to you if you prefer communicating with him directly."

"But, incomprehensible creature that you are, would you rather confide in Mr. Auverne, a comparative stranger, than in me, whom you have known since you was a child?"

"Strangers haven't it in their power to strike as friends can. Yes; I would rather tell all to Mr. Auverne, and have you learn it through him. Let us consider that as agreed upon. How long will it take to drive from here to the station-house?"

"Confound the station-house! you've nothing whatever to do with it at present. Understand that I do *not* consider it agreed upon that I am to learn from any superfluous go-between what it is my fixed purpose to learn from yourself, if at all."

Lucy sighed drearily.

"Why should you be so exacting? I am not so strong as you think me. I am not accustomed to hard words; they hurt me; why should you compel me to submit to them?"

"Will you never comprehend that you have nothing of the sort to dread from me? Are you so used to being imposed upon that you can't take an honest man

at his word ?   Didn't I tell you that I would listen as a
friend, to what you have to tell me ?"

"But I would a thousand times rather you listened as
a stranger."

"As a stranger let it be, then, if that will suit you
better."

"You cannot make yourself a stranger; I cannot
think of you as such."

"Perhaps not; I think I have some trifling claim on
your acquaintance, if not your regard, owing to some
slight favors I was able to render your mother; and
which, I presume, have not entirely escaped your memory."

Vigilant as was her guard, here was a movement
so unexpected, that, taken by surprise, she was forced
from her position, abandoning her outer line of defence.

"I have not forgotten what my mother owed to your
generosity; she must have sadly tried your patience
at times, as I have tried it since.   You have a claim on
my gratitude, and on my confidence, too; you shall
have it, however reluctantly it may be given.   Where
shall I begin ? at the very outset of my acquaintance
with Monsieur Menrice ?"

"At the very outset, if you please."

"It was you who first introduced me to him, when I
was little more than a child, as my music master; and
I always liked to laugh and chat with him because he
was lively and agreeable ; natural enough, wasn't it ?"

"Perfectly so ; what next ?"

"The first time his attentions became so marked as to
be seriously annoying, was a couple of days before you
went off with your company.   The circumstances were
so trivial, and his words so lose their meaning on repetition, that I am not sure of being able to explain to
your comprehension.   He went to St. Marc's Hospital

with Miss Barton and myself, she wishing to present a
bunch of flowers to a patient. Amongst them was one
he called love-in-disguise; it came from your own conservatory."

"I never had such a plant in my collection. What
was the blossom like?"

"The petals were something like those of a pansy,
only all of one color, a rich deep purple."

"With a row of barbed thorns so fine you would
never see them"——

"That is it; I thought them stinging nettles, and
when I got one in my finger, through incautious handling of the flower, I said thoughtlessly that the very
name of the plant was enough to condemn it, as true
love had no need of a disguise, and might openly express itself like any other honest emotion. This he took
as a sort of challenge to make me a declaration, at least
so he said, when he called on me the day you left. I
can't tell you how it all came about; he was so much
deeper than I, that I often found it difficult to make out
his precise meaning; and it is impossible for me to describe what I never clearly comprehended. He seemed,
before I was aware of any such intention on his part, to
take it for granted that there was a tacit agreement or
understanding between us, and all I could do or say
wouldn't shake him out of this conviction."

"But if you knew the assumption to be unfounded,
why didn't you contradict it outright, and let him know,
once for all, that he was laboring under a total misap-
prehension regarding the facts of the case?"

"That is what I tried to do; but he only shrugged
his shoulders and said, 'Mademoiselle does but affect;
Mademoiselle is not so obtuse;' and, as I didn't want him
to think me a downright simpleton, I did affect to comprehend matters about which I was really quite in the
dark."

"But why should you be so anxious to stand well in this man's good opinion, that you were willing to make any sacrifice to effect such a purpose?"

"All owing to a foolish habit I have of striving to please my friends. I have learned a lesson, I think, that will cure me of such folly for the future."

"I am sorry to hear you speak in that way; and should regret still more to see you exchange the open, winning, unsuspecting manner that has always seemed one of your best charms to me, for a cold, repellant, suspicious demeanor entirely foreign to your real character. Choose wisely the friends on whom to lavish your regard and your confidence, and then you cannot trust too unreservedly, or strive too earnestly to win the approbation you crave."

"But there is the difficulty," objected Lucy. "Are mistakes in such choice always to be avoided? Did you never make such a one yourself?"

Mr. Caruthers actually blushed.

"I will not drag you to the confessional and then decline obeying your summons to the same, Lucy. What will you say when I tell you that I did once seriously intend making Miss Brandon my wife?"

"If any other had told me this I could not have believed it of you, Mr. Caruthers."

"Neither would I have believed, save through your own admission, that you could have jilted me for that glib-tongued Frenchman."

"But I thought you a very paragon of excellence, too noble and upright to stoop to any species of deceit."

"Just what I thought of you, Lucy Sears. Since we live in glass houses let us not throw stones at each other; it is worse than useless; it is unsafe and full of danger."

"You really did care for this Miss Brandon, then, after all?"

"Not a straw. I was proud of her beauty, grace and

intelligence, and thought they would do great credit to my handsome establishment. You know I always sought your society in preference to hers, or that of any other person. She wearied me unspeakably with her interminable raptures about the sayings and doings of old poets and playwrights that were dead and in their graves centuries ago. As though there wasn't enough to think about in these stirring times, without pottering amongst the dry-as-dust relics of a past that has had its day, and might as well step aside and give the present a chance. There was another thing that made her presence almost irksome to me, and that was the consciousness of the false part I was acting toward her. I don't see how your stage actor can play the lover to perfection when it is only make-believe, and must say that I found it much more like work than play, the only time I ever tried it; besides, it irritated me to that degree that I was repeatedly guilty of treating Miss Brandon with a lack of consideration, not to say a positive harshness, that she was far from meriting at my hands. There, my confession is ended; you see by my frank unreserve that I am acting no double part with you, so proceed freely and unrestrainedly with your own story."

"I saw a great deal of Monsieur," she resumed, with an alacrity and animation she had not previously exhibited, "and, to tell the plain truth, his companionship was the only solace I had. You do not see what need I had of solace; I will explain. I had lost my own self-approval, I had sunk in my own estimation; for I knew, after the sacred promise I gave you, on the day of your departure, that I was a base, unworthy ingrate to violate it. Monsieur was the only person who overcame my scruples and reconciled me to myself, so he was always welcome. He so persistently assured me that you and I were wholly unfitted for each other, through disparity of years and diversity of taste and disposition, that I was more than half persuaded that he was right—while I was with him. Left alone again, the upbraidings of my own conscience were absolutely insupportable, until he persuaded me anew that there was not the least occasion for such self-reproaches. My health failed; I felt more than ever the need of kindly sympathy; and he was the only person in the world from whom I was always sure of receiving it."

"There you do me injustice, Lucy. If I did not write you as soon as you could have expected to hear from me, it was because my duties were arduous, and my time not at my own disposal. When I did send you a letter, as kindly worded as I knew how to make it, you never answered it."

" I wrote you an answer, but it was never sent."

" How was that?"

" I was putting on my bonnet and scarf to carry the letter to the office, when Monsieur Meurice came in and read your name on the envelope. 'This reminds me,' said he, 'that I have also to write Mr. Caruthers, and it is best that he should hear from us both at once. He was one of my most useful patrons when I first came to this country, and he is not to think that I am capable of making an ungrateful return for past favors. Undoubtedly you have informed him that, being convinced that a union between you would not be conducive to the happiness of either, you terminated the engagement and took the initiative in fostering the attachment and encouraging the advances of one without whom existence would be to you a blank. Let me read what you have written, and I will but reiterate the same; surely he will not refuse credence to the concurrent testimony of two impartial witnesses.'

" I couldn't endure to have him read the letter, so I tore it up, and there was an end of it."

" Did not Mrs. Thornton perceive the pernicious influ-

ence that was gaining sway over you, and warn you
against yielding to it?"

"She gave me no warning, but she treated me with a
distant coldness that repelled my confidence, and often
spoke in a way that reminded me most painfully of my
blameworthy conduct toward yourself. One warm day
we were sitting together in the hall, the door open so
that the air might draw through the outer blind, which
was closed, when she began comparing your character
with that of Monsieur Meurice, greatly to his disadvan-
tage. I never heard her so cutting and severe. She
had another listener, too, although neither of us knew
it at the time. Monsieur, himself, from the steps where
he was waiting for a break in our conversation before
ringing, heard every word that passed between us.
After that, he insisted on placing me beyond the reach
of what he called Mrs. Thornton's intermeddling and
officious tyranny, and gave me no peace until I consented to remove to a boarding-house of his own selection. It seems incomprehensible to me, now, that I
should so readily have complied with all his suggestions,
however unusual. I can only think of a rashly venturesome fly that has incautiously approached a spider's
web, unaware of the danger, until hopelessly entangled
in its toils.

"Miss Barton called on me by his invitation, and
in his presence congratulated me on my approaching
nuptials. I denied, point blank, that there was any occasion for such congratulation. She turned to Monsieur
with a look of qestioning surprise. He bent on me a
look of the most bland and tender forbearance, as he
said : '*Mignonne douce*, she is indisposed with *agacement*
of the nerves, and nothing shall be spoken of to her annoyance. Does she affect publicity, we are open-mouth-
ed to all the world; does she choose rather to screen
herself, like the enchanting Undine, in draperies of

12*

transparent reserve, we are silent as the grave.' I did
not wish to make myself ridiculous, and so gave up all
attempts at denial or remonstrance.

" Then came news that my uncle had been instantly
killed by the accidental explosion of a mortar on board
one of the gunboats in which he had sailed with the
great naval expedition. Next we heard that you was
seriously if not fatally wounded, and my last hope
seemed to centre in Monsieur Meurice. My health
broke down completely, and I was scarcely able to
leave my room. The physician he called in recommended change of air and scene, and proposed a sea-voyage
as my surest, if not my only, chance of recovery. What
were you saying, Mr. Caruthers ?"

" That the whole plan was a detestable and nefarious
league against a defenceless and unsuspecting woman, and
I would to like pay the conspirators in so vile a scheme
their just dues. Proceed ; unravel the rest of the plot."

" I caught at the idea of change with an eagerness I
am at a loss to account for. I had been so miserable in
that boarding-house that everything connected with it
had a melancholy cast, and I longed to get away. The
doctor said this craving for change was generally found
associated with a debility like mine, and that it would
disappear, my wretchedly low spirits also, under the re-
novating effects of the bracing sea air. It was he who
proposed my marriage with Monsieur previous to undertaking the voyage. I had gone too far to recede. I
seemed to have lost all power of volition, and resigned
myself passively to the current of events. I was too
weak to resist.

" We were to have been married at the Church of the
Messiah ; but the doctor objected that the publicity and
fatigue would necessitate too much exertion for one in
my feeble state, so it was decided that the ceremony
should take place privately in the boarding-house par-

lor. He promised to be present, but sent excuses and regrets at the last moment, on account of pressing professional engagements, so that not a single person was present at the wedding excepting the clergyman who officiated on the occasion."

" Did it not occur to you, Lucy, that this was a very singular way, to say the least of it, of conducting a ceremonial of the kind?"

" Certainly it did; but you must remember that I was very singularly circumstanced. I was too weak to receive a crowd of guests, even if I had had a father's house to invite them to, instead of being the waif I was; and as I have already told you, the doctor had decided that the effect of appearing in a crowded church was one I ought not to undertake."

" Who was this doctor?"

" Nobody I ever saw or heard of, before or since his attendance on me. His name was Denton."

" Another humbug, I'll be bound. Was ever a woman with the slightest claim to ordinary sagacity so easily hoodwinked and entrapped? Did it not strike you as unusual that there were no published bans, and that no marriage certificate had been procured?"

" Marriage certificate! I never saw such a document in my life. I thought it was the intended groom who always looked out for that sort of marriage preliminary. Do women generally go round hunting up ban and certificate? I never heard of such a thing."

" Quite likely; it is not every woman who is so unfortunate as to place herself in the power of an unscrupulous adventurer who is ready to trample under foot any law, human or divine, that interferes with the accomplishment of his own selfish schemes. Did the seavoyage answer your expectations?"

" Far from it. I was scarcely able to leave my stateroom during the entire passage."

"And Monsieur; did he devote himself constantly to the pleasing task of beguiling your hours of their tediousness?"

"He was not intentionally neglectful; but it would have made him ill, so he said, to be shut up as I was; and I couldn't go on deck or into the saloon, where he spent most of his time."

"You met him when meals were served, of course."

"No, indeed; I could not go down the cabin stairs; it made my head swim to try. He sent me, by the stewardess, such delicacies as were procurable on board a steamer, but I scarcely tasted them. I cannot tell you how thankful I was when that tiresome voyage was over, and I could get the sound of tramping feet and jarring machinery out of my head.

"We had a lovely suite of rooms at Paris, overlooking a charming court-yard with vases and statues and fountains. Monsieur was very kind and attentive, and the shop-windows—O they were fascinating beyond description! Such satins! such embroideries! such laces! such shawls!—such splendor of coloring and magnificence of material I never feasted my eyes on before. And the price a mere *bagatelle;* I trimmed my underskirts with flouncings that I wear for sleeve draperies now. My thoughts being diverted from myself by all this novelty of display, I rapidly improved in health, strength, and spirits.

"We were out for a walk, one day, Monsieur and I, when we accidentally met an acquaintance of mine, a brother of an old schoolmate, Emma Ford. I was delighted at the sight of a familiar face, and at sound of the language I had been brought up to speak and hear. Monsieur professed to be equally delighted, and invited, even urged, Mr. Ford to dine with us at the hotel; and after he had accepted this invitation, insisted on his remaining with us for the evening—so he staid. We

were all three in high good-humor, or at least, I supposed we were—I have learned, since then, not to rely
too strongly on the evidence furnished by appearances.
Monsieur ordered a little supper at ten, and after that
had been discussed, left us for awhile, from an unavoidable cause of absence. so he said. When he returned,
Mr. Ford was teaching me to play, with a curiously
painted set of cards, a game called 'Fates.' We offered to throw up the game when he came in, as an odd
number would have spoiled all ; but he so cordially insisted on our finishing it, that we kept on.

" I had not the remotest idea that anything had gone
wrong until after our guest had taken leave. The door
was scarcely closed behind him, when Monsieur began
to rave like a madman. No protestations of mine
calmed his rage in the least. No denunciations that he
could heap upon me seemed in his opinion too severe.
He said I would find that I had a very different-person
to deal with from that uxorious Caruthers; and swore
that he would be the dupe of no woman's coquetries.
He bade me rue the day in which I changed his friendship to an enmity that would overleap all difficulties in
the pursuit of revenge. He was terrible in his wrath ;
a cold, cruel gleam in his eyes; his lips drawn back
from his teeth ; and his words coming so fast, in his
own tongue, that I was not always able to catch their
full significance. He concluded by warning me not to
try his patience too far, or he should be driven to a
method of retaliation it was at any moment in his
power to make, by disavowing a marriage whose validity he defied me to prove.

" That was the first time that the singular circumstances attending our marriage occurred to me as a
matter of doubt and apprehension ; and I lay awake
the whole night thinking them over. I could not make
up my mind that Monsieur really had the power of ful-

filling a threat whose accomplishment would have left me—nobody ; but his violent exhibition of temper, with his unjust and intemperate language, had taught me to fear and mistrust him ; and I looked forward with a sinking heart to the prospect of repeated bickerings and altercations I had every reason to expect.

" He went out next morning, directly after break-fast, saying that he was going to spend the day with a friend ; but I had an uncomfortable suspicion that he was lurking somewhere in the vicinity, in order to play the spy upon my movements. Mr. Ford called accord-ing to agreement, to pay his parting respects before his departure for Bordeaux. Of course I declined seeing. him.

" Soon after he went away there was a light knock at my dressing-room door. On opening it, I found the trim little maid, Cynthine, who always answered my bell, standing outside.

" ' Is Madame quite alone ?' she asked, with a mys-terious air.

" ' Quite alone,' I replied, not a little surprised at her intruding upon me without being summoned.

" Stepping inside the door, she pushed it together behind her, and held out a letter, saying that she had been requested to place it in my own hand when no one else was present. Suspecting some trick on the part of Monsieur, and not wishing to lend my aid in furtherance of any such artifice, I hesitated about taking the letter, and asked where she got it.

" ' From a discreet youth, who ran away before I had time to ask his name,' she answered, with a smile, half saucy and half demure ; ' and if I can be of any ser-vice, Madame may command my utmost discretion.'

" She dropped the letter in my hand, and tripped away.

" I scarcely heeded her words at the time they were

spoken, but I afterwards recalled them, greatly to my own advantage.

" Cutting the envelope, and unfolding the large sheet of paper it held, the first words that caught my eye were, ' private and confidential,' written in a bold, firm, masculine hand, and inclosed in brackets. It was but the work of an instant to turn to the signature, which was that of Lawyer Auverne. I knew it must be a matter of grave moment that would induce him not only to write me, but to take the pains he must have taken to convey the letter directly to my own keeping."

" Not so difficult a matter as it might seem at first thought. Mr. Auverne has a nephew who is studying surgery at Paris, and your letter was doubtless sent under cover to him. Do not let me interrupt you longer."

" The lawyer wrote me that he had received a letter from Monsieur Meurice, postmarked New York, and dated the very day we took passage by steamer from that city, directing him to sell the house you deeded to me, even at a heavy discount on its original cost and real value, and pledging himself to obtain my written sanction to the procedure whenever it should be needed. Mr. Auverne protested most earnestly against putting my name to any paper Monsieur Meurice might request me to sign. The remainder of the communication convinced me that his threat of disavowing our marriage was no idle menace, but a fearful weapon that he really had the power to wield against me. You will agree with me when I tell you what that remainder was.

" When I read that Mr. Auverne had just been instrumental in sending a fellow, calling himself Ned Franzelman, to the penitentiary, for going round nights breaking windows, and making a very good thing of it by turning glazier daytimes, and setting the glass that, but for his handiwork, never would have needed setting, I couldn't see what that had to do with my case. It was not until I reached a paragraph informing me that Abednego Witherspoon, the man who married us, and Ned Franzelman were one and the same person, that I waked up to the full enormity of Ned's delinquencies. It seems that he had owned a flat-boat, by means of which he had plied a very profitable trade on the Mississippi, until that river fell into the control of the insurgents, and he was driven out of employ. Then he turned his hand to any sort of occupation that came in his way; nothing came amiss, only provided it was sufficiently remunerative. He could pick a lock, or preach a sermon; give good advice, or follow evil counsel; expatiate with unction on the just deserts of all wrong-doers, of whom he was chief, or practice a trick with loaded dice; but he could bring no satisfactory proof that he was a regularly ordained minister of any established persuasion.

"The perusal of this letter left my thoughts in a perfect whirl. The ground I was beginning to believe secure, seemed once more sliding from under my feet. The reason for Monsieur's kindness and devotion was all explained; he would cajole me with fair words until my fortune was his, and then he was at full liberty to cast me off, when and how he pleased. If he is free to cast me off, I said to myself, then am I equally free to go; but oh! the fearful price of accepting such freedom. I thought of meeting those from whom I had received notes of congratulation as Madame Meurice, after having resumed the name of Lucy Sears. It never occurred to me that, in forsaking him, I was exposing myself to the crushing sort of blow you gave me, or I should have shrunk still more from the trying ordeal I was forced to pass through in order to escape the false position into which I had been artfully lured. The ties that bound

me to this man had already become hateful and galling
to me ; but not on that account would I have dreamed
of rending them asunder ; not until I found that they
were bonds basely forged, to be as basely riven when
they had served the selfish designs of their forger, did I
fully and firmly, with such deliberate resolve as in my
intense excitement I was capable of forming, decide to
throw off the name I had no right to bear, and to flee
from a bondage to which I had been subjected through
fraud and deceit.

" I never was accustomed to the responsibility of
thinking and acting for myself in matters of importance ; and, alone as I was, a stranger in a strange city,
I was sadly perplexed as to the safest and speediest
means of carrying out my plan, undetected by Monsieur
Meurice. In this strait, I bethought me of Cynthine's
offer of assistance, and made up my mind that I could
not do better than to avail myself of the 'discretion'
she had been so ready to place at my service. Ringing
for her, I explained so much of my intentions as was
necessary to win her to my interests, and then secured
her hearty coöperation by the present of a blue muslin dress, with a lovely set of turquoise ornaments to
match."

" You did excellently well for a novice ; what
next ?"

" I had not the means at hand for defraying my
travelling expenses on the voyage home."

" A serious drawback that ; you could not have had
one more so."

" I had to place more confidence in Cynthine than I
originally decided on. I did not dare to go myself to a
pawnbroker's, from fear of being seen and followed by
Monsieur, so I was obliged to trust my diamond brace-
let to her, and she disposed of it for little more than
half its real value."

"You had reason to be thankful that you got that amount, or ever laid eyes on the girl again, with such a premium on dishonesty as that in her keeping."

"I know nothing of her trustworthiness in general, but she proved faithful and grateful in my case, I will say that for her. Fortunately, she had a brother who was a *voiturier*, and one of the hotel porters as sweetheart. I did not like to run the risk of having my trunks carried out by the main entrance, lest they should be discovered by Monsieur Meurice, and my whole plan of flight be frustrated. Cynthine seemed to have an intuitive perception of all the exigencies of the case, and to find means for obviating them with a readiness and facility of which I was wholly incapable."

"A French woman for an intrigue," sententiously interpolated Mr. Caruthers.

"But there was no intrigue in my way of effecting my escape," remonstrated Lucy, with a look of perturbation and distress.

"I did not mean to assert that there was anything of the kind, only that your maid evidently thought there was, which made it the same thing for her, rendering her a much more valuable auxiliary than she might otherwise have been. Let me hear how she overcame the difficulties of extricating you from a position more perilous than you seem to have been aware of; for if Monsieur Meurice had once suspected your purpose, he would have moved heaven and earth to thwart it."

"I was fully aware of that; and my dread of doing anything to arouse such suspicion on his part, almost unfitted me for taking the needful precautions for insuring the success of my plan. My own trunks were left undisturbed in the closet, and a couple of new ones, of much cheaper make, were procured for me by the porter already mentioned, for which I paid exorbitantly."

"Of course the fellow looked out for his commission," remarked Mr. Caruthers, with quick mercantile comprehension.

"He marked the cards, in a coarse, legible hand, with the assumed name, Clarice Godefroy, under which I was to travel, and tacked them to the trunks, which Cynthine packed in a linen closet leading from the landing, carrying my wearing apparel there as she needed it. While she was thus occupied, I sat in the parlor, listening to every step in the corridor, ready to give her warning at the first intimation of Monsieur's approach. If he had come in, I never could have retained an appearance of even tolerable composure, and my agitation must have betrayed to his quick perceptions that something unusual was going on; and he would not have rested a minute until he had found out what it was. A rap at the door sent my heart to my throat, and me to my feet. I gave Cynthine a signal to keep out of the way, and went to the door, where a shop-boy handed me a box of embroidered neck-ties that Monsieur had just purchased, proving to me that he had not left town as he had asserted his intention of doing. This made me more than ever anxious to get away before his return; and dragging Cynthine out of the linen closet, where she had fled at my signal of danger, I begged her to hasten preparations for my departure by every means in her power. We were not again interrupted. My baggage left by way of the servants' hall.

"I was all ready to start when Cynthine placed a crumpled scrap of paper and a pencil in my hand.

"'One moment, Madame, before putting on your gloves. Henri says, will you be pleased to write down the name of the city you are going to, and he will drop you a line, directed to Clarice Godefroy, if anything should happen, in the course of the day, which that lady ought to be made to know.'"

"Grateful for the girl's kindly forethought in my behalf, I gladly complied with her request.

"Going down equipped only with reticule and para-
solette, as if for an ordinary shopping expedition, I
entered a hack, called for me by a servant from the
nearest stand, and was set down at a fashionable milliner's, where I bought a few trifles to account for my
appearance in the shop, which I left by a door opening
on a different street from the one by which I had entered. Satisfying myself that I was neither followed
nor observed, I walked rapidly to the corner of an
obscure lane, where I met the *voiturier* with the conveyance specially provided to take me to the railway
station, where my trunks had already preceded me. I
was so relieved when the cars moved off at a rate of
speed that promised soon to put a safe distance between
me and the city from which I had fled. Several slight
detentions occurring on the way, put me in an agony
of apprehension that Monsieur might take advantage
of them to pursue and overtake me. That whole journey was one fever of apprehension, and I did not feel
safe from pursuit, even when I had reached a Havre
Hotel. I scarcely ventured outside my room, until
after the servant I had sent to the office brought me a
letter that greatly allayed my fears. In it I was informed that Monsieur had returned to the hotel shortly
after my leaving it. Then my dressing-room bell rang,
and Cynthine obeyed the summons. He asked how
long I had been out, and she told him; where had I
gone; she put her discretion at my service, and knew
nothing; when would I return; she was wholly ignorant on that point. He dismissed her with a plain
intimation of displeasure at her want of communicative-
ness. She had hardly reached the foot of the stairs
when the bell rang again, with a sudden and angry
peal. How came it, he asked, that my bureau drawers

were nearly empty, and where was the key to my dressing-room closet. Once more she placed her discretion at my service, and left him as wise as she found him. He sent for the landlord, who was very bland and very much at Monsieur's service, but in despair at being unable to make return pertinent to his inquiries.

"When Cynthine went down a second time, she found her brother waiting to tell her that he had successfully carried out his part of the agreement. She told him of the new turn affairs had taken, and he determined to watch Monsieur's movements if he should leave the hotel. He soon came out, went to the coach-stand, and drove off in the very hack that had been ordered for me a short time before. He was not gone long, returned in haste, remained but a few minutes, and started off once more with a valise in his hand. The *voiturier* kept trace of him until he saw him fairly on his way, by rail, for Bordeaux.

"I breathed more freely after learning these particulars; but lost no time in taking passage, by steamer, for New York. From that place I went directly to Mrs. Thornton, who, notwithstanding my previous disregard for her wholesome counsels, has treated me with a gentleness and forbearance for which I can never be sufficiently grateful. I had thought to find with her a more peaceful asylum than I shall find anywhere, at least anywhere in this part of the country, while I am forever haunted by this constant sense of dread and apprehension."

"What is it you fear now?"

"That Monsieur will cross the sea to urge his claim on my hand."

"But he has no such claim rightfully to urge."

"I know he has no rightful claim on my hand; but I have, or might have such a one on his."

"What claim, pray?"

"Mr. Auverne says that if I should take a solemn oath in presence of a magistrate that our marriage, according to my most sacred belief, then and since, so long as I bore the name of Madame Meurice, was legally solemnized, it would, so far as he could see, be no longer void. Oh, Mr. Caruthers! could that man, by taunts or by threats, force me into speaking words I would as soon die as utter?"

"Remember, Lucy, that such words would ensure you a respectable standing in society, and spare you much bitter mortification."

"I do remember it, and further, that such words would give him the power to harass and torment my life out, until my fortune was his—fatal gift, that splendid mansion of yours to me—and then the sooner I died the better for both it would be. I quail at the bare possibility of dragging out an existence so wretched. No arts, no persuasions, no reproaches, no stratagems shall ever wring from my unwilling lips words that would condemn me to such a fate. Take back your house. I thought, no longer ago than this morning, that I would keep it between me and the possibility of want; it was a poor resolve to retain a golden lure for Monsieur. If you will allow me the value of the set of diamonds you gave me in happier days, I will take the name under which I safely crossed the Atlantic, and bury myself in some eastern town or village, where, in strict seclusion and retirement, I may find the peace and rest which are all that is left me to hope for in the way of happiness."

She started from her chair with a sudden cry of affright.

Mr. Caruthers turned his eyes in the direction of her glance, and saw only a young hospital physician standing in the door-way.

"Would you like to have your arm freshly bandaged, sir?"

"Not just now; drop in again in the course of an hour."

The doctor withdrew.

Mr. Caruthers bent a look of fixed and searching scrutiny upon his pale and trembling companion, who was wiping the large drops of beaded sweat from her brow. His last doubt vanished; it could be no counterfeit terror she was enduring.

"What startled you so, Lucy?"

"I thought it was Monsieur standing in the doorway," she faltered; "the silky moustaches were exactly like his, the height and figure quite similar."

"Supposing it had been he; what harm could you fear from him while you are under my care?"

"You advised me to take steps that would render my marriage valid, and I would as soon be advised to throw myself into the river. This never-ending terror is driving me out of my senses; how shall I escape it?"

The question was addressed rather to her own perturbed thoughts than to him, but he made prompt response.

"By giving me the right to defend you against the world, Lucy. I renew my offer of heart and hand, to be taken this time, if at all, for once and forever."

She looked at him intently, through softly gathering tears, and read in his face only a friendly expression of lively sympathy and tender commiseration.

"You were always generous to me, never more so than now; and I will not take advantage of your generosity to inflict upon you such a burden as you would soon find me."

"You mistake me entirely, Lucy. It is to no prompting of compassion that you owe this renewal of a previous offer. You are still for me *the* one woman in all the world, and your refusal would dash to the earth hopes the dearest I have to cherish."

"Weigh your words well, Mr. Caruthers. I broke faith with you once; could you unreservedly trust me again? I know what it is to be watched and suspected; I could not endure it from you."

"Let the past take care of itself; the future is all that remains to us. My proposal has sufficiently attested my confidence that there is a happy future in store for us."

"You forget the stigma attached to my name."

"So much the more reason for your taking mine."

"But what if Monsieur Meurice should come to this country in pursuit of me?"

"Let him cross my path, and see how he comes out."

"You have overlooked the opposition you will be certain to encounter from your own family. I met Miss Dian in the street, a few days ago, and she crossed to the opposite sidewalk to avoid recognizing me."

"If Dian cannot treat with respect and courtesy the lady bearing her brother's name, he can forego the pleasure of her society, without any heartrending sacrifice of fraternal regard, that's a sure case. Now, Lucy, have done with raising all these objections for me to combat and overcome. Be reasonable, and come to my—oh-h! I had forgotten that this once strong right arm of mine is useless now. Come back to me, and we will bear and forbear, each with the other; for I am inclined to believe that only through mutual concession and forbearance can any union be made a source of happiness to those bound by its compact."

CHAPTER XVIII.

AN OLD ACTOR IN A NEW GUISE.

IT was Lily Barton's twentieth birthnight, and toward the invited guests who had assembled in honor of the occasion, she displayed a courtesy and urbanity that yielded her a most pleasurable return. In this quiet festal scene, the demeanor of those gracing the same by their presence was more deeply marked by an all-pervading sadness than quite befitted such an assembly. There were sunny smiles and mirthful sallies on young lips, while knots of grave men insensibly collected and spoke in subdued tones of the late disasters on the Rappahannock, criticising government moves and military measures with an outspoken freedom that, under despotic sway, would have consigned the speakers to guarded fortress or dungeon cell.

In an arm-chair, speaking to no one, his eyes bent somewhat wearily on the floor, sat a discharged officer, the arm he wore in a sling telling why he had left his country's service. A light, noiseless step drew near.

"You are not enjoying yourself, Kilby; I am sorry I persuaded you to come."

"I am not sorry I came, if you are spending a pleasant evening."

"It will be pleasant no longer; I cannot enjoy what makes you uncomfortable."

"Not uncomfortable, Lucy; though I must say there is no place in the world for me like a certain lolling-chair drawn up before a grate full of flickering fire-light, and somebody in the lady's sewing-chair opposite, who keeps still as a mouse while my head runs on business cares, and chats with me when I'm chatty."

13

"I will return that handsome compliment by proposing that we go home at once. You shall get off that tight dress coat, which I dare say hurts your lame arm. It is not very late, and you can look at the dancing firelight, while I read aloud to you from the evening paper just what you always first search out—latest news by telegraph, doings at the brokers' board, and the advertising columns."

"What! talking of going away so soon," broke in the young hostess, who had approached them unperceived. "I appeal to you, Mr. Caruthers, to say if it is doing as you would be done by to make the first move toward breaking up my party at this early hour. For a wonder, shoulder-straps and velvet facings predominate over wreaths and spangles to-night. Then do not add to the list of uniformed wall flowers by carrying off an elegant dancer, and the only bride my party can boast. Leave her with us another hour, will you not?"

"Assuredly, if she wishes it; it was she, not I, who proposed leaving. I will go up to the card-room and see who is there."

He put his words in effect.

"I have a bit of news for you," said Miss Barton, drawing Lucy within the shade of heavy draperies curtaining a window; "but first let me tell you that you have really achieved a triumph to-night. Miss Caruthers' cold eyes have often been fixed on you, and the courteous, respectful attention you receive from others will, in time, have weight with her and overcome her prejudice against you. Now for my news. I have discovered, by meeting her in the street and inquiring her out, that the young lady who received us the day we went to St. Marc Hospital together, was not Miss Barr, but the veritable Miss Brandon, who once came so near proving a successful rival of yours. She was lately married, I hear, to one of our returned volunteers, who is maimed for life; shocking, isn't it, to think of the horrible risks our soldiers run? The newly wedded pair are living at a mortally lonesome, pokey, out-of-the-way place in the country, where Mr. Auverne, who knows all about them, says they are a perfect picture of Arcadian felicity. Are you curious of one who formerly threatened your own supremacy?"

"They, and all others, are heartily welcome to their own Arcadia, so long as mine is left uninvaded."

"Then you hang out no beacon light to warn inexperienced navigators off the dangerous shoals of matrimony."

"I have seen no such shoals, at least since my real marriage—of mock ceremonials it becometh not me to speak."

"You are naturally yielding, I think; but whatever thwarts my purpose I oppose with a stubborn resistance, which is part of my nature. The very idea of being bound by a solemn vow to obey would, I fear, be a powerful incentive to open revolt. Is it always easy, even for you, to have your own wishes a secondary consideration, to be set aside on the instant, if such whim happened to seize the fancy of your right royal liege and master?"

"You do not state the case fairly. My liege lord is so doubly pleased to see me pleased that I must be heartless and ungrateful not to prize his pleasure more highly than my own."

"Have a care, or, wearing your bonds so lightly, you will tempt others to risk the same. I must tell you what an insufferable noodle I have been making of myself this whole blessed evening. You remember the gentleman in whose favor I robbed your flower-stand on my way to St. Marc's."

"I recollect the robbery, not the gentleman."

"Well, he sent me a lovely bouquet this morning,

from which I took this blush-rose at my bodice. Now, I am so much afraid that he will either over-value the compliment or be repelled by my boldness in bestowing it, that I have persistently avoided him ever since his entrance, not having so much as changed words with him yet. I wish you would look about us, and tell me if he is anywhere in this room; for I would not, on any account, have him suppose that I was looking for him with the purpose of singling him out as an object of special attention."

"Do you expect me to recognize a stranger at first sight, when you have not even described him to me ?"

"Excuse my stupidity. He is dark and slight, with a bearded chin, brilliant eyes, and a highly spirited, intelligent cast of countenance."

"That description will apply to many persons present; you must be more definite."

"He is the handsomest man in the room."

"That won't answer; tastes are so apt to differ. Tell me something that he wears."

"A captain's uniform."

"There goes one; its wearer is a sandy-complexioned man, with coarse, bristling sorrel hair, a decided squint of the left eye, and "——

"You malicious creature, you know that is not the person I refer to. He has a clear. olive complexion, with an abundance of dark, glossy hair."

"That must be he who is making his way toward us with another gentleman. Do not speak or you will be overheard, as they are quite near."

"I have been doing my best, ever since my arrival, to find or make an opportunity for greeting the hostess; but fate has not until this moment befriended me. Allow me to present my friend, Mr. Clermont—Miss Barton. As he is a stranger in the city, I took the liberty of bringing him where I knew he would be amply repaid for coming."

" Any friend of yours is most cordially welcome.'

" Thank you. And now as I claim your hand for the next redowa, you would be showing my friend a mercy by introducing him to a partner."

" Certainly ; Mrs. Caruthers, Mr. Clermont."

" I am charmed to make Mrs. Caruthers' acquaintance. Permit me the pleasure "——

He offered his hand, and both couples joined the dancers.

" I think, although your name is unfamiliar to me, that I must have met you, or some one nearly resembling you, before," remarked Lucy to her companion, who, although the redowa was over, and he must have seen that his presence was not particularly desired, still maintained his position at her side.

" These chance resemblances are sometimes sadly perplexing," he carelessly rejoined.

She was constrained and unrestful, but unable to account for her uneasiness. Without a look or a word amiss, he had created an unfavorable impression on her mind. His very tones, the turn of his head, the touch of his long, slender fingers, had jarred those subtler chords of being whose manifestations it is so difficult to catch and imprison in plain verbal description. He was perfectly at ease, graceful, fluent, self-possessed, apparently quite unobservant of her embarrassment and brief malapropos rejoinders. With scant apology, she crossed the room to escape him.

She had nearly succeeded in regaining her disturbed composure when her hand was hurriedly grasped, and Miss Barton asked, in a guarded whisper :

" Have you not penetrated his disguise ? Beware of Monsieur Meurice !"

" Beware !"

The word seemed hissed in the ear of both.

Miss Barton turned with a look of surprise, Lucy with one of uncontrollable terror, in search of the speaker who had pronounced this single word of sinister warning. Behind them stood Mr. Clermont, an open photograph album in his hand, intently scanning a pictured face, that of Lucy Sears in bridal robes, with orange wreath and floating veil. She gazed at him with the intensity of growing conviction. The silky moustaches had disappeared, the hair been dyed to a deeper shade, and the foreign accent sedulously banished from his speech ; but despite all these attempts at disguise, Lucy knew that the man whom of all others she had most reason to fear and dread stood before her.

" Open a window, a lady is fainting," cried one gentleman to another.

" It is but a momentary giddiness that will be over in an instant," explained Miss Barton, supporting her friend, and striving to screen her from observation.

" Permit that I make myself of service," said Mr. Clermont, offering his arm.

Miss Barton declined this proffer of aid in Lucy's behalf, courteously but decidedly, never once leaving her until she saw her safely seated in the cloak-room, when she went in search of Mr. Caruthers, with a request from his wife to start for home immediately. He was found deep in a game at whist; interruption in such case was not to be thought of, and Lucy decided to remain where she was in preference to returning to the drawing-room, and thereby risking the chance of a second encounter with her relentless pursuer.

" Half an hour ago," she said to herself, " my path for the future lay bright and smiling before me ; now the very foundations of my happiness seem crumbling at my feet. Of what did he bid me beware but of his own evil self? If we could only get away from this ill-starred entertainment."

She raised her eyes with a quick, startled glance; surely something in the room had been slightly moved. Yes; she could not be mistaken, some one from the landing outside was slowly and cautiously pushing open the door, which had been left ajar. Her heart beat fast. What the cause for this caution and stealth !

"Who is there?" she asked, with forced calmness.

"Ah, you are here then. May I come in?"

A sickening thrill crept over her, as she replied :

"Certainly not. This room is appropriated to our use; your hat-room is on the opposite side of the stair-case."

Disregarding this prohibition, Mr. Clermont crossed the threshold, closed the door behind him, and leaning his back against it, stood regarding his companion with a look of fixed and determinate resolve. She shivered as though chilled by a biting wind. Partially mastering the tremor that shook her frame, she rose and approached the presuming intruder.

"Let me pass, Monsieur, I will go to my husband."

"No need, sweet love, he has come to you."

He laid his hand familiarly on her shoulder, and she shook it off, with a gesture of loathing and repugnance that kindled a fiery gleam of anger in his eye.

"It is at Madame's option; of the friendship or of the enmity, which chooses she?"

"I care not which so I may but be free from your presence," she desperately replied.

"Have a care, my fair lady ; for every word humiliating that you on me inflict, to yourself shall be returned with the usance most rigorous exact. Carry yourself loftily as you may, I will bow to the very dust that look which has had the temerity to meet my own with scorn. Retract; it is not yet too late, and permit that I, in this salute, do seal the pardon "——

He paused abruptly, for a slight noise made him aware that the handle of the door against which he leaned had been cautiously turned. Before she was aware of his purpose, he had softly turned the key in the lock, and by a very slight exercise of strength, drawn her to the opposite side of the room.

"You have no right to detain me against my will; no right to be here at all," she earnestly remonstrated. "I will not submit to such imposition ; I will call for help."

"And brave scandal! Madame has of the courage one grand overplus to dare so much."

There was a rap at the door.

"It is only I, Lily ; let me come in."

Lucy attempted to dart past her detainer, but he caught and held her fast by both wrists ; held her also by a look that riveted her own as a basilisk glance. He even smiled with malicious amusement at her ineffectual struggles to release herself.

"My pretty wren pecks at the hand that bars its cage —a hand kind as strong, and more ready to caress than to cross. Fail you to discern the good will screening you from the impulsive rashness of yourself? How of it with a stranger to be found closeted? Ah, Heaven, what indiscretion."

An indignant blush burned on her cheek.

"You taunt me with the cruel strait to which you have purposely brought me."

"I had not of the choice any other. Suggest a place more suitable for the renewal of our interview, and this one terminates on the instant."

"I shall do nothing of the sort ; you may be sure of that."

"Then the suggestion must come from myself, or this meeting be prolonged until the relations between us to subsist for the future be defined most accurate precise."

"There are no relations to subsist between us for the future."

" I venture not on the rudeness of to contradict ; but who lives shall see, and who wins shall wear of triumph the smile."

There was the sound of a man's step on the stairs.

" Leave me, I beg of you," she entreated, wringing her hands in a perfect fever of apprehension.

" The word is yours to say—where next to meet."

" Nowhere."

" Very good. *I* can afford to defy the appearances. Sit down, there is no haste; we will not fatigue ourselves."

" I will appeal to my husband for protection."

" That is—to myself."

" You know better. You defied me to prove the legality of a ceremony that was neither more nor less than a fraud and an imposition."

" Very correctly stated. I did thus defy you to the proof, in the heat of angry passion ; but not thus safely could you have defied me ; for the proofs were in my possession, and are so still."

" What proofs ?"

" I will tell you at our next meeting."

" Such meeting, with my consent, will never take place."

" Be not a great deal positive, so you shall yield with finer grace. You shall retract ; I· have reason. You will not provoke the alternative fatal that from your refusal might result. Weigh well my words. Flatter not yourself that they are lightly spoken. An earnestness terrible is in my heart. You shall meet me in the afternoon of to-morrow, when it has the hour of five, in your garden, by the path of shrubbery leading from the billiard-room."

. " I shall not."

13*

"As Madame pleases. Will she do me the favor to hand this card—the card of Monsieur Meurice—to her vaunted protector; and to him say, with my compliments, that Monsieur awaits with impatience a call from his old patron."

Lucy shook from head to foot as she caught the look of malevolent hate on the face of the speaker, and felt that there was no crime of whose performance he was incapable.

"What harm are you meditating against Mr. Caruthers?" she asked, in tremulous tones.

"He has made his will; made you his heir, I learn. Our second tour shall be performed in a style of splendor that shall strike all eyes."

She felt that death would be preferable to the fate his words darkly suggested.

He perceived that he was holding her in the bonds of deadly fear, and hastened to strengthen such bonds.

"My word of honor, he shall give me the satisfaction due the injured honor of a gentleman, or I spit at his honor of the base-born canaille; I heap on him of the insult unbearable gross. Sacred faith, but he will fight or some contractor of the funerals shall have a job. Did Madame chance to hear of one garoted in the street the last dark night, not much for motive mercenary; but for to wipe out a stain of honor, for to revenge? Meester Caruthers shall have of the advantages every one. If he says swords, of them we will choose; and if but one arm he can use, I but one shall make to strike."

He saw the color fading from her cheek, noted her sharply drawn, gasping breath, and counted his final success as certain.

"Hark!" she exclaimed, in a startled whisper, "what is all that noise on the stairs?"

"It is only the gentlemen going down from the card-room," he coolly rejoined. "The guests will soon begin to leave ; your decision speedily must be made. You will meet me as I proposed ?"

She bent her head in token of acquiescence.

He left her—left her to her own bitter self-upbraiding for a step she had seen no practicable mode of avoiding save at the risk of consequences she dared not brave ; to a vague but oppressive sense of wrong-doing, for which she was wholly at a loss to account. Worst of all to bear was the thought that she was shut out from her husband's sympathy. This weight of wretchedness must be borne without confession or complaint, for a revelation of its cause to him would but precipitate a hostile, perhaps a fatal, encounter. She was like a bird fluttering in the meshes of a fowler's net, and finding no mode of escape. Then what if M. Meurice should really be able to establish the validity of their marriage ? In that case, Mr. Caruthers' very generosity in providing for her by will, in case she should survive him, might prove the fatal gift that was to work the ruin of both. The probability of M. Meurice being able to produce such proofs of the legality of their union as he asserted to be in his possession, she would not for an instant admit to herself ; but the very possibility of such an event completely unnerved her. He had promised that at their next meeting such proofs should be forthcoming. She was not to be taken in by any fresh chicanery. She would be very wary ; his word should pass for nothing ; his proofs must have a base more substantial than that.

These all-engrossing reflections were interrupted by the entrance of Miss Barton, who, on observing her friend's troubled face, grasped her hand, whispering hurriedly :

" Insolent Gaul ! I knew how it would be. I missed him from the drawing-room, and came to warn you, but he was beforehand with me. I was in such dread that some of the others might come up, which d····

would have suited his purpose well, and did my best to
prevent it. How smooth he is, with his iron hand
gloved in velvet. Be on your guard ; take every precaution to prevent a second encounter like this; promise me that, Lucy."

The latter was spared the necessity of reply by the
announcement—" Mr. Caruthers' carriage waiting."

The drive home was a silent one.

Mr. Caruthers, who was weary ot the crowd, the light,
the music, the mirth he had not enjoyed, accounted for
his wife's unusual taciturnity by supposing that she was
as weary as himself. When she offered to read aloud
to him anything he might wish to hear, he declined the
offer ; and insisted, with kindly authority, on her immediately seeking needed rest. This very consideration
for her comfort smote her as an unmerited return for
the concealment and tacit deceit she was practising toward him.

It was long before she slept. From her first light
slumber she was awakened by an appalling dream. She
was standing on the verge of a frightful precipice over
whose beetling brow some demoniac power was impelling her with resistless but subtle, magic power; while
Mr. Caruthers, who with difficulty maintained his foothold on a jutting crag at her side, in striving to hold
out to her a helping hand, was momentarily in danger
of being dashed upon the sharp and jagged rocks plainly
discernible in the yawning chasm scores of feet beneath
them. She awoke with a cry of affright, and so vivid
was the sense of reality inspired by the dream, that it
was with a strong feeling of relief that she assured herself there was no occasion for her groundless terrors.
But was there no occasion ? As the occurrences of an
earlier portion of the night crowded back upon her memory, she could not answer this self-asked question in
the negative.

Restless, apprehensive, a prey to harrowing doubts

not unmingled with compunctious misgivings, she rose, and in wrapper and slippers, paced to and fro with compressed lips and contracted brow. Tears and sobs came at last to her relief, and groping her way with blinded eyes, she stumbled against a chair and overturned it.

"What does ail you, Lucy? Why did you cry out in your sleep?"

"I had a bad dream, Mr. Caruthers."

"But you are not dreaming now. What are you poking about there in the dark for?"

"I am feeling very miserable," she replied, in confusion, endeavoring to suppress all tokens of emotion.

"You are not quite as strong as you once were, and danced too long, is that it?"

"When I spoke of feeling miserably, I did not mean that I was ill."

"But you must be, or you wouldn't take on in this way; for you are not given to being hysterical, or to giving way, like some high-strung women, to attacks of nervousness that I never could have patience with. You were gay as a lark before we went to the party; something must have gone wrong there, what was it?"

She was utterly at a loss for a reply.

"Now I think of it," he resumed; "I see what it is you are brooding over, and giving yourself all this needless trouble about. You can hide nothing from me."

He paused an instant, and she waited breathlessly for him to proceed.

"The fact is, Lucy, you women, to say nothing of thin-skinned men, are so over-and-above sensitive, that you fret your hearts out about trifles that aren't worth the breath they cost to mention; there was young Sharp, who had his nose put out of joint for the whole evening, because, having set up for a wit on a small capital, Lily Barton took no notice of a very passable

joke of his, for the sole reason that she was all eyes and
ears for somebody else; and here are you, who, I did think,
had more sense, acting in the high tragedy line, because
that high-in-the-instep sister of mine turns you the cold
shoulder.   If I don't care a straw for her condescend-
ing airs, why should you?   We can do without her as
long as she can do without us.   I shall not lose any
sleep on account of her absence, if you'll only learn not
to mind it, and be bright and cheerful as you have been,
making my home the pleasantest place in the world
for me."

His hearty, self-confident tones subdued her agitation,
and restored to her a tolerable degree of composure.
She drew a stool to the side of the low French bedstead,
and seating herself, leaned her throbbing head on his
strong, broad shoulder.

"I have had more than you think to trouble me
to-night, Kilby, and I prize your kind words more
deeply than you are aware.   Whatever happens, or
whatever others may say of me, you will not turn
against me or bear me in other than kindly and charitable remembrance."

"I wish you knew my heart, Lucy, and then you
would know that my constant study is for your good as
much as for my own ; that every plan of mine includes
you as well as myself; and you would rest secure in my
regard, not taking molehills for mountains as you do
now."

He proved the sincerity of his conviction that her
troubles were of the molehill stamp, by resigning himself, with brief delay, to the soothing embrace of the
balmy god.   Calm and peaceful his slumber; but
neither calmness nor peace came to solace the restless
watcher who at his side kept sleepless vigil.

CHAPTER XIX.

THE CLANDESTINE INTERVIEW.

PUNCTUALLY at the appointed hour, Lucy was in the shrubberied walk, according to agreement; M. Meurice was also punctual.

"Is Meester Caruthers at home!" was Monsieur's first question.

"No," was the reply; "he dines at Delmarq's with a customer whom he would not bring home with him on account of my severe headache."

"Uxorious; very good. Around your finger very little you shall wind him while the moon lasts; for my benefit, too; for my benefit, I make oath. I of it am a great deal much please."

He looked at her fixedly to mark the effect of his words.

She was calm, with firm self-repression; her face betrayed nothing of her thought.

"I do not yet comprehend the nature of your demands; when I do so, I can decide whether to accept or reject them."

"*Diable!*—thousand pardons—the decision, it with you rests not. I have decide already; it is for you to submit without condition. Comprehend you now?"

"I may be able to do so when you explain to me what it is you require."

Her cool imperturbability surprised and slightly disconcerted him. A more subtle gleam came to his eye, and his manner assumed a more wary alertness.

"Of which would Madame be first informed, of the concessions I demand as the price of my silence, or of

the claim that gives me the power to exact such concessions?"

" Your demands first; let me know the worst I have
to dread."

" I have had of the misfortune to contract debts in
anticipation of a contingency which did continge never.
Not to myself was the fault. On whom it does belong
let it fall. But to my muttons. This indebtedness must
have of the cancelment sure and speedy. Without delay
immediate, the means you must procure. A thousand
francs, scarcely a couple of beggarly hundreds in your
sordid currency decimal, is what you shall procure for
me this hour."

" Impossible; I have not that amount at my disposal,
and even if I had "——

" There is no such word as impossible when I say
sha'l," he almost fiercely interposed. " I must have of
the money or of its equivalent. There is Madame's
jewelry."

" I will not part with it. I see no reason for doing
so."

" Then of the reason I shall make you to see; through
compulsion, force you my claim to recognize. Attend,
it is the claim of a husband over his lawfully wedded
wife."

" I deny the claim. This is not the first time you
have tried to dupe me with false words and treacherous
arts. Thanks to your precepts and example, I am older
in worldly wisdom than I was when first I gave you my
confidence—a confidence withdrawn forever. If experience has been a harsh teacher, it has not been
a profitless one to me. I will take nothing you say on
trust."

" Very wisely resolved, most sapient skeptic. I do
not contradict; I prove."

He handed her a slip of paper, and she changed color

on examining the same. It was, with the exception of
the groom's and one other name, very nearly an exact
counterpart of the marriage certificate Mr. Caruthers
had playfully insisted on her examining, and was evidently a genuine document.

"Name any other proofs you may require, and of
them you shall have all."

"Prove that it was a regularly ordained clergyman
who wrote this certificate, and who performed the ceremony which you know, as well as I, was not binding in
law."

Monsieur shrugged his shoulders, with a complacent
smile.

"I will not argue the point; it has of the consequence
far too little. What imports it so long as I have of the
proof abundant that the itinerant priest was a Justice
of the Peace, regularly appointed in this county, and his
term of appointment as yet unexpired."

Lucy's face whitened to the very lips.

"Can such an official take the place of a clergyman
on such an occasion?"

Without a word, Monsieur took from his pocket a
small volume, holding it so that she could read from the
title page: " Revised Statutes of this Commonwealth."
Turning to a chapter headed " Marriage and the Solemnization thereof," he directed her attention to the following question and reply:

" By whom may marriages be solemnized ?"

" By a Justice of the Peace within his county, or by
an ordained minister of the gospel throughout the
State."

"I have only your word for it that this Mr. Witherspoon, or whatever he calls himself, is a regularly appointed Justice of the Peace," she persisted, still animated by a hopeful degree of incredulity.

"Ah, faithless fair; nothing wilt believe without the

evidence dual that the doubting apostles of law do insist on?
You shall no longer have for the doubt one suspicion of
excuse. If you wrongfully believe not the word of myself, the word sacred of one of your sect you shall have.
He stops with me all the days at the Hotel Ironside.
He has the house of himself neighboring that of Meester
Witherspoon, whom he knows always since he is one
small boy. Come with me, and your own ears shall
listen to the testimony corroborative of a person in holy
orders, very devout."

This proposal, after some persuasion on his part, she
finally acquiesced in, and accompanied him to the hotel
already mentioned.

After leaving her for a few minutes alone in a private
parlor, he returned, accompanied by a heavy featured,
stolid looking man in a home-made suit of kersey-grey,
his knit-yarn stockings showing plainly above his strong
pegged brogans. In movement he was slow and deliberate, in manner somewhat positive and overbearing,
like one accustomed to the submissive respect of his as-
sociates, and in appearance sedate and eminently respectable.

"Deacon Brown, Mrs. Caruthers," carelessly announced
M. Meurice.

Lucy hesitated at thought of addressing a stranger on
matters of vital moment to herself. Monsieur, with
ready tact, paved for her the way to such address.

"All the facts you can inform this lady, Deacon, of
this neighbor of yourself, Witherspoon, with whom I
have had of the dealings will be to her of interest, and
to me of the obligation for to requite."

"Wal, so I reckoned by a word you dropped in the
bed-room up-stairs. I've knowed him ever since he was
a little shaver fishin' for pollywogs with a crooked pin
baited with a bug, and I can't say as I ever seed much
harm in the chap, though he might have been a trifle

wild in his younger days, but turned out likely enough
when he growed up, and went to meetin' regular, and
was a tongney man, always ready to hold forth at con-
ference meetings; and if our pulpit didn't happen to be
supplied, not a man anywhere round could fill it to better edification than he."

" Did he hold any public office when the house of himself neighbored your own," adroitly queried Monsieur.

" I disremember, and should say he didn't, leastways
nothing more than a.Field driver—I know he was that,
for he put as likely a span of shotes as I ever raised in
the pound—or a Justice of the Peace, and I know he
was that, because he married Jake Stilts to Patience Little; and though they was awful incompatible, and always
having spats, she a-threatening to drown herself, and he
a-thinking it wasn't a bad idee, they had to tough it out
the best way they could, for they was as safely yoked as
though a minister had tied the knot."

" Have you of the proof sufficient?" asked M.
Meurice.

Lucy replied by rising to leave.

" Hold on a bit," said the Deacon, " I believe I've
got an affidavit swore to before the Justice; that will
tell the story. No, it is up-stairs in my great coat
pocket; I'll be back in a jiffy."

He left the room, returning, after a few minutes'
absence, with a plethoric wallet in his hand, from which,
after considerable fumbling, he drew a paper worn and
creased, and unfolding handed it to Lucy, who, after a
glance at its contents, read carefully the concluding
lines, which ran as follows:

" Sworn to before me, this 20th day of September,
1860.

" ABEDNEGO WITHERSPOON, *Justice of the Peace.*"

" Was he your neighbor so lately as 1860 ?"

"He was, Marm, excepting when he went down river once in a while on a trading vy'ge."

Lucy turned quickly to M. Meurice.

"Can you tell me, Monsieur, whether Mr. Witherspoon has more than one alias to his name?"

"Ah, then Madame has heard of this affair so dolorous unfortunate; of my poor friend's arrest on a charge fraudulent, false; of his being dragged off amongst the vile contrites and riffraff miserables. Should his own name, that had of the esteem, be pollute by sounding with that of this rabble and scum? The law clutched him, his name it could not clutch. He took the only way of saving that from disgrace by making another do duty in its stead. If you have of the information sufficient, we will make our *adieux* to this worthy man with thousand thanks and greatly oblige."

She could hear the loud beating of her own heart as she passed down the steps of the hotel to the side-walk.

"My faith, but incredulity you no longer can conserve; two responsible witnesses not of testimony conflicting, what more of the proof can you require?"

"If you are deceiving me, M. Meurice, it is the cruellest deed of your life."

"If Madame still inclines to doubt, I scorn further to protest; if my word of honor is not veritable to be believed, to make oath is nothing better."

She turned toward him, a look of piteous appeal on her white and troubled face.

To this mute appeal he replied,

"There is no use of quarrelling with the fate which alone has made you miserable. Where you cannot resist with success, submit without demur; that has of the true philosophy. Meester Caruthers to you can deny nothing; why should I be subject to those disagreeables, the creditor's importune, when you so easy shall release me from such beastly insolence?"

"Do not distress me any more to-day. I am half crazed already. I must have time to think."

"You of it shall have ample. At what hour do you breakfast?"

"At eight."

"Very good; one hour earlier I will met you in the garden. Attend my coming; I am not patient of the delay."

She left him without reply.

"Peste!" he mentally ejaculated; "she veritably thought to baffle and foil one as thoroughly versed as myself in the wiles and the guiles, the crooks and the turns of the finesse feminine, intricate. Fancied, did she, that I would relinquish of the advantages, like one donkey despicable, at a pleading look from one whose beauty is only so-so; one without style, without manner, of culture little, and of spirit less. By concealing from her husband, as she may continue to call him if these spirits importune are laid to rest, these planned interviews clandestine, she has given me the wedge to effect the separation of themselves; for if she threatens to expose me to him, I against herself can turn the threat. As *diplomat*, she counts for nothing. If she dare me too far, I plan a surprise, one grand *tableau vivant;* in the foreground frantic lover, weeping wife; in the background, jealous husband, gaping servants, gathering crowd. Faith of Meurice, but it is inimitable! One hint of it to Madame shall be enough. Fairly caged, fair dame. A wealthy merchant shall be my banker. Let me see; how large a sum shall be placed to my credit? What is woman good for but to serve us? For what sole purpose was she created but to subserve the interests of man, while he of Godlike front has of the interests to subserve multifarious? I am of my being fulfilling the purpose while forcing her thus to fulfill the same. *Vive la diplomatie.*"

Sadly the victim of this diplomacy wended her way homeward, going directly to her sleeping-room on reaching the house. As she sat with bowed head, searching in her own mind for some mode of extrication from the strange and perilous position in which she found herself, the deepening lines on her brow, and the painful compression of her lips, showed that she sought in vain for any satisfactory solution of the problem set her to solve. She had done all she could, unaided, to test the authenticity of the proofs M. Meurice had brought forward to establish the legality of their marriage. The idea of consulting Lawyer Auverne presented itself, but was quickly set aside; for she felt that in the present case she could not count on the lawyer's silence, as every consideration of friendship and fair dealing would lead him to reveal the whole affair to Mr. Caruthers, and what might follow she shuddered to even conjecture. It is through me, she thought, that comes his great danger. If I was out of the way he would be safe. I owe him some reparation for the grievous wrong I once gave him in return for his love and trust; I owe him some requital for the generous kindness that has never let me know a want. How little M. Meurice knows of my real character if he supposes I would remain here on his terms. It would be bigamy, a criminal offence. Neither will I yield myself to his guidance, even though it were ten times sanctioned by law; I see too plainly where it would lead. I would as soon brave plague and pestilence as the pollution of his presence.

She went slowly down to the conservatory, sighing drearily as she caught sight of a showy exotic, with its gorgeous petals and its hidden thorns. Then, with a softening glance, her eye ran over many-hued roses, clustering oleanders, fragrant heath and orange bloom; stalks close strung with blue and purple bells, or bearing the snow-white chalices of perfumed lily-cups—ran over them longingly and lingeringly, as one looks on cherished favorites for the last time. This was the only leave-taking with living creature that she could permit herself.

Back once more to her room she made her way. Taking from the closet a small enamelled travelling-bag, she folded and placed therein a couple of the plainest dresses in her possession, together with a few additional articles of wearing apparel, and almost the entire contents of her work-box. From the satinwood box containing her jewelry she took only the miniature of which we have before had occasion to speak, in its costly setting of gold and pearls. The chain attached to the miniature she had already thrown over her head, when, after a moment's pause for reflection, she as quickly removed it. It might prove the means of her detection, and she dared not take it. Of the original she could take no leave; but upon the pictured face her tears rained fast as she murmured over it tender words of parting, and a final " God bless you—Farewell !"

Half blind with weeping, she nevertheless counted accurately the contents of her purse, which she found to contain a larger sum than she had expected, and knew whose generous hand had added by stealth to its store.

Thus furnished with the means of providing for her immediate needs, she fled in the deepening shades of eventide—fled from her warmest and truest friend, seeing no other safe and justifiable course to pursue in the cruel extremity to which she had been reduced.

Mr. Caruthers, utterly at a loss to account for his wife's sudden and inexplicable disappearance, left no means untried to trace her flight; but despite his efforts, aided by those of the police, whom he had summoned to his assistance, weeks went by and the mystery was not cleared up.

CHAPTER XX.

REJECTED PROPOSALS.

Lucy Sears, or rather Lucy Searls, as she had called herself since interpolating a single letter in her maiden name, plied her needle industriously in the low-ceiled basement room that had become the scene of her labors for a livelihood. It was not yet dusk in broader, lighter thoroughfares; but in this dark and narrow alley she was obliged to sit near, and bend toward, the window pane to obtain the light needful for the prosecution of her task. The room was a front one, but its single window was mostly below the scant strip of sidewalk, so that there was little temptation to look forth at a prospect comprising dirty boots and leggings, the property of passing pedestrians, or a scrap of dingy brick wall, the vested right of the owner of the tenement across the way.

Lucy's companion is scarcely a proper subject for description, presenting no salient points for the narrator to seize. If she had ever had in her composition anything brighter than neutral tints to boast, they had long since been washed out of it by a life of uncheered, unvaried and laborious monotony. She was considerably past middle life, very deaf, and very taciturn. If she had likes and dislikes, preferences or aversions, she never expressed them; but what she had to do, set herself about with a dull, mechanical persistency, such as is sometimes manifested by a broken-down convict on a creaking treadmill. As Lucy looked at Miss Moodey's face, so joyless, so impassive, so unexpectant, she wondered if she had ever learned individually the full meaning of the words recreation and sympathy. It was not without a vague feeling of dread and oppression that the younger woman looked forward to the prospect of her own life becoming a hopeless blank like that of the elder.

From the entry above came harsh, discordant sounds from children wrangling over a disputed toy; for, small as the house was, it was occupied by two families.

A man's step was heard in the diminutive basement-hall outside. Miss Moodey rose without the slightest change of expression on her cold and rigid face, and passed into the adjoining kitchen to commence preparations for tea.

The man came in—a man with a large, loosely-knit frame; a broad, thick hand with swollen joints; an awkward, shambling gait; coarsely cut features, with a weak, receding chin; lips full but not closing firmly; and pale grey eyes, the white greatly predominating over the color of the iris, which opened and shut with much deliberation. For good or for evil, he was evidently not one of the swift workers in this hurrying world.

"You are home early to-night, Mr. Moodey," Lucy remarked, her busy fingers scarcely pausing in their work.

"A trifle earlier than common," he slowly enunciated, after duly deliberating his reply. "I shut up early; we all on us did, on account of the funeral of an officer—one of the Black Plumes."

Lucy turned pale, and her nimble fingers grew suddenly still.

"Did you learn the officer's name?"

"In course I did; it was in everybody's mouth."

"Be so kind as to tell me what it was."

"Lieutenant Weldon."

A sigh of relief unconsciously escaped her; and she bent her eyes once more on the long strip of plain cash-

14

mere which she was surrounding with a figured bordering.

She was much changed, even more in manner than in looks. The pretty affected ways and sprightly coquettish airs wherewith she had once sought to charm, had now given place to a quiet, subdued, womanly demeanor that well became her; no longer striving to attract, she had grown doubly attractive.

" It is too dark to sew now ; you will only strain your eyes. Put by your work till the lamp comes in," good-naturedly remonstrated Mr. Moodey.

" I will go for the lamp myself."

" No ; it will be here soon enough. Do take time to breathe; it is enough to tire a person to death to be always in such a hurry as you are."

" You forget that with all my hurrying I can little more than pay my way."

" There ain't no occasion for you any more than paying your way, as I can see."

" If I should at any time be unable to get work, I should be thankful then that I had made hay while the sun shone."

" Oh, I'll look out for that; you shall have work enough, either from my shop or somebody else's."

" But I might lose my health, you know, and be unable to work on that account."

" Wal, in case of sickness you don't suppose that I'm the man to turn a woman out of house and home, whether she could pay her board or whether she couldn't —not by a long chalk. I like to have you here. I don't have to hollo at you as I do at Gelly "—his sister's unabreviated name was Angelica—" and you don't never fret and stew on account of its being lonesome here, as one of your gad-about highflyers would be sure to do. You ain't one of them kind, nor nothing like it. You are of the kind that attends to their own affairs, and lets other folkses alone; and they are always found out, because they are worth the finding. If a woman is only worth the finding, she can't be hid so close but she'll be found, and by the right one, too."

"Do you really think so?" asked Lucy, a little startled by this positiveness of assertion.

"True as I am sitting in this chair," he gravely asseverated. "It ain't the girl that spins the most street yarn, and is forever showin' off in a crowd, that gets married the soonest. There was Judith Foss, always upon the go, and Judith Foss will be cut on her gravestone, I've no doubt. Then again, there was Almiry Hunt, who was brung up in a place there wan't no road to; but, bless you, that didn't make no difference; her feller come down stream in a wherry; got snagged; had to call on Ben Hunt to help him out of the fix; got a sight of Almiry wading in the pond after duck's eggs; and struck up a bargain with her right straight off the reel. She was a saving, thrifty home body; them's the kind for my money."

Highly satisfied with this labored exposition of his views on a subject by which, in bachelor meditations, he had been considerably exercised, Mr. Moodey, assuming an attitude of comfortable negligence, sat complacently watching the deft fingers that once more busied themselves with needlework. Absorbed in her own thoughts, Lucy had nearly forgotten the presence of her observer, when he remarked, with emphasis:

"You be awful spry; that's a fact."

"It is well for me that I am so," she quietly rejoined.

"Then you think a nimble sixpence is better than a slow shilling; but a body is richer for having them both in these times, when a man is reckoned up according to his money value; don't you see?"

Lucy replied by an amiable affirmative; though not

catching, in the least, the drift of his meaning. He
hitched his chair a little nearer her own, so as to speak
in a lower and more confidential tone.

"So you think, Miss, that the spry sixpence might
put up with the slow shilling because it was worth the
most; is that so?"

"I dare say, and glad of the chance," she returned,
abstractedly, tired of a conversation which had neither
point nor interest for her, and wishing she could afford
a room and a light all to herself.

"I see a young woman on my way home, buying
some vilets and chamomile blows, or what looked like
'em, and she seemed so tooken up with the weeds that
I thought I would buy you a few, there is so little
worth looking at here, and you don't never go nowhere
else," said Mr. Moodey, with some hesitancy and embarrassment of manner. "I went into the shop where
they kept all sorts of garden sarce and green herbs
a-growing. The storekeeper cut me off anything I
asked him to, that was in the flower-pots; and as true
as I'm alive, the feller had the face to ask me a dollar
for 'em. I was so riled up at the idee of having made
such a blasted jackanapes of myself, that I'd a great
mind to fire 'em in the feller's face and smash a flower-
pot, to come up with him. They are out in the entry;
you can get 'em if you want 'em."

She hastened to act on this permission, returning with
a lovely bouquet in her hand. She sat down and examined it with critical appreciation, a soft smile playing
over her lips as she recognized favorite after favorite of
the Caruthers conservatory. The flowers were very
welcome to her through power of association; not a
thought had she to spare for the donor.

"I wish she would look at me like that," thought the
neglected Mr. Moodey, as with some vague purpose of
connecting himself with his gift in her mind, he drew

his chair beside her and attempted to describe the varieties composing his floral offering.

"Them yaller roses is the Chiny Sophrony, so the
chap I bought 'em on said; and I thought I'd remember the names o' purpose to tell you."

"Chinese saffrona," corrected Lucy to herself, without a look at the speaker.

"And that bunch of red blows, that is full equal to a
hollyhock any day, is only a highbred pennyrial; an
edicated weed, you see."

"Hybrid perennial," she mentally corrected.

"And this that smells the best of the lot, is nothing
but a 'darnation pink,' the feller told me so."

She did not hear him.

As day after day passed by, she grew more and more
expert with her needle, and thought this the reason
inducing her employer to trust her with more elaborate
and more remunerative species of needlework, entertaining not the remotest suspicion of the fact that she
received double the amount for her labor that he paid
others for the same. Relieved from the dread of finding herself unequal to the task of earning her own livelihood, her brow was gradually clearing from the look
of apprehension it had worn, and the faint color brightened in her cheek.

Her employer treated her with unvarying kindness,
giving many a practical proof of increasing good-will.
Her dresses were too light and delicate for her new
position, and he brought her home a soft, brown Thibet,
marked down much below cost, on the plea that it was
old-fashioned, and a little shop-worn; while the shawl
of tartan plaid in which she occasionally treated herself
to a short walk in the precincts, between daylight and
dark, cost more, fresh from its maker's loom, than when
it came into her possession. For this kindness she
strove to make suitable return, by standing between

him and many a petty household discomfort to which
he had become too much accustomed to think of reme-
dying. Not worth noting down are the trifling ways
she took of making her presence agreeably felt; he
only knew that his own dwelling was a pleasanter place
to stay at than it had formerly been ; and that, conse-
quently, he spent more hours there than had been his
wont.

Previously to Lucy's coming, he had now and then
borrowed a newspaper of his tenant overhead; and
spelled, by slow, laborious process, through a few of its
more striking paragraphs. Now he rarely came in to
tea without his evening paper, which she read aloud to
him, the only drawback to his enjoyment of its contents being indicated by his repeated remonstrance, " I
can't take in the words so fast; they all run together,
without you keep each one separate on its own hook ; I
do wish you wasn't quite so awful spry."

One evening he took the unusual step of bringing
home a book, a small, pocket volume, exquisitely bound
and gilded. She expected to be asked to read it aloud,
but her expectations were not realized. Hour after hour
he sat poring over the volume with an intensity of
application that denoted the deep interest his studies
inspired. Even his newspaper was forgotten. Lucy's
curiosity was piqued; she resolved to improve the first
opportunity for a peep at his new acquisition. He
seemed resolved to baffle her purpose. Some one called
him to the door, and with him went the book, his finger
between the leaves. He was even obliged to leave the
house, but pocketed the volume before starting.

Her chance came at last. On his return he resumed
his studies with unflagging zeal. By an adroitly
planned glance over his shoulder, she caught this head-
ing of a chapter, in large capitals: " Elegant forms of
marriage proposals for bashful Bachelors."

She was much amused at her discovery; it seemed so odd that a man so inelegant by habit and choice as Mr. Moodey, should be interested in elegant forms of any sort. Had she but known the end and aim of this novel literary pursuit, she would have been anything but amused at it, as she afterwards learned, to her cost.

One afternoon at dusk, as Lucy was folding up her work, preparatory to her short walk, Miss Moodey being up-stairs, her employer, having returned earlier than was customary, entered the room with an appearance of haste strongly at variance with his usual deliberateness of movement.

"Sit down, Miss Searls, I have something of the greatest importance to say to you."

She obeyed, dreading to be informed of the loss of steady employment, or a reduction in its price.

To her utter consternation, he, with considerable difficulty, being somewhat weak in the knees, knelt before her and propounded the following ominous query:

"Would the addresses of a lover be agreeable to you?"

A quick flash of resentment burnt on her cheek; but in an instant she reflected that he was ignorant of the cause that to her made his words seem like an insult.

"I cannot for a moment listen to such a proposal, Mr. Moodey; I have highly valued your kindness, I may even go so far as to say your friendship; but I cannot keep them on terms to which it is impossible for me to accede."

"Never mind the terms, I won't be hard about them. Hear me out, will you? I do hereby offer you, without the least expectation of any money equivalent, in proof of an attachment as adorable—blast it all! where be I?—to the lovely being I hold of all the earth most adorable, my heart and"——

Lucy sprang to her feet, leaving her discomfited adorer kneeling before an empty chair as his sister entered the room. The not over light step of the latter, Lucy had heard on the stairs, and sprang aside, hoping to terminate a scene whose exposure could lead to nothing better than embarrassment and mortification for its principal actor. Mr. Moodey's lack of agility rendered him unequal to the occasion. In striving to rise hastily, he grasped the leaf of a small pine table to aid his efforts, and said perverse article of furniture, being probably under the influence of one of the spirits malign, tipped earthward, administering to its informal assailant a smart rap over the head as both fell to the floor.

Miss Angelica, startled out of her habitual taciturnity, was surprised into inquiring the cause of this strange concatenation of mischances.

"Only a broken table leg that I can't mend," he bellowed in her ear, after struggling to his feet. "Step round the corner, and speak to the old-broken-furniture man to come and repair it, will you?"

She started without an added word.

Nothing daunted, the would-be wooer once more assumed the offensive by drawing his chair as nearly as the laws of space would admit to that of the reluctant object of his devotions.

"A poor beginning makes a good ending," he confidently remarked; " and you must overlook what ain't jest according to rule; for I never went a-courting in all my life before. You see, it makes a feller feel kind o' sheepish jest at the outstart; but the ice once broke, a man that ain't got much of the gift of the gab, can hoe his row with the best on 'em. You jest consider that the ice is broke, and I shall be as happy as a clam at high water. That's the talk; silence gives consent. You needn't say nothing. I ruther like to see a young damsel kind of offish ; it's a deal better than to see one right on hand, and ready to do more than half the sparking herself, like that brassy-faced Pawliney Hotchkiss. She took all manner of roundabout ways to figgle me into popping the question ; but old birds ain't caught with chaff ; and thinks I to myself, if I can't do my own courting, it can go undid."

"I wish you would hear what I have to say, Mr. Moodey. Although it would be a pain to me to hurt your feelings, and although I should be very sorry to go away from here, still "———

"My stars, you ain't going away ; don't be scaret before you are hurt. Now that I've fairly made up my mind to take you for better or worse, I don't want to put it off by no manner of means. I always count the cost before I start, but when I do start, I go ahead like a house a-fire. I'm ready to start now, and I'm going ahead. The fust thing I do will be to give the folks overhead notice to quit, so that we can have the whole house to ourselves. I suppose that will make Viles, next door, who is tight as the bark of a tree, living awful stived up, and letting every spare inch of room, even his cellar-closet, to an apple and candy woman to sleep in, think we are mighty stuck up : but as long as I can pay my honest debts, he is welcome to his thoughts ; I shan't knuckle under to nobody."

"Mr. Moodey, will you please hear what I have to say ?"

"After I've had my say comes your turn, in course."

With a look not wholly resigned, she assumed an attitude of civil attention.

"There is Gelly, who has grown rheumatic and stiff in the joints, and takes on about having to tote things up and down stairs so much ; she can go out to Brother Silases' farm, where we was all brung up, and where they will be right glad to have her knit footings for the

14*

farm hands, and look after the young ones. Not but
that we could git her back here if we should ever want
her, you know. Speak out, now's your time. Be as
perk as you please, but don't go to being contr'y like a
critter that won't haw nor gee, if you don't want to
make me real put out with you."

" I should be very sorry to offend you, after all the
obligations you have placed me under by furnishing me
with employment, and granting a forlorn outcast, as I
came to you, the shelter of a home ; but "——

" You talk like a book. I am glad you have the
gumption to understand what a heap of obligations you
are under to me. It isn't one man in a thousand that
would have lifted you out of the gutter, as a body might
say, and put you right in the clover, as I have did.
How could I tell but what you'd make off with the
spoons in my cupboard, or even my money-pus, when
you never brung me no recommendation whatsomdever?
It was odd, to say the least on't, to see a woman with
hands as white as milk, and not the sign of a finger-
prick on ary finger, left to shift for herself, with nary a
friend nor relation to speak a good word for her. It
looked as though she had been used to a good home ;
and if she had been turned out of it, who was to blame
for it? That is what most folks would have asked in
my place; but I kept mum, and didn't ask no questions,
and don't ask none now, only if you will have me, and
that isn't hard to answer, I'll bet a copper. Speak out,
for so far, our talk has been like the handle of a jug, all
on one side."

" Mr. Moodey, even if I were not personally averse
to the acceptance of your proposals, which I gratefully
appreciate as the highest proof you can give of confidence in my worth, however appearances may belie
me, still "——

" Botheration ! what in thunder are you driving at ?

Are you crazy as a loon to talk of being averse to my proposals? Ain't you tooken my meaning yit? Don't you understand that I'm offering to make you my honored wife?—you that ain't got an extra suit to your back but what I've sold you at less than cost—you that ain't tough, and can't no more stand it to rough it through this shoving, scrambling crowd of money-changers, without somebody to give you a lift over the steepest places, than a down-south wood-lark could · winter on our bare prairies. Let me tell you that I don't take up with you, Jack at a pinch, because I can't do better. I know of more than one likely young woman that would jump at the chance of saying ' yes ' to such a question as I've give you the chance to answer. There is Pawliney Hotchkiss, as tough as a knot and as smart as a steel-trap, if she is ruther for'ard, who could do more hard work in a day than you in a week. There is Phebe Shooks, too, with a heap of tin that would furnish up the house tip-top, and put a new front, that it needs bad, to the store ; to say nothing of Deacon Barns' daughter, and the deacon pop'lar, and one of the pillars of the church, and all the custom he could bring me. But I won't talk hard to you; for I've seen enough of the rough-and-tumble of life to find out that molasses catches more flies than vinegar. If you'll only try to make things comfortable, and be kind o' chipper about the house, and never snap me up nor be snarly and scratchy tempered, I shan't mind if you don't bring me the fust red cent. I will do all the earning, and all you'll have to do, will be to take care of what I earn, and see that nothing goes to waste. You can work for the shop whenever it suits you, as, in course, you will want something to take up your time, as you ain't given to gadding all over creation like some folks I could mention. If housework don't agree with you, I'll git a little yaller girl to come and go at your beck

and call, and you may dress up and sit in the best front
room every day of your life."

He paused, beaming radiantly upon her at thought of
his own unparalleled beneficence.

" You are very good," faltered Lucy, who was beginning to fear her dauntlessly persistent wooer, and to be
seriously apprehensive of the effect any ill-judged word
on her part might have on her future prospects; "but I
tell you decidedly that I cannot marry you ; my hand
is not at my own disposal."

" Not at your own disposal? what do you mean by
that? that you've got another feller?"

He waited for her reply, but she gave none. Her
silence convinced him that he was right in his surmise.

" A poor shote," he muttered contemptuously, "to
leave you to shirk for yourself in this way, and never
once come nigh you. A cut-throat gorilla, perhaps;
our troopers will soon clear the State of them vermin.
I don't care a end of tobacco what he is, or where he is,
if he will only keep away from here. I said I wouldn't
ask no questions, and so I won't, only that one I spoke of."

" You have my final answer," Lucy firmly but gently
persisted.

" Then you are standing most awfully in your own
light, I can tell you that, young woman ; and if you
don't find it out, and that right soon too, I'll lose my
guess."

Lucy trembled at the sudden change in his tone and
manner, the former harsh, the latter stern, as he uttered
this prediction of evil omen.

" I hope this subject may never be renewed, Mr.
Moodcy, that it may be forgotten, and everything go on
the same as before it was broached."

" Wal, I reckon not. I can hire my work better done
for less money. There is Phebe Shooks could do as

much as you and Gelly both, and not think it was no great shakes nuther; and my store needs a new front with a plate-glass window bad. How much do I owe you?"

"Only a trifle."

"You may live to see the time when you won't think a fifty-cent greenback a trifle, but that is your hunt, not mine. You are welcome to your night's lodging, and you can finish that cambric set you are at work on to pay for your breakfast."

She drew one long breath, then applied herself steadily to the completion of the task assigned her, her thoughts busy with the wretched experience she had endured, before reaching her present asylum. She called to mind the incidents occurring directly after her flight from home; the obscure inn where she had passed the first night thereafter; the shouts and stamping of a drunken vagrant who had been shut into the lock-up, directly beneath her chamber window for safe keeping; her terror at finding that her door was without fastening of any kind, and her attempts at improvising some such safeguard, resulting in breaking her scissors' points. Vividly also came back to memory her first essays in the search for employment; the paper she had bought of a newsboy, and the various applications she had been induced to make by its column of "Wants." At one shop she had been dismissed with a gruff churlishness from which she shrank sensitively like one wholly unused, as she was, to such style of address; while at a second, courteous regret was expressed by its proprietor at being unable to furnish employment, even to those who had been long in his service, and at a third she was directed to a distant part of the city in quest of a situation she was wholly incompetent to fill. Toward nightfall she had been sent to Miss Moodey, and, her brother happening to be in the house, he had, after a couple of days' trial of her skill with the needle, engaged her to do such light shop work as came easily within the scope of her ability.

When she had finished, folded and laid away the cambric set, she took the evening paper as usual, and commenced reading aloud to the employer who was hers no longer. He was evidently in no enjoyable mood, and her reading seemed rather to annoy than interest him. In the midst of an article selected expressly for his gratification, he abruptly left the room, and taking his hat from the entry table, strode out of the house. She did not see him again that night. Next morning she arose before any one else was astir in the house. She was strongly inclined to steal away without leave-taking of any kind; but on second thought was forced to the conclusion that this would be construed as an expression of resentment, which she neither felt nor desired to have unjustly attributed to her. Accordingly, the usual hour for breakfast found her seated at table. Mr. Moodey kept his eyes fixed on his plate, whose contents he disposed of with a great show of appetite. Lucy sipped her coffee without even the pretence of eating. Both rose at the same instant. She went round to his side, but without seeming to observe her, he stalked into the entry, and began hurriedly to thrust his arms into the sleeves of his store-coat. Not to be repulsed, she followed him into the entry, standing quietly by his side until he had no longer a shadow of excuse for fumbling with his coat buttons.

"I wish to thank you, Mr. Moodey, and to bid you good-bye."

"Good-bye," he curtly responded, starting for the outer door without noticing the hand she held toward him. He turned the handle to the latch, then hesitated, looking back to her a little ruefully.

"It's all your own doing," said he; "you wouldn't

have me; but for all that, you can refer to me if you ain't got nobody else to speak up for you."

She was at his side in an instant, a look of deep gratitude on her face, her little hand resting in his broad palm.

" I shall always remember this kindness, Mr. Moodey, for it is little enough I may receive from others."

" If the world does not use you well, come back to me."

He closed the door heavily behind him, and the parting was over.

Once more Lucy went forth a homeless wayfarer, seeking some mode by which to obtain needful shelter, food, and raiment.

—◆◆◆—

CHAPTER XXI.

ADVICE GRATIS.

A SECOND time our houseless wanderer has secured for herself a place of shelter which she calls home—a cheerless place it is, too ; a skylighted attic room with bare floor, a narrow cot with palm-leaf mattress and scant covering, and the single wooden chair in which she is constantly seated, save at meal times and during the hours of nightly rest.

The various articles of boys' wearing apparel strewn over the bed plainly indicated the occupation to which she was applying herself. Perseveringly she stitched away at the Grecian jacket she held in her numb fingers, pausing occasionally to chafe them into warmth ; for the day was chill, and through the narrow door to her room came but a faint glow of warmth from the open stove in the hall three stories lower down. There were no means for lighting a fire in her chamber, and even had there been, she would not have permitted herself the luxury of a separate fire, although the hacking cough that so often interrupted her work rather increased than abated in severity. By such slow, insidious approaches did it undermine her strength, that when, one morning, she found herself unable to leave her bed, she could scarcely believe that she was really ill.

"I must get up ; I *must* finish this suit of silver grey, as it is for a customer on the first floor whom I dare not disappoint."

Repeatedly, resting her head on her pillow, she strove to go on with her task ; but was as often baffled in the attempt, and was finally forced to abandon the futile effort.

Next day she was able to sit up, wrapped in her shawl ; but her needle was an implement beyond her power of grasp for more than a few minutes at a time.

The suit of clothing she was so desirous to finish had come to her, folded in a newspaper. This she removed, glancing occasionally at any short article that happened to arrest her notice. Thus it chanced that her eye fell upon an advertisement inserted at the behest of one Dr. Irlingham, solely, thus ran its purport, in the interest of suffering humanity. The most obstinate cases of cough, with attendant symptons of lassitude, depression, wakefulness, and kindred disarrangement of vital action, had disappeared as if by magic beneath the marvellous efficacy of the treatment which had constituted the advertiser one of the most distinguished benefactors of his race. Testimonials to this effect had been received and could, if needful, be produced, from some of the highest mag-

nates in the land, from New England's rock-bound coasts
to California's golden placers; men who had been
snatched from the very jaws of disease, and restored to
a state of robust vigor never previously enjoyed. The
great medical desideratum, the most serious want of
the age, had at last been vouchsafed to the unwearied
scientific research, the laborious investigation, the patient and protracted experiments in combination, analysis and effect, that had finally resulted in a new method
of cure, at once eradicatory and invigorating, acting
entirely in harmony with every vital law, both organic
and functional—always an aid, never a hindrance, to the
benign processes by which nature seeks to repair the
ravages of disease. In order that no one might be deprived of the benefits of the wonderful remedies, it was
a cruelty to withhold from the suffering sick, from the
fact of being unable to afford the large fees with which
his more wealthy patrons liberally rewarded his invaluable services, the doctor had set apart Wednesday afternoon of every week in which to receive patients of limited means, when all who called at his office might rely
on obtaining a full and accurate diagnosis of the disease
from which each was suffering, together with professional advice, free of all charge to applicants.

"It is Wednesday afternoon," thought Lucy, "and I
would very much like to know whether I am only a
little ailing or really ill. What is there to prevent my
consulting the doctor? It can do no harm, and will
cost me nothing more than the effort of a long walk. If
I find it to be too long, I have only to turn back."

She started; the clear, bracing air invigorated her,
and the walk was accomplished with much less fatigue
than she had anticipated.

A small boy admitted her to an ante-room leading to
the inner professional sanctuary, and in this hall of admission she was desired to wait for the termination of

an interview with another patient, who soon made her
appearance, in the form of a red-faced Irish girl, who
gave vent to her dissatisfaction by this muttered protest :

"Two-an'-saxpence for a plaster, or a poultice, which
ivir ye calls it, to put on mi arm, to aise this raging
pain in mi tooth. Bi St. Patrick's day in the mornin'
but it's an impersition, when it's mysel' could get the
whole thing, ache and all, dhrew out for a quarter ; bad
cess to it, but that is twice more nor the old shell is
worth !"

Lucy was shown into the presence of this distinguished
benefactor of his race. He was a man of severe and
awe-inspiring dignity, as became one of faculty so pre-
ëminent. The closeness of his scrutiny startled her
with the impression of having met him before. An
attack of coughing forced her to turn her head aside,
and he improved the occasion by drawing a thick Vene-
tian blind over the window.

With an air of grave and weighty deliberation he
pondered the symptoms of her case, which he seemed to
comprehend, aided by a very slight amount of information obtained from her. A stethoscope was next
brought into requisition, the following announcement
proclaiming the result of his auscultation :

"The case is one that will require great care on your
part, eminent skill on mine, to prevent the formation of
tubercles on the lungs, incipient stages of such formation being already unmistakably discernible. I can at
present do nothing more than arrest the progress of the
disease ; and when I have counteracted and subdued
the abnormal action of the entire respiratory organs, I
shall be better able to decide whether your ultimate recovery be within the bounds of possibility. You have
neglected yourself too long ; had you come to me a few
weeks earlier, your disease would have been perfectly

amenable to active treatment, and even now I am not prepared to assert that it will not yield to appropriate remedies. I will put you up some medicines which will act as alleviatives, if not of direct curative power. It is something to be made comfortable where it is impossible to secure at once the renovated vigor of perfect health."

Some tiny powders, neatly folded, and a couple of phials filled with a liquid compound, he was doing up for her, when a sound from the ante-room attracted his notice. He paused to listen.

" He is busy and not to be disturbed, sir," said the boy by whom Lucy had been admitted.

" Busy or not, he will see me, and that with little delay," persisted a second speaker, in cool, determined tone.

" It is my orders not to admit any one when he is engaged with a patient, and I can't break rules," remonstrated the boy.

" Stick to your rules, and I will admit myself," said the new comer.

The doctor passed hastily into the ante-room, carefully closing the door behind him ; but the latch not catching securely in the socket, the handle turned, leaving the door ajar, so that Lucy could not avoid hearing what passed between the speakers in the adjoining apartment.

" Dr. Denton, if I have been rightly informed," was the first salutation that caught her ear.

" Dr. Irlingham at your service," blandly corrected the doctor.

Lucy had started and changed color at the mention of this name, Denton, calling to mind her impression of having seen him before—an impression since obliterated by the overpowering anxiety excited by his alarming account of the state of her health.

"I have good grounds for believing," persisted the first speaker, "that you are the same person renting the small office in"——

" Leave the room," broke in the doctor, addressing small boy, who made his exit accordingly.

" Now, sir, I will listen to what you have to say."

" I simply repeat my assertion, that you are the same person passing under the name of Denton at the small office in the rear of the Ironside Apothecary shop."

" Allow me to ask what induced this surmise on your part ?"

"It is no surmise, but a certainty. I went to the office I have already mentioned in search of Dr. Denton, and found only his assistant or accomplice—suit yourself to terms—who informed me that you was only there at stated hours of specified days; but when I threatened him with a caning if he didn't tell me where you was ordinarily to be seen, he prudently divulged."

" A most singular and high-handed mode of procedure, upon my soul."

" Don't try the outraged-dignity dodge on me; that cat won't jump. My object was to find you, and I generally succeed in any deliberately-formed purpose of mine."

" Your success in the present instance shall be rewarded by an explanation it will cost me but a trifling waste of breath to make. When old Dr. Denton retired from the profession, I paid him a handsome bonus for the office he vacated, and for the practice that went with it. This practice was, in medical parlance, a *specia'ty ;* and when those afflicted with the special ailments he had for many years successfully treated came to me for relief, mistaking me for the man to whom they had been recommended by those he had cured, I let the mistake pass uncorrected, as it harmed no one and benefited me."

"That it benefited you, I have not a shade of doubt; whether or not it harmed any one is an open question."

" I beg your pardon, it is not an open question ; my time is too valuable to be thrown away in profitless altercation. I have already deigned a more ample explanation than any mere stranger is entitled to expect. If you desire medical aid, command me, sir ; otherwise I will return to my interrupted duties."

" First there is a little account to be settled between us. I would like the amount of your charges against my niece, Roberta Fay."

" I'm too busy to attend to it now, as I cannot spend time to look over my books."

" I can await your leisure ; but this room I do not leave until our account is squared."

" Very well, if you can wait, I will set aside all considerations of mere personal convenience while complying with your demands."

" I can wait," was the laconic response.

After a brief absence the doctor returned, saying :

" Here is your bill, sir."

Then followed a brief silence, broken by the exclamation :

" Three hundred dollars ! for what ? You never visited my niece twenty times."

" I do not charge for visits, but for entire course of treatment. It was a very obscure and complicated case, requiring a great amount of study ; and the medicines which I supplied were difficult to procure, and of the costliest description."

" I understand their value quite as well as yourself, and refuse, point blank, to pay the bill."

" Then I will give it to a lawyer for collection."

" You can't be too quick about it. When I found that it was Arnold Clermont who recommended my niece to apply to you for advice, I at once suspected a systematic course of fraud and imposition, with the extortion naturally accompanying that style of sharp practice."

"Arnold Clermont! what do you know of him?"

"I have practised for the last ten years in the Paris hospitals, and one learns strange secrets in that sort of confessional at times; however, that has nothing to do with the present case, and I never play the part of informer, unless it be to subserve the purposes of justice, or to protect the interests of society."

"Who are you?"

"Dr. Chillingford is the name, and the only one, I answer to. Thanks to the medicines supplied by you, portions of which my niece still retains, and to her account of herself, I am able to furnish you with a tolerably exact analysis of the mode of treatment adopted in her case. She was on her way to a private concert, where she had a solo to sing, and being somewhat hoarse from the effects of a slight cold, she was induced, by an acquaintance, to procure a box of your pulmonic wafers to clear her voice. She added to her cold by exposure, became feverish, and you was sent for. Instead of prescribing the simple emollient drinks which were all she needed, you greatly exaggerated the gravity of the case, thoroughly alarming my widowed sister— the most credulous creature alive—by allusions to diptheria; and ended by administering quinine and other powerful tonics, until her system was toned into a violent fever. When this had burned itself out, and nearly all the victim's vitality with it, instead of striving to repair the wasted tissues by some light form of nutriment, you gave her calomel until she was salivated, and every tooth in her head was loosened. To fill up the measure of your iniquities, you stilled her restlessness by various preparations of morphia, and when her nervous system was so completely shattered that her sight grew morbid, imaginary goblins and phantoms flitting about her bed, you coolly inquired if insanity were hereditary in the family.

"I found her too weak to raise her hand to her head, doomed, in all probability, to become a life-long invalid. I have heard of overworked army surgeons whipping off a leg to save the care and attention necessary to the restoration of the mutilated member, and of young practitioners who were far too ready to use the saw, the lancet, and the ligature, for the sake of acquiring expertness in handling the same ; but never so wanton a disregard of the most ordinary laws of hygiene as you have exhibited in the present instance. Such inhuman malpractice, persisted in for the sole purpose of extorting exorbitant fees from profitable patients, ought to be a legally indictable offence ; but there is still a corrective for this species of empirical fraud—public exposure. I am well known in this city, where I was born and bred ; if I cannot otherwise procure the insertion of an article in the daily papers, I can afford to pay for such insertion. I make no threats. Leave that little bill for collection whenever it suits your convenience. Good day, sir."

When Dr. Irlingham came back to her, Lucy noticed that his eyes were lit by an angry flame, and his features working with rage. He walked about the dimly lighted room, seeming scarcely aware of her presence.

"I am in haste," she ventured, as a reminder, being anxious to escape before his attention was again specially directed to herself, "and would like the little parcel you were preparing for me."

"Thank you, certainly ; I will attend to it," he abstractedly replied.

She saw that his hand was unsteady as he folded the

paper about phials and powders, and knotted the small
pink cord binding the same; handing them to her
with the remark, " Advice gratis; only your medicines
to be paid for; five dollars you are indebted to me."

She could ill afford the outlay; but so anxious was
she to leave the office without being recognized, that
she hesitated not a moment in complying with his
demands.

" I shall expect to see you one week from to-day,"
said the doctor, " unless you should become worse,
in which case I am to be immediately informed of the
fact."

It is hardly necessary to state that she left, firmly
resolved never to repeat her visit.

In the evening, her boarding-house-keeper came up to
Lucy's room, making inquiries for her health, and
advising her to consult one of the boarders, a physician
formerly renowned for skill, but who had, years since,
retired from active practice.

" We all consult him for little ailments," pursued
Miss Lunt; " for since his son threw up a profitable
business and enlisted as private in a regiment of volunteers, Dr. Croyland is more glad to see us than when
he had Leonard with him every evening."

Lucy readily acceded to Miss Lunt's proposal; and
the latter, after conducting her to the doctor's sitting-
room, introduced her and withdrew.

To his questions, few and adroitly worded, Lucy
readily replied; and then requested his opinion as to
the ingredients of the liquid compounds she had a couple
of hours previously obtained from Dr. Irlingham.

Her newly selected advisor took the phials, critically
examining their contents, an odd smile curling his lip
the while.

" Can you tell what they are composed of?" she
asked.

"With sufficient exactness to answer all practical purposes. I should pronounce the liquids to be highly spiritualized solutions of molasses and water, colored with red saunders, and tinctured with sassafras and cardamom seed to cover the smell and taste. Let me avail myself of the privilege conferred by age and experience, by earnestly warning you against the pernicious practice of dosing yourself with drugs in any form whatever. You need nothing of the sort. Your cough is nothing serious. Your ills will cure themselves in time. Keep yourself in cheerful spirits ; exercise as much as you can without fatigue ; and have no apprehensions for the future. I beg your pardon ; if you have formed a clandestine marriage—I would not for an instant be guilty of the disrespect of supposing you single—you should at once insist on its acknowledgment. The kindness of my motives will, I trust, excuse the plainness of my speech. Should you desire to consult me again, my advice, whether friendly or professional, is freely at your service."

With a heavy step and heavier heart, Lucy returned to her room, and sat down face to face with the new aspect of affairs the physician's disclosure had presented to her.

"Have no apprehensions for the future," she repeated. "How can I help such apprehension? I can just support myself by working steadily ; but, when I cannot work at all, with additional expenses, too, what is to become of me?"

She rose, closed the door to her room, turned the brass button constituting its fastening, wrapped herself in her warm shawl of tartan plaid, drew her chair beside the bed, and, folding her arms across the pillow, rested her head thereupon, giving way to one of those passionate outbursts of weeping that exhaust the physical energies without bringing solace to the sorely laden spirit.

15

When her grief had had its way, she strove to rouse herself from the apathy succeeding it.

"This is not obeying the doctor's directions and being cheerful," she said to herself. " I ought to be glad that my cough is nothing serious ; but I am too miserable to be glad of anything just now. It won't mend matters to gloze them over even in my own thoughts. It is a thorny path that first false step of mine has forced me into, and I must follow it as best I can, not disguising from myself the fact that it was my own misdoing which brought me to this forlorn pass. No matter how unworthy the conduct of M. Meurice, his wrong-doing doesn't palliate mine. It was only through treachery to another that I placed myself in his power. My conscience does not accuse me falsely when it tells me I did my best to attract the notice I coveted, while caring nothing for him by whom it was bestowed—that I strove to win admiration simply from love of admiration—a game as unsafe as ungenerous for any woman to venture on ; but, since I made the venture, I must even take the consequences I cannot escape. Where is the use of fretting and worrying about what can't be helped? I must not waste my strength in this way, for my strength is all I have to depend on now—now, when I feel the need of kindly care as never in my life before. I will not think of this; my energies shall be put to better use."

She dried her eyes, opened the door, lit her lamp and set it in the chair, folded her shawl, and, placing it on the floor as a seat, resolutely went to work on the suit of boys' clothing which was nearly completed. Weakness soon compelled her to relinquish the vain effort of proceeding with her task.

After a few minutes' reflection, she went down four flights of stairs to the kitchen, where, in a corner, cleaning plated dish-covers, sat the trim, buxom German girl

who performed all acts of household service with such a
ready graciousness that one was disposed to ask them as
a favor rather than demand them as a right. To her
Lucy made appeal.

"I know, my good Minchen, that you have more than
enough to do, but I am sure you will give me a slice of
bread and a glass of water when I tell you I have eaten
nothing since breakfast."

"Eaten nothing since breakfast," said the good-natured
cook; "that isn't right. No one can work and fast both
at once. Sit here while I toast your bread quite nicely.
Then I shall pour you out a cup of broma. See how
bright the cup is. I like my block tins to look like
silver, so I always give them a rub with silver powder
whenever I dry them with a towel; that is the way
Madame Müller taught me—I lived with her since when
I was a child—but she had real silver, and such beautiful
ways. She paid my fare when we came over to this
country, and I thought to live with her always, but she
died, and I have been with Miss Lunt ever since. She
is kind to me, but not like my lost mistress. There,
your cocoa has warmed by the steam from this kettle;
you must have a clean napkin on a corner of the table,
with toast and a bit of cold chicken left from dinner.
Does it look inviting?"

"I am sure it does, you dear, good Minchen, all the
more so from your kindness in being so willing to get it
for me."

"Shall I go away, or stay and wait on you?"

"I shall require no waiting on; but there is no occasion for your leaving; you are so cheerful that I like to
hear you talk."

"That isn't the reason I like to listen to every word
you say, which is because you speak to me as one lady
speaks to another, and that makes me think of dear
Madame Müller, who hadn't one way of speaking for

the gentry and another for poor folks, who feel the difference if they say nothing. If you wouldn't mind, I would like to ask why you didn't come down to dinner and to tea."

" Because I felt so miserable I preferred going without my meals—I didn't miss them much—to meeting all the boarders at table."

" That is too bad ; if you feel no better to-morrow, you shall not come down, and you shall be served equal to the very best. I will find time to make you a soup so very nice as you shall not often see. I learned to make it in the old home-land ; listen, you shall know. A bone so slowly stewed all the morning, so carefully skimmed, then vegetables, celery, anything, chopped very fine and stewed very much all the same, salt and pepper you know very well without me, all to be strained, and the soup put back in the stew-pan, with bread-crumbs one half tea-cupful, and mace and macaroni. You shall like the German cookery, I know, and I shall bring it up to you myself."

This expression of simple good-will deeply moved its recipient, and she desired in some way to testify her appreciation of the same.

Unfastening from about her neck the narrow linen band answering the purpose of collar, she handed it to the girl.

" It is hardly worth the giving, but I am poor like yourself."

Minchen drew back.

" I thank you all the same, but I am well paid for all I do here ; I have money laid by out of my earnings."

" But money will not buy kindness such as you have shown me, Minchen ; and I had thought you might be pleased to accept a proof of kindness, trifling though it be, in return."

"I am much bound to you," returned Minchen, no longer declining the proferred gift.

Strengthened by food, consoled by the ready sympathy of one whose fortunes, humble as they might be, were, nevertheless, superior to her own, Lucy went back to her attic room, plying her needle diligently until her task was completed.

CHAPTER XXII.

CHANCE ENCOUNTERS.

As Lucy sat, next day, pondering over the ways and means by which her expenses might be lessened, her income augmented, arriving, it must be confessed, at no very satisfactory result to her cogitations, she bethought her of the small amount of jewelry which had once been her mother's, but was now indubitably her own. It had not occurred to her to take it with her on forsaking her former luxurious home. Was it yet too late to remedy the oversight? To be sure, the rings and buckles were old-fashioned and ill-designed, but some of the settings were heavy, and could readily be disposed of as old gold. How to obtain possession of them, that was the question. The box containing them she had herself placed on the top shelf of her dressing-room closet, and presumed they had remained there untouched ever since. If she could but gain admission to the house unperceived, there would be little difficulty in the way of accomplishing her purpose. She determined to make the trial.

Possibly some vague desire of obtaining positive assurance of Mr. Caruthers' welfare; of looking once

more on the home to which, in thought, she often involuntarily returned with longing, lingering regret, may
have influenced her decision; if so, not even to herself
did she acknowledge such motive.

It was nearly sundown when she set forth, a thick,
brown veil effectually screening her features, in prosecution of her plan.

The distance from her boarding-place to the more
fashionable part of the city was so great that, deciding
the walk to it would consume more time than she had
to spare, she entered an omnibus, which set her down
within a square of Mr Caruthers' stately mansion. The
rear garden gate leading thereto, she entered without a
shadow of hesitation; for even if discovered by one of
the servants, she wore not an article of dress that could
provoke recognition, and had only to ask if Mr. Hun-
ter, the gentleman next door, lived there, to account
plausibly for her intrusion.

Fortune seemed to befriend her, for she made her
way undiscovered, to the rear angle of the conservatory.
A sash was up to air the plants, which were dripping
with water, showing that they had just been showered
from the hose still lying in coils on the perforated marble floor. The man in charge of the floral department
had evidently been called away in the midst of the
showering process, and was liable at any moment to
return and drop the sash. Not an instant was to be lost.
She darted through the conservatory into a narrow passage used only by the servants, and up a side staircase
rarely used at all. When nearly at the top of the
stairs, she stopped, rooted to the spot. Directly in front
of her, but with his back toward her, stood the colored
florist, whose temporary absence from his sphere of duty
had afforded her means of ingress, disentangling a ball
of coarse twine, with which to fasten some creepers
to their trellises.

Lucy's courage almost failed her. Should she fly while still the way of escape was open to her? More than half resolved to make the attempt, she turned to retrace her steps, when a new complication presented itself in the shape of a house-maid coming along the passage, trolling snatches from a popular minstrel melody to which the florist roared in hilarious response—

"Lubby Rosy, Sambo come,
Don't you hear the banjo tum, tum, tum?"

The bearer of broom and dust-pan hushed her voice and entered the conservatory.

Lucy's heart beat high. Between these two horns of a dilemma what but a bare possibility remained to her of escaping both? She crouched, breathless, upon the stairs. Her last chance of escape seemed vanishing when the maid came to the foot of the stairs calling out in high dudgeon,

"Here, Lonzo, you miserable brack sheep; didn't you tell me to go an' sweep up de leaves, an' habn't you dun gwine made such a swash, there ain't no doin' nothing in such a puddle?"

"Don't waste your bref, lubby Rosy, a-chiding dis chile; but jus cum and help discumstrangle dis drefful snarl wid your lubly, limber fingers."

Lucy was calculating the chances of being handed over to the police on the charge of entering a dwelling with intent to steal, and the slender probability of being able, in such case, to conceal her identity, when her apprehensions were partially lulled by the saucy response.

"I'se got oder fish to fry. When dis darkey gets in a snarl she jes gets out on't, no tanks to nobody; but some gemman's fingers is all t'umbs, and dey's so tick skulled, so tick skulled. Hi, hi."

"Gets in a snarl an' gets out on't, does she? we'se see 'bout dat; we'se see 'bout dat," muttered the incensed Lonzo, moving off at a quick pace toward the stairway leading to the kitchen domain.

Once more Lucy breathed freely. To the last speaker's diversion from his original plan of procedure, and to the favoring darkness of the unlighted staircase where she crouched, she owed her escape from detection.

Rapidly completing the ascent of the stairs, she cautiously made her way to the chamber from which her dressing-room opened. To her inexpressible chagrin, she found the door between the two rooms locked, and the key withdrawn. There was no help for it; she must leave without accomplishing the design for which she had risked so much. She had nearly reached the door, in pursuance of this intent, when the sound of a firm, manly step ascending the front staircase defeated her purpose. She just had time to conceal herself behind the silken curtains depending from the canopy over the bed, before Mr. Caruthers entered the room, dropped the draperies over the windows, turned on the gas which had been dimly burning at his entrance, sat down at a marble slab beneath the burner, and commenced assorting some papers which he drew, one by one, from a large gutta-percha envelope he held in his hand. Coming to a written schedule, he unfolded it, reading the names and commenting thereon in an under-tone, as his listener had heard him do on a previous occasion. Here is a sample of his style:

"Eben Whipple—five hundred—good, but slow pay; needs looking after. Peter Stringer—two thousand, charged off to profit and loss—no calculator—goes in at high figures and gets aground when the tide turns— no nerve; never can hold on for prices to rise—no caution; sells right and left, his profits eaten up by bad debts. He had better clerk it by half, I'll write and tell him so; take ten cents on a dollar, and wind it up. Chase and Longwood—up to sharp practice—can pay but don't mean to—property enough, but held in some other person's name. Have no idea of being jewed out of three thousand by them. Will put my account in the hands of a clear-headed lawyer who lives near them, and if that don't open their eyes and bring them to terms, they will get law enough before they get through with it. I can stand the expense as long as they can."

Lucy was in terror lest one of her attacks of coughing should come on; but again fortune befriended her, or otherwise, as the event might have proved, and the irritability of her throat was scarcely felt for the time.

So apparently absorbed was Mr. Caruthers in the furtherance of his own projects, that she ventured to move slightly so as to obtain a side-view of his face. He looked so strong, so resolute, so well able to defend her from any adverse blow, whatever the quarter whence it came, that instinctively the desire arose within her to give her weakness the prop of his strength.

"If I could only reveal to him my real motives for deserting him," she said to herself; "only explain to him why I was compelled to leave, I should at least regain my old place in his esteem, be comforted by his forgiveness, and reassured by his counsel. It cannot be. I must not deceive myself; his esteem would not content me; nor his counsel, however kindly, still these miserable longings for more heartfelt and endearing sympathy. Further than that, such a course on my part would but endanger his safety. Well I remember his look as he said of M. Meurice, 'Let him cross my path and see how he comes out.' What deadly malignity, too, had gleamed in the eyes of Monsieur, as he told

15*

her of the man who was assassinated in the street for revenge.

"If I confess all to Mr. Caruthers," she reflected, "his first step would be to call M. Meurice to account, and where it would all end, Heaven only knows. Am I to be a source of contention, of bloodshed perhaps, between these two? Never. Both are safe in my absence, safe let them remain. Whatever happens to me, my conscience shall be burdened by no fresh misdoing. It is no more than right that everything should go on the same; that I should not even be missed here; but it is hard, harder than I could have believed, to bear. Imperative duty forbids that my heart should flow out to him, but he knows no such stern check to faithful remembrance of me."

Tears of tender regret, which she strove to repress, half fearing them to be wrong, welled up to her eyes.

There was the sound of a second and lighter step on the stairs. The door opened, and Miss Dian Caruthers, in superb walking costume, entered the chamber.

"They told me you was in the house, Kilby, and as I am in a hurry, I preferred looking you up myself to waiting the slow movements of a servant. You will go with us to the Irlinghams to-night."

He shook his head.

"Really it is insufferably tiresome of you," she remonstrated, "now that you have so far recovered the use of your arm as to dispense with a sling, to stay moping at home in this absurd way."

"You jump to hasty conclusions. I have an engagement that calls me in another direction."

"Defer it, then; for I assure you this evening's entertainment is well worth attending. There are to be private theatricals, and Dr. Irlingham himself is to take the part of the 'social bandit' in the new drama entitled, 'Every man for himself, and the de'il take the hindmost.' With his talents, he will personate the character admirably; he can be so elegant and ingratiating in demeanor, or so dark and stormy, as the exigencies of the scene may require."

"I can find enough of that sort of personation in real life, without going to see it acted in plays."

"I see how it is, Kilby. You have been the sport of a heartless coquette's whims and caprices, and it has embittered you toward all the world beside. It does seem strange to me that you, who are usually so self-poised, so judicious, so little apt to be blinded to your own interests by any undue ascendency of feeling over interest and judgment, should exhibit the weakness of taking deeply to heart the desertion of a woman who was never worthy of you—a woman of scarcely average intelligence, of no remarkable personal attractions, fickle and false; a mere human butterfly, with about as much sense of moral responsibility as one of those light-winged, brainless insects."

Lucy drew a hard breath through her firm-set teeth, a burning spot of red on either cheek. She had not an instant to wait for Mr. Caruthers' rejoinder:

"You forget, Dian, that it is my wife of whom you are speaking."

"Forget it! I wish I could," she impatiently retorted, "as well as the fact that she has given the busy tongue of scandal an excuse to prate of the affairs of a family never before debased by such prating. She has made our honored name that, within my memory, never knew a stain, a theme for coarse innuendo and dishonorable allusion; and yet she, having found her way to the one weak spot in your heart, which knowledge she artfully and selfishly turns to her own advantage, brands your name with infamy; and you are too blind to see this, or too weak to defeat the machinations that make

348

you the puppet of a light woman's will. Perhaps no one has told you of the rumors that are rife on the street, and have even reached your servants' ears; perhaps no one dares mention them to you, but I dare to speak what it is for your interest to know. Report says that Mrs. Caruthers did not leave the city alone. The music-master with whom she used to flirt at every opportunity was seen to leave your garden the very afternoon she left your house."

"Hush! Dian, there are some things which, even from a sister, I will not bear. Bring me no lying rumors, I will not give them a thought. Though appearances were a thousand times against her, I would sooner suspect them of deceitfulness than suspect her. Until she is proved faithless—and such proof, in my opinion, her worst enemies will never succeed in bringing to light—my faith in her remains unshaken."

"If you are still so credulous, so ardently desirous of being imposed upon, that this is the ultimate decision at which you have arrived, why, even be consistent and cherish your fond delusion till the clear light of truth shows you that it is such. By all means use every effort to trace her flight; and if facts warrant a separation, I trust it may be final, and your release from her toils complete. In the meantime I am willing to do anything in my power to make your life more tolerable than it seems to be at present. If you desire it, I will come and take charge of your household, as I did before this ill-starred marriage of yours."

"Thank you; I am at home but little, my servants are trustworthy and efficient; and as for company, I have neither time nor inclination for it, and have the less need for any one to preside at table or in the drawing-room."

"The time was, Kilby, when my society was not irksome to you; but I will not speak of that, since it annoys you. The time may come when a sister's presence will be not only tolerated but welcomed. Since you will not come with me, I must go without you."

She left, and her brother returned to the employment her entrance had interrupted.

Tears, wrung forth by the violent alternations of feeling occasiond by the above dialogue, fell, drop by drop, from Lucy's brimming eyes. The conflicting emotions by which she was agitated it is impossible to describe. The sister's scathing strictures had cut her to the quick, but their effect had been greatly softened by the brother's chivalrous interposition in her defence. " No matter how much appearances may be against me," she said to herself, " he sooner trusts me than them ; and his faith in me strengthens my faith in myself. I cannot see my way very clearly, or very far in advance; but so far as I do see it, I will walk as circumspectly as though he were with me watching every step."

He was writing rapidly on a small-sized commercial sheet when the bell rang for tea. He rose, on completing a sentence, and left the room, locking the door after him, and taking the key from the lock. She was startled and unable to account for a procedure so unusual. Waiting until the sound of his retreating footsteps had ceased on the stairs, she emerged from her place of concealment and approached the slab at which he had been writing. Piles of United States bonds, easily recognizable through their prevailing tint of green ; notes and acceptances, filed in bands of labelled paper ; certificates of railway and mining shares, with other documents of kindred stamp, sufficiently explained the reason for his leaving the door securely fastened, little drea ning whom he had thus made prisoner. This was the hour on which she had calculated for escape ever since his entering the room, and by how slight a mischance had her purpose been thwarted. If he stopped to look at

the evening paper after tea, as was his custom, it
would make the hour late for her to be out in the
streets alone. She was anxious and restless, the sense
of close imprisonment growing momentarily more oppressive, when her eye was caught by the following
composition, on which Mr. Caruthers had been engaged
when interrupted by the summons to tea:

"*Description of Personal Appearance.*

"Mrs. Caruthers is five feet three inches in height,
with light, curly hair, very pleasant blue eyes, a clear
complexion, and a color in the cheeks not dark enough
to be called red; a straight nose; small, white, even
teeth, and dimples in cheek and chin. She is low spoken,
and slenderly built, having sloping shoulders and a
long, slim hand and foot. She walks without any
swinging of the arms, or superfluous movement of any
sort, with an easy, gliding motion, like one who gets over
the ground with the least possible effort. Her dress
I cannot describe, as I find nothing missing from the
wardrobe she left behind at the time of her mysterious
disappearance; but her tastes were elegant and correct
in matters of dress."

Lucy turned away with a smile half sad half pleasurable on a face too pale by far to tally with the above
description.

"However much they may strive to prejudice him
against me, he still thinks me worth the seeking,"
thought she, "and I will never prove less worthy than
now."

She walked toward the mantel, when a new painting
hanging above it attracted her gaze; it was a full-length
portrait of herself in bridal attire. It must have been
copied from the photograph recently taken, she assured
herself, and colored from a miniature on ivory, painted
several years previously.

Passing on to the bureau, she pressed the spring to the satin-wood box, exquisitely carved and polished, in which her jewelry had formerly been kept, when it flew open, disclosing its contents more neatly and methodically arranged than they had been at the time of her departure. The ticking of her watch attested the fact of it having been wound up. A gold hair-pin that she had left minus several pendants, had been skilfully repaired; and a safety-chain added to a pearl brooch. There, fastened by a clasp of quaint workmanship, was the string of gold beads that her mother's mother had worn, and that she had sometimes used entwined with strings of pearls to adorn her own braided tresses. She drew the beads about her neck, and fastened the clasp at her throat; but after a minute's consideration, unclasped and removed the acquisition with such alacrity secured, saying to herself:

"It would be missed, and one of the servants suspected of purloining it. Even if it is rightfully my own, it is not right that I should take it in a way which would subject others to wrongful suspicion. It is easier, as I have learned through bitter teaching, to take the first wrong step than to retrace it, or to tell where it may lead."

Closing the box resolutely, she returned to her position behind the bed-curtains.

The minutes passed slowly; but after an absence that seemed to her much longer than it really was, Mr. Caruthers came back to the room, and seating himself at the slab, read over what he had written, and threw it aside with the muttered comment:

"Too fine by half. What do they know or care of a lady's gait, or her taste in dress?"

Taking a fresh sheet, he wrote awhile, then restoring his papers to their envelope, left the room with them. She waited until she heard him leave the house, before

venturing down-stairs. The hall was very light as she stole noiselessly across it. Cautiously drawing back the spring lock, she turned the handle, when, with a creak, the door swung back on its hinges; closing it hastily, she fled through the vestibule not an instant too soon, as she was convinced by the cry of a startled servant:
" Who's dere a-tamperin' wid dat lock ?"
The clock from a neighboring church tower was striking eight as she gained the sidewalk. As she peered apprehensively at the dark shadows cast by projecting angles and broad curves, she felt that the perils of her rash undertaking were by no means safely overpassed. If the omnibus office could but be reached, the worst would be over; for by the conveyance there procurable, she would be set down within a few doors of her boarding-house. The office was reached, her foot on the step, her hand on the latch, when the sound of voices in loud and angry altercation within caused her to hesitate and look through a glass panel of the door to ascertain the cause of the disturbance. Three or four young men sat smoking on a bench inside, while near the middle of the room, two men of maturer years stood confronting each other with mutual interchange of looks anything but conciliatory.
Said the shorter but more powerfully framed of the two :
" Unless the extinction of slavery is to be the price of our conquests, not one snap of my finger would I give for victories so fruitless. War, still war, shall be our battle-cry—who cries peace shall find that for him there is no peace—till this corroding rust is scoured from our national escutcheon. You say, sir, that, considering our superiority of men and means over those of the insur-gents, our arms have not been proportionately blessed. Granted; but why has disaster so often resulted from our best-planned campaigns? I reply, because there

are traitors at the North in league with traitors at the South—because the North does not band itself together as one man, and say to this accursed institution, 'Die thou shalt, and die thou must.' We must wipe out this foul stain before we can look for a blessing from on high."

"What would you have, in Heaven's name? A larger human sponge than the couple of hundred thousands we have already used up in this fierce fratricidal struggle? Can it be that the great 'I Am,' of mercy infinite, withholds his blessing that myriad hecatombs of fresh victims be offered up in sacrifice?"

"You are ready enough with your arguments; but I, for one, am for no temporizing policy with rebels, no compromise with traitors. This wicked and causeless rebellion, and slavery with it, must be crushed at all costs and all hazards. Right *must* prevail in the end."

"In the end, I grant you, but the end is not yet. While human nature is what it is, we must cultivate broader and more catholic charities. Religious tolerance—our fathers learned that lesson through many bitter teachings of Providence, and to us have transmitted it—is not the only kind of tolerance we have need to know and to practise, so long as the rain descends on the just and the unjust, and the tares are permitted to grow with the wheat."

"Then we are to let traitors in arms work out their designs in subverting the best government the world ever saw, through fear of rooting up the wheat with the tares; that is, through fear of harming the true and loyal men undoubtedly to be found under rebel rule."

"You purposely pervert my statement, knowing, as you do, that I came home on brief furlough, to be cured of wounds gained not in crying 'War, war!' but in doing my duty where hard blows are struck and brave lives are risked and lost in the nation's service; knowing, too, that within the week I rejoin my regiment. First and foremost, down with the rebellion, say I, and then down with everything, North and South, that stands in the way of a reconstruction of the glorious old Union, under the grand old Constitution our fathers framed."

One of the smokers hissed; a second cried, "Down with all Copperheads;" and, incited by these demonstrations, the shorter of the two speakers suddenly, with his clenched fist, aimed a blow at the taller, who, by a movement as sudden, and far more dexterous, parried the blow, and, seizing his assailant by both arms, pinioned them in a vice-like gripe to his sides.

Lucy stopped to see no more. Convinced that this was no place for a woman to await a conveyance, she sped swiftly down the narrow street and joined the throng passing down a broad, well-lighted thoroughfare. Soon leaving this, she entered an alley lighted at either corner by a single lamp, and directly after became aware of following footsteps, very nearly keeping pace with her own. Whether she hastened or retarded her steps, those of the person behind her accommodated themselves to her movements. She crossed to the opposite sidewalk, and her unknown pursuer unhesitatingly copied her example.

With a sigh of relief, she passed into a street brilliant with lights from shop and lamp, where she felt the protecting influence of numerous respectable-looking pedestrians. Among the numerous footfalls she could no longer distinguish that of her pursuer, and was about to congratulate herself on having escaped him, when a man took and maintained his place by her side. When passing beneath a street lamp, she succeeded in obtaining a view of his face, and recognized Dr. Irlingham.

Had he also recognized her? was the question she in-

stantly asked herself; and, in the interest of M.
Meurice, was he seeking to trace her to her place of
abode? If so, she must leave no means untried for
eluding his pursuit. But what possible means of escape
were at her disposal? At first, she could see none which
gave the slightest promise of proving effectual.

In passing a church, a stream of persons poured forth
from its vestry. Adroitly separating herself from her
attendant, she passed rapidly along in the shade of the
building, thus placing a string of passers-by between
herself and him. A new discovery: but a short distance in front of her walked one to whom, if driven to
extremity, her appeal for aid would not be made in
vain.

Her pursuer, baffled for but brief time, resumed his
place at her side.

"Take my arm," he said, peremptorily, "or you will
be lost in the crowd."

She no longer delayed her appeal to the tall, loose-
jointed individual who, with shambling gait, was making
his way before them.

"I am out later than I intended to be, Mr. Moodey,
having been unexpectedly detained; may I walk with
you as far as you are going my way?"

"In course you may, and as much further as you've a
mind to," was the hearty response. "Golly, I'm right
down glad to see you, and no mistake. I guess we'd
better lock arms, its easier to keep step."

She complied with the suggestion, and had the satisfaction of seeing Dr. Irlingham pass them, without turning his head, and disappear around the nearest corner.

No more danger of seeing him again to-night, thought
she; for he must hurry home and prepare to personate
the "Social Bandit" he acts to the life.

"I have something particular to say to you," confiden-
tially imparted Mr. Moodey to his companion, "as soon as

ever we can git out of all this hubbub; here is a nice
still street, what do you say to turning down it?"

"It is our nearest way, and I am too tired to walk
farther than I can help," she languidly assented.

"I've been sorry more'n fifty times that I sent you
away from our house; but I'll tell you what, you come
back, and we'll make up as good as pie. Don't you
mind nothing about the rig I run on when I was put out
with you for giving me the mitten right straight off the
reel. That was all bunkum; I don't care no more for
Pawliney Hotchkiss than I do for the fifth wheel of a
coach. Her temper is the reg'lar kyan pepper sort, and
she's a real tyke, if there ever was one. As for Phebe
Shoots, Gelly got her down to our house to stay a few
days, and she was so highty-tighty, and so full of her
pranks, that I couldn't get a minit's peace of my life,
and dropped her like a hot potater. Money isn't all,
and smartness isn't all, when a man is looking out for a
wife; it's something to find one that can be peaceable
and contented at home, without forever scooting round
the streets to show herself off, and putting on the purties
for outsiders, and all in the dumps if something in the
company line isn't going on. I'm willing to take all the
blame to myself for what has come and gone. I never
seriously made up my mind to git married before; and,
as it was ruther late in the day, I hadn't no time to lose,
and was in such a consarned hurry that I went a-head
like a down-river steamboat, a-gitting the horse before
the cart, a-popping the question before the sparking had
been gone through with at all. Now, if you are willing
to start fair, and try it all over again, I be. What do
you say?"

"That I thank you for your good opinion of me; and,
that you have shown me so much real kindness, it deeply
pains me to "——

"You needn't go no further. I don't owe you no

grudge, but I don't want to hear all that lockram over again."

They walked on in silence.

"I leave you here," she said, withdrawing her hand from his arm, on reaching a place whence their separate ways diverged.

"I don't mind going out of my way, if it will oblige you, Lucy."

She was touched by this kindly offer, after the second repulse with which she had been compelled to check his advances, and declined his escort in grateful terms.

"It's awful lonesome down to our house, Lucy, won't you come and see us sometimes?"

"Whether I come or not, Mr. Moodey, I shall never forget your kindness or cease to be thankful for it."

There was something really pathetic in the tone of his exclamation, "It's all over with, now," as she turned from him, leaving him to pursue his way alone.

On reaching her boarding-house, Miss Lunt followed her up to her room.

"You are out late to-night, Miss Searls."

"Yes; I was unexpectedly detained."

"Detained, where? if I may make bold to ask."

"At a house where I went hoping to obtain some articles of value that once belonged to my mother."

"You withhold name, street, and number, designedly so, I suppose."

Lucy bowed; Miss Lunt's manner was not calculated to invite confidence, being cold, prying, suspicious.

"I do not like to see young persons guardedly cautious of betraying any clue to their past life," she dryly remarked; "it looks as though there were something in that life that wouldn't bear the light of inquiry. Did you come home alone?"

"I had a friend with me a part of the way."

"Ah! 1 may be more fortunate in my present question perhaps. Who was this friend?"

"The man from whose shop I obtained work before I came here."

"Umph! where did you live when you worked for him?"

"I boarded with himself and sister."

"He was a single man, then."

"He was."

"Why did you not continue to procure work from him after you came here?"

Lucy hesitated, embarrassed for a reply.

"Because I wished the acquaintance between us to be wholly broken off."

"Why was that?"

"Because he had professed for me a regard I could never, under any circumstances, have reciprocated; and offered me lover-like attentions I was forced to discourage."

"You mean that he made you an offer of marriage."

"I do."

"Was he respectable?"

"Entirely so."

"Then I should most certainly advise you to encourage a renewal of his offer, and that with as little delay as circumstances will admit of."

"Impossible."

"Give me his name, and I may be able to bring about a better understanding between you."

"I thank you; but there is already a perfect understanding between us."

"Then I have nothing more to say on that point; but, on another, I have considerable to say. Have you any friend to whom you can refer me for assurance that your previous life has been irreproachable?"

"I am not, at present, in communication with any

of my friends," Lucy sadly replied, her eyes filling with the bitter sense of humiliation this question conveyed.

"I am sorry to hear it; for, without a satisfactory reference of the sort, you cannot longer remain with me. I have had a long talk with Dr. Croyland, who thought you might have some explanation to make that might justify my keeping you, but, as you vouchsafe not a word in your own vindication, you must submit to the natural consequences of such reserve. I shall tell the seamstress who has applied for your room that she can have it later in the week. I never was called a hard landlady by any of my boarders; but the respectability of my house is all I have to depend upon, and, even if so inclined, I could not afford to be lenient where that is concerned."

Lucy was too much overwhelmed by this new and unexpected blow to make any attempt at self-justification, and, serenely self-approving, Miss Lunt withdrew.

CHAPTER XXIII.

CONCLUSION.

STILL again our homeless outcast has been successful in obtaining shelter, and the employment by which she hopes to earn her bread.

In a small, lonely, out-of-the-way dwelling, at the foot of a shelving bluff overlooking the river, sat Lucy Searls, busily engaged in stitching on the visor to a soldier's cap. A straw matting on the floor, a bed in the corner, a braided rug on the hearth, a looking-glass in rudely carved walnut frame, a light-stand and a couple of cane-seated chairs, completed the furniture of the room she occupied.

The door opened, and a woman of lank and meagre frame, with features shrivelled by age, but eyes still bright, sharp and piercing, came in and sat down near a window looking out upon a limestone ledge, its monotonous surface here and there diversified by a stunted, leafless shrub protruding from cleft or crevice.

"You work too steadily, Miss Searls; you will soon wear yourself out at this rate. You cough more than is good for you, and you haven't so wholesome a color on your face as you had that first night you came here, and had such hard work to persuade me to take you in, which isn't to be wondered at, considering that I'm timersome and shy of stragglers, living all by myself, so far from neighbors. Harboring strangers is what I never did make a practice of; but I haven't been sorry for breaking through my rule this time, for you are quiet and easy satisfied, and don't bring no end of company to nasty up the steps and scraper, and track dirt into the house. I'd as lives have you here as not, as long as I don't lose nothing by it; and that is why I tell you that you mustn't stick to work from morning till night, day in and day out, if you don't want to make yourself down sick abed. What's to become of you, then? I'm sure the poor-house, or them genteeler places they call houses of refidge for indigent females, wouldn't suit the like of you."

Lucy's heart sank; but she had already learned, in her brief experience of struggling for a livelihood, to make no appeals to compassion on account of her comparatively destitute and dependent condition; least of all, would she have betrayed to the woman who had long been accustomed to make the pleasure of petty accumulated gains the primary object of her life, any signs of apprehension regarding her own ability for self-maintenance.

"By sewing all the time, excepting at dusk," resumed the Widow Smallmain, in a cold, hard, calculating tone, "you just make out to earn two shillings a-day, and that just pays your board. Where are your clothes to come from? I don't wish to be a-meddling with what ain't none of my business, but I must say that I should be a deal easier in my mind if I could see a little clearer how you are to pay your way."

Lucy gave her needle so vehement a thrust that it snapped short off in the resistant leather.

"There, child, now see what you have done. You must learn to be more careful; for even the breaking of a needle is no light matter when a person hasn't the means for buying another."

"I am not so destitute as your words would seem to imply. I need no clothes or sewing materials, at present; if I did, I have the means for procuring them. If I can earn my board I am perfectly satisfied; and if I should, now and then, have to give up work for a few days at a time, you needn't be afraid of meeting with any loss on that account."

"You don't say so! I'm a deal easier in my mind to know that you ain't really obliged to live from hand to mouth. I reckon you have been used to a profitabler trade than cap-making, and have laid by a spare penny for a rainy day."

The speaker waited for either a denial or confirmation of her surmise, but this allusion to her past life had awakened memories by which Lucy was too deeply moved to venture an immediate reply. When she did speak, it was in a tone studiously calm and restrained.

"I owe you many thanks, Mrs. Smallmain, for your kindness in procuring me work sufficient to defray your

16

weekly charges ; any small additional expenses I can pay
myself."

"That's the best news I've heard this many a day ;
for the fact is, I'm a little pinched to get along in these
times of high prices, when you can't have sugar to your
sauce, or a gown to your back, without eating or wearing a tax along with it. If you've got means to hender
it, I'm sure, after all I've done for you, giving you up
my best spare room, and drudging for you as I ain't
used to doing for nobody, you won't see me come to
want. If I should get really hard up, it's comforting to
know that I could borrow a five-dollar bill and get out
of the fix. I bought them candles you sent for, and
give two of them little ten-cent greenbacks and a postage
stamp for 'em ; you might as well fork over a quarter,
as I had to go a whole square out of my way to patronize
the tallow-man, and the extra wear of shoe-leather ought
not to come out of me."

Lucy drew out her purse, and handed her creditor the
required amount, the last silver coin in her possession.

"There is nothing like paying up prompt for what a
body must have ; and that is what I'm always trying to
ding into my nephew's head," said Mrs. Smallmain, with
an approving nod at her boarder. "I don't preach what
I don't practice neither. For instance, it's a sight cheaper
to buy flour by the sack than by the pound, as I have
done lately ; but I wouldn't buy the sack till I could
scrape together money enough to pay for it. Wal, I've
got enough now, into a dollar or so, and, if you've
a mind to advance that on your week's board, it will
make matters all straight. Much obleeged to you ; I
knew you would be accommodating after all the pains
I've took to help you to an honest living. I've been
meaning to speak to you about coffee ; it's got so dreadful high and skurce that I've concluded to use roasted
barley in place of it ; and tea has riz so that I've been

thinking of making it out of sage or spireal—there's lots of it up garret, if you wouldn't turn up your nose at such herb drink."

"Whatever suits you will suit me, Mrs. Smallmain."

"I'm glad to see you so reasonable and considerate. If you'd only said, 'I can put up with it,' that would have sounded kind of hash and fault-finding, and I couldn't put up with that nohow. There is one other thing that I might as well mention now it's on my mind. I agreed to do your plain washing, and I won't back out of my agreement; but white petticoats, with tucks all round, and serpentine trimming into the bargain, I won't sweat myself over for nobody. Folks that want to rig up in that style every day may do their own starching and ironing for all me. I should recommend your buying moreen, or something of that sort, that don't need doing up every week."

"I will attend to it as soon as I am a little over my hurry with this case of caps, which I promised to return as soon as I could possibly finish them."

"That will answer every purpose. You see you don't lose nothing by accommodating me. Since I've found out that you mean to do about what is right, I shall put up with some things, if they ain't quite so easy."

The speaker left the room, on economic plans intent, and seated herself by the kitchen fire, too much absorbed in her own penny-saving projects to listen to the pleasant drone of the tea-kettle humming on the hob.

It was nine o'clock when Lucy set her last stitch in her taskwork for the day. Then she took up the newspaper—bought of the milkboy twice a week, a day old, at secondhand—kindly loaned for her perusal, and tried to interest herself in its contents; but so vividly was she thereby reminded of an elegantly furnished apartment where she had, in times gone by, read aloud to an attentive and indulgent listener, that an aching sense of forlornness and isolation weighed down her spirits. She was about to lay the paper aside, when a name that seemed to burn through her eyes and brand itself in characters of fire upon her brain, caught her startled gaze. With quickened breath and bounding pulse, she read as follows:

"Arrest and Execution of a French Spy in Confederate Employ.

"A man of prepossessing and even elegant appearance, who has been closely watched for a month past, has been discovered visiting our arsenals, dock-yards, camps, and fortifications, where, under the pretence of being an official inspector in the Federal service, he has contrived to pick up a vast amount of valuable information, relating to our means of defence, as well as to the movements of our army and gunboat fleet; all of which information has been, it now seems, regularly transmitted to the enemy.

"Suspicion reached its climax when the aforesaid individual was detected in the act of drawing a plan of the earthworks intrenching the position held by a division of our corps, when he was at once arrested and placed under guard. The search which was immediately instituted, brought to light sufficient evidence of collusion with the enemy to subject him to rigorous confinement on the accusation of being a rebel spy.

"Amongst his effects were found rough draughts of letters addressed to various Confederate officers, high in rank, detailing the plans of the southwestern campaign, and suggesting measures for foiling the same, with much additional matter tending to the success of the insurgents and to the national disaster.

"Our informant, a gentleman of unimpeachable veracity and high intelligence, in regular correspondence with this journal, further learns that Arnold Clermont, the rebel emissary, belonged to an influential family of Normandy, of considerable note under the old *régime*, but that during the present imperial rule, his estate was confiscated and himself exiled, for some political offence of whose exact nature we are left in ignorance. Thus it would seem that, even in his own country, he was an accomplished and unscrupulous intrigant.

" For a year after coming to this State, he supported himself under another name, probably assumed from motives of family pride, by giving lessons in music; he having been previously an amateur pianist of no mean proficiency.

" The latter part of the year 1860, and the whole of the succeeding one, he passed in New Orleans, where he did military duty in the City Guard, with the rank of brevet major, and where also he joined a secret order of knighthood pledged to the overthrow of the present Government, and to the established supremacy of the so-called Confederacy.

" Sometime during the past year, he made, under an assumed name, and in violation of his sentence of perpetual exile, a short visit to his native land; but a letter from a southern officer, incautiously directed to his real address, placed him under the surveillance of the police, from which he escaped by speedy flight.

" So clear and conclusive was the evidence of his guilt, that, after being tried by court-martial, sentence of death was passed against him ; and he has, ere this, paid the penalty of his crimes. May the summary manner in which justice was awarded his deserts act as a warning to others suspected of treasonable intercourse with the enemy.

" A certain M.D., of wide-spread notoriety in his profession, was so deeply implicated in the affair that his arrest was ordered; but on instituting search for the culprit, it was discovered that he had suddenly decamped, leaving his tradesmen's bills unpaid, and numerous creditors minus their dues. His name we refrain from divulging, for the present, as the direction of his flight is more than suspected, and those who have the matter in charge do not yet despair of effecting his arrest."

"Thank Heaven, I had no hand in it," ejaculated Lucy, as with eager, yet shrinking gaze she read the article to its final word; "but, right or wrong, I cannot mourn for him."

For a half hour she sat motionless, thinking over the change thus effected in her own prospects, and the new line of conduct now open for her to pursue.

"There is no longer any valid reason for withholding any portion of the truth from Mr. Caruthers," she decided; "and when he knows all, I cannot think he will give me up; it would be too terrible. I cannot go to him, it would seem too much like claiming in his home a right which is not mine to claim, but I can write."

She lost no time in carrying this resolve into effect. All sense of fatigue was lost in the trembling anxiety with which she indited the following:

"DEAR MR. CARUTHERS:—Now that I am free to explain to you the cruel combination of circumstances that drove me from the happiest of homes, I am very anxious to see you, and to explain. When you know how I have been tried, and all I have suffered, working for my bread, as I never was taught to do, with no one to be glad if I succeeded or sorry if I failed, and these heavy secrets a dead weight on my spirits all the time, I hope you will not blame me for taking the only course that I thought right, and that promised to secure your safety.

"Even though I can plead no claim to your indulgence, save that of friendship and your unpaid guardianship of a penniless orphan, still you cannot leave me without a hearing, without being told that your desertion would place me in a position so cruelly false that I cannot look forward to it with anything like calmness or resignation.

" I know that you still care for me by the faithfulness —it is not wrong for me to tell you this, now, nor how hardly I have striven to master such remembrance— with which my thoughts turn ever to you.

"The time will be long till I see you here in the small brick cottage, at the foot of Mallow's Lane, which leads from Grove-Spring Avenue.

" I need not write you more as my hold on health is not firm ; and I am tired with sewing all day. Resting in the assurance of soon meeting you, I await your coming with patience."

She signed her name simply " Lucy ;" to what other could she lay claim !

Early next morning, she posted the above herself, awaiting the reply with a degree of unrestful impatience she vainly strove to overcome. For the first time, the caps on which she was employed were not neatly finished; and she received Mrs. Smallmain's strictures on her bungling seams with an unaffected indifference that strongly moved the ire of that notable dame.

One day, two, three, went by without bringing any tidings to the anxiously expectant Lucy ; and she grew sick with hope deferred. On the fourth day of this wearing suspense, she was forced to lay aside her work, to close the eyes that had been sleepless through the previous night, and to lean her aching head on the back of a chair.

Mrs. Smallmain repented her of her harshness, on seeing that Lucy was really too ill to work, and trundling a
hard hair-cloth sofa into her room, she graciously devoted it to her use. She couldn't help reflecting, however, in her capacity of economic housekeeper, that if
Lucy couldn't work, her board would be paid all the
same; and that an occasional bowl of herb tea was not
expensive fare to provide.

On her hard couch Lucy uneasily reclined, when the
sound of a manly step, quick, firm, decisive, in the outer
room, sent a glow to her pale cheek, an eager light to
her lustreless eye.

" She is too sick to see anybody, and she don't want
to see no company nuther; she has too much to do when
she can sit up, for wasting her time on visitors," Lucy
heard, in Mrs. Smallmain's high-pitched, shrewish tones;
" hows'ever, I'll speak to her, and let her know you are
here. if you want me to."

" Which is her room?" was the question impatiently
asked.

"That one; I will speak to her if you are bent
on "——

The door to her room opened and closed. Mr. Caruthers bent over her, raising her head to his shoulder as
tenderly as though she had been an ailing child, an
expression on his face no woman could misinterpret;
for the moment her content was boundless. Replacing
her head carefully on her pillows, he was the first to
speak :

" Unless you had very good cause for leaving me as
you did, Lucy, I shall not find it easy to forgive the
anxiety, the suspense, the agony of apprehension I have
suffered on your account. Then your letter—I was out
of town when it came, and only received it on my return this morning—instead of clearing up matters, made
them darker than ever. Not wrong to tell me that you

still cherish my memory; that's a riddle beyond my guessing. Entreating me not to desert you, when the reverse has been the case, and it was you who deserted me. Lucy, I never gave you the slightest occasion, by deed, word or thought, for writing to me as you have written."

" I did not intend to convey the impression that you had. The fault was wholly mine ; I broke faith with you, in the first place, in direct opposition to my own better convictions, and "——

"Don't rake up that old story ; it's past and forgiven."

" Bear with me this once, for from that one false step dates all my misery. I thought I had escaped its consequences when I found you was willing to reinstate me in your confidence and your regard, letting the past be as though it had never been; but the past was not so easily to be blotted out. I had suffered so severely through the deceptions practised by M. Meurice, as he called himself, that I had come to abhor deceit, whatever guise it took, and I did not intentionally deceive you when I told you "——

Her abrupt pause in her sentence was caused by the entrance of Mrs. Smallmain, who, knitting-work in hand, deliberately seated herself by the window commanding a view of the bluff.

Mr. Caruthers turned toward her, pointedly remarking, " I called purposely to see this lady, madam."

" So I supposed, sir. Don't stop to mind me; go on with your talk."

" I beg your pardon, but as our conversation is to be strictly personal, it would be simply tedious to an uninterested listener."

" Never mind me, sir. I'll resk being tedious. I reckon you wouldn't think I was uninterested if you knew all the pains I'd took to put her in the way of earning

16*

an honest living. To be sure she is kind o'tuckered out, sticking so close to work as she has along back, but it will come easier when she gets used to it. She ain't fit to see nobody to-day, and if you will come out in t'other room I can convince you that she is getting along fust rate, considering that cap-making is a new business for her; and don't need to put herself under obligations to nobody, which is what a young woman shouldn't never stoop to."

He turned quickly to Lucy.

" Have I wearied you ?"

" Not in the least."

He rose, politely held open the door for Mrs. Small-main to pass; with a courteous wave of the hand dismissing the reluctantly departing widow from further attendance.

" What was you saying, Lucy, in regard to not having intentionally deceived me ?"

" That in telling you my first marriage was not legally binding, I fully believed that I was speaking the truth, as I did but repeat the opinion of Lawyer Auverne that it was, to use his own words, null and void."

Mr. Caruthers looked doubtingly at the speaker, as if half inclined to question her sanity.

She caught the look, and rightly interpreted its unspoken language.

" You are mistaken; I have not been crazed by my trials, as you will perceive when I have told you all. I met M. Meurice, under another name, at Lily Barton's birth-night party "——

" Ah! it is your foolish habit of keeping things to yourself, and acting on your own judgment, that is always getting you into trouble. Why couldn't you have put matters on a right footing by telling me of this meeting at once ?"

" Have patience and you shall know why. I was so

overcome on finding out whom I had been dancing with that I nearly fainted, and went up-stairs, wishing to start directly for home ; but as you were engaged in a rubber at whist, I did not wish to make a commotion by interrupting the game ; and to avoid Monsieur, decided to remain in the cloak-room until you was ready to leave. He had the audacity to follow me there ; and in spite of my entreaties that he would go, insisted on remaining until I had named a place for a second interview."

" Was you so unwise, so beside yourself, as to accede to such a proposal from such a man ?"

" Consider my position ; locked in a room with a person to whom I had just been introduced as a stranger ; one so utterly destitute of honor that he was ready to sacrifice me, you, or any other obstacle that came in the way of the selfish, inhuman design he had in view."

" And that design was what ?"

" To extort money from you through my agency ; but I did not know that at the time. Let me go on, and you will see how I arrived at the conclusion that such was the fact. He said he had proofs, which he offered to produce at our second meeting, fully establishing the validity of our marriage—mine and his, I mean —and when I still refused to appoint a place to meet him, he threatened to force you into a hostile encounter, reminding me of the provisions you had made by will in my behalf, saying that our second trip across the Atlantic should be made in better style than the first. Then he threw out dark hints against your life, in case of your refusing to accept his challenge, and the malignant scowl on his face when telling me of a man garroted in the street, one dark night, from motives of revenge, I shudder to think of still."

The face of her listener wore an expression of indifference nearly amounting to contempt.

"I have heard men talk before," he said calmly; "and have had to deal with too many crooked customers in my day to be easily scared by hard looks or hard words either; besides, your determined assassin doesn't threaten, he strikes. So you met the villain again."

"I did, at the foot of your garden, when he furnished such clear proofs of our having been really married that, much as I wished to do so, I did not dare to doubt their genuineness; and proposed that I should wring money from you to pay the price of his silence. He little knew me if he supposed that by any inducement he could urge me into the pursuance of a course so monstrous, so wholly unjustifiable that it could lead to nothing but misery and wrong doing."

"But the proofs: they may seem less conclusive to me than they did to you."

"He assured me that the marriage ceremony, although not solemnized by a regularly ordained clergyman, was binding, as it had been sanctioned by a regularly appointed justice of the peace. I refused to credit his mere assertion, when he invited me to go with him for proof to the Ironside Hotel, where he introduced me to Deacon Brown, a townsman and neighbor of Mr. Witherspoon, who fully corroborated the statement of M. Meurice, and further confirmed its truth by showing me an affidavit (whatever that may be) sworn to before Abednego Witherspoon, Justice of the Peace, in 1860."

"In what town was this affidavit sworn to?"

"I did not see the name of any town on the paper shown me by Deacon Brown."

"What sort of a looking man was this Brown?"

"A short, thick-set, broad-shouldered man, with dark, bushy hair, and a deep scar over the left eye, quite near the temple."

Mr. Caruthers rose hastily, and drawing on his

gloves, started for the door; but paused before reaching it, detained by an imploring gesture from Lucy.

" Where are you going?"

" To hunt down that story before it is many hours older."

" But whatever you learn, you will come back and break the news to me yourself; you will not leave me long in suspense; and you will come *yourself*."

He returned to the seat he had just quitted.

" Let me tell you that, although I am not given to making fine speeches to please a lady's ear, what I say I mean; and I do say that I will leave no means untried to place you once more in the home that is as dreary as all the rest of the world in your absence. If I find that there is any foundation in fact for the statement of M. Meurice, I will consult Auverne immediately as to the practicability of your procuring a divorce."

" Haven't I told you? M. Meurice is dead, or I should not have ventured to write you."

" Indeed! that simplifies the matter very materially. But are you sure of what you say?"

" Please reach me that newspaper on the stand, and you shall see how sure."

Supporting her head on her hand, she read aloud to him the article already transcribed, remarking at the conclusion of its perusal:

" Clermont seems to have been his real name; Meurice only an assumed one."

" Clermont," repeated Mr. Caruthers, " I have heard the name before. I have it now; Miss Barton stopped me in the street to tell me that you had met M. Meurice, under the name of Clermont, at her party; but her description of his personal appearance did not coincide with that of Monsieur; besides, I was sure you would have mentioned such an occurrence to me if it had actually taken place, and dismissed it from my thoughts as too improbable for belief."

Lucy was inattentive to this last remark, her next words proving that her mind still dwelt upon a former one.

" I do not see how the death of M. Meurice materially simplifies the matter. I have studied the Statutes of our Commonwealth, which I obtained as soon as I could after my second interview with him, and, as nearly as I can make out, my marriage with you was not binding, if the first was in force at the time the second was consummated. I have pored over this little law book hours and hours, when I ought to have been abed and asleep, and, oh, Mr. Caruthers, I am not your wife."

" Don't distress yourself in this way; dry your eyes; leave everything to me, and rest satisfied that all will come right in the end. If the first ceremony was not in accordance with due regulations of law, we will go to another State and have it quietly repeated. Your consent I take as a matter of course; for you couldn't have the heart to condemn me to the probation of a second wooing."

Lucy was too deeply moved to venture on speech, save through the eloquent looks replying to his own.

" Is that man an acquaintance of your'n?" tartly inquired Mrs. Smallmain, soon after Mr. Caruthers' departure.

" He is a highly valued friend," laconically responded Lucy, who was strongly desirous of being left to the undisturbed luxury of her own meditations.

" I needn't ask you to tell me who he is, though you hadn't the manners to introduce me; and said plain enough, under my own roof, too, that my room was better than my company," spitefully announced the slighted widow. " I know him by sight, no thanks to nobody; for I've seen him at my nephew's, the nephew that you are making caps for, the nephew that hires his store of Mr. Caruthers. A powerful rich man he is too, and lives in such a grand big house, that you could put the whole of this one in his best company room on the fust floor. It strikes me that he is an odd friend for a young woman that makes caps at a shilling apiece, to have. I'll tell you what, poor sewing girls shouldn't make rich acquaintances; it looks bad, it makes them feel above their station, and it don't turn out well."

"I supposed that as long as I paid my board-bill promptly, and conformed to the strictest rules of propriety, I might be permitted to receive an occasional call from a friend without question or comment," returned Lucy, with a show of spirit she would have been incapable of assuming an hour previous.

"There is where you are entirely mistaken; I'll be mistress of my own house as long as I have one; and I'm not going to be put down nor run over by no young upstart whatsomdever. Whoever comes under this roof has got to toe the mark, if it's the grand Mogul himself; and I tell you, once for all, I won't have no rich man coming and rushing into your bed-room, after my telling him you wasn't fit to see nobody, so you may as well make up your mind to it fust as last. Either he has got to make himself skurce or you have, that's the long and short of the matter. If he comes again, you needn't see him. Leave it to me, and he won't come where he isn't wanted again, I'll warrant you."

"He came this time because I sent for him; he will come again, and I must see him," Lucy strenuously insisted.

"If you do, I can tell you the very next thing that will come to pass; you will pack up and be off, bag and baggage."

Lucy bore this intimation with composure, devoutly hoping that the speaker might prove a true prophetess.

No expression of angry resentment could have provoked her to wrath as did this mute indifference.

"You carry your head so high, Miss Searls, that I can't help thinking you've found some way of making a living—an honest one, I hope—independent of your needle; for if you ain't, you'd better jest look and see which side your bread is buttered on. I run hither and you to git work for you, and I got it, and I can take it away again. As true as I'm setting in this chair, if out of this house you go, not a rag belonging to my nephew goes with you."

" Thank you for reminding me of the subject : if I should leave you suddenly, it would be inconvenient, perhaps impossible, for me to comply with the terms on which I agreed to work for him."

" I hope you remember what those terms were ; he was to pay you for making each case of caps when it was finished and sent back to him, not before."

" I have a perfect recollection of the agreement, and have no intention of evading it; if I am unable to make the whole case of caps he sent me last, I will ask nothing for those already finished."

" Fractious !" was the only word vouchsafed by Mrs. Smailmain, as she went out of the room, banging the door after her.

It was nine in the evening before Lucy heard the welcome step for which she had long been listening.

Disregarding the attempts to delay his entrance, Mr. Caruthers made his way straight to Lucy's side.

" Good news, my dear; Anverne put me on the right track at once, and I found that fellow, Witherspoon, faithfully and laboriously engaged in his country's service."

" Enlisted ?"

" Not he ; but pegging away at soldiers' boots in the penitentiary. He did serve once as Justice of the Peace in an aguish swamp called Snakes Lick, hundreds of miles down the river, and his term of appointment expired years ago, so that story is—bosh. Auverne has a shrewd suspicion that Deacon Brown is a comic actor, who has been in the city on a theatrical engagement the past season, as he patronized the Ironside Hotel, and has a scar over the left eye near the temple, as you described. Come, let us go home; it is late, and I have not yet had my tea."

" You forget that I have not been able to sit up five minutes through the day. I can hardly raise my head from the pillow."

" Never mind that ; you can lean back in the carriage, with my arm for support, if you need it."

" But my clothes; I haven't strength to get them together."

" Never mind them either; they don't amount to much ; but without you, I do not leave this house. And now that I am in an authoritative mood, I may as well tell you that there is one exaction which I shall most stringently insist on your complying with; it is, that you shall give me your unreserved confidence, in return for my own, never withdrawing it unless I give you just cause for such withdrawal."

The beaming smile irradiating Lucy's face showed that what he had termed an exaction, presented itself to her in the light of a coveted privilege.

THE END.

www.ingramcontent.com/pod-product-compliance
Lightning Source LLC
Chambersburg PA
CBHW030905270326
41929CB00008B/588